CATALOGUE OF CYCLES

PART I—ECONOMICS

By

LOUISE L. WILSON

FOUNDATION FOR THE STUDY OF CYCLES, INC.

Pittsburgh, Pennsylvania

FOREWORD

The idea of a catalogue to list all allegations of rhythmic phenomena regardless of discipline was first suggested in 1941 by the late Alan Gregg, at that time Director of Medical Science at the Rockefeller Foundation. Doctor Gregg felt that such a list complete with bibliographical references would provide an essential base for comparative cycle study. It would provide a place where a worker in one field, who had discovered a cycle of a particular length, could readily find all the other fields in which cycles of the same wave length had been alleged.

Doctor Gregg's idea was warmly seconded by Wesley C. Mitchell of the National Bureau of Economic Research and by Ellsworth Huntington of Yale, both of whom, like Doctor Gregg, were Directors of the Foundation for the Study of Cycles, until their deaths.

Various matters prevented the realization of this project from 1941 until now. The venture, however, is now under way. Volume I, dealing with allegations of economic cycles, is presented herewith; other volumes, dealing with allegations of cycles in other disciplines, are in the process of preparation.

It is believed that the entire compilation, when complete, will fill a long-standing need.

Edward R. Dewey
Executive Director

FOUNDATION FOR THE STUDY OF CYCLES, INC.
124 South Highland Avenue
Pittsburgh, Pennsylvania 15206

INTRODUCTION

This volume, which records allegations of cycles in economic data, is the first of a series of monographs dealing with allegations of cycles in all aspects of the natural and social sciences. No attempt has been made to evaluate the significance of cycles listed. References have been limited to material in the libraries of the Foundation for the Study of Cycles, the Carnegie Library of Pittsburgh, the Carnegie Institute of Technology, the University of Pittsburgh, and in otherwise conveniently available sources. The references have been further limited to allegations of cycles of specific wave length.

In this presentation, references have been listed alphabetically by subject matter under the following main headings:

> Commodity Prices
> Stock Prices
> Other Financial Data
> General Business
> Agriculture
> Building Construction and Real Estate
> Manufacturing
> Services
> Miscellaneous Economic Activity

Under all alphabetical sub-headings, the references have been arranged by cycle length, unless otherwise noted. An exception has been made when one single reference lists more than one cycle in the same phenomenon; in such instances, the reference has been arranged according to the shortest cycle length alleged.

Contained in each precis is the name of the time series involved, the period of the cycle, and the author. In addition, when available, the following statistics have been included in each precis: the time interval over which the cycle is alleged to exist; the locale involved; the nature of the cycle (whether rhythmic or average); the amplitude of the average wave; the date of an ideal crest or trough; information on whether or not the cycle continued to move in the ideal pattern after discovery; indication of whether or not the author included charts, figures, or data in his work; and any other pertinent information supplied by the author.

This volume has been amassed for the following reasons: (1) it calls attention to the very large number of economic phenomena in which rhythmic fluctuations (or cycles present on the average) have been alleged; (2) it calls attention to the very large number of wave lengths that have been alleged; (3) it provides raw material for a comprehensive checking program to determine the significance of the alleged cycles; (4) it indicates wave lengths common to various economic phenomena; (5) it provides a bibliography of economic cycle allegations; and (6) it provides a list of cycle lengths in economic data which can be compared with cycle lengths alleged to be present in non-economic phenomena which will be found in subsequent volumes (in preparation) of the Catalogue of Cycles, in order to see, if and when identities or seeming identities appear, whether or not an interrelationship may be possible and to find, when possible, the cause of the various behaviors.

Because economics is within the framework of everyone's interest, this field was selected as the base of the first volume. Contained herein is a history of the well-being (or lack of well-being) of all human beings.

The word "alleged" has been used deliberately to indicate that no significance has been ascribed by the Foundation to any of the various cycles to which the author refers; in truth, any cycle present merely on the average is suspect, and even a rhythmic cycle may be present by chance. The results of this compilation must speak for themselves; any conclusions drawn from this material must be regarded as personal and any deductions derived must be founded on the intellectual integrity and scientific competence of the investigator-reader.

The Foundation hopes that this study will make an important contribution to the literature of economic cycles and prove a forerunner of many similar studies from which society can obtain information and guidance for the solving of serious problems incident to the interpretation of economic activity.

Credit should be given to Erlenne Fails, Catherine Herzel, and Helen Shirk, who did some of the preliminary library research; to Mary Montanari, for the charting; and to Joan Andersen and Marge Copeman who, respectively, typed and varityped the manuscript.

Louise L. Wilson

TABLE OF CONTENTS

COMMODITY PRICES

COMMODITY PRICES

APPLE PRICES

1

A 10-year rhythmic cycle in Apple Prices, U.S.A., 1890–1940, is alleged.

There has been a tendency for apple prices to move in cyclical swings averaging about ten years in length with high prices recorded about 1900, 1910, 1920, and 1930. Low prices were reached about 1895, 1905, 1915, and 1925. These swings differed in length and strength, but they persisted throughout the 50-year period.

Woodin, 1941. (Figure)

BARLEY PRICES
(see GRAIN PRICES)

BEAN PRICES
(see GRAIN PRICES)

BEEF PRICES
(also see CATTLE PRICES)

2

A 1 1/2 – 4 1/2-year rhythmic cycle in Beef Carcass Prices, U.S.A., 1896 – 1925, is alleged.

Movements of cattle cycles and beef carcass cycles, as analyzed by Hopkins, followed like patterns, but the amount of such movements sometimes varied considerably. Highs in beef carcass prices occurred in February 1899, June 1902, July 1904, June 1908, April 1910, August 1912, August 1914, September 1917, February 1919, October 1920, and December 1923. Lows were recorded in June 1896, January 1901, April 1904, October 1905, August 1909, June 1911, September 1913, April 1915, March 1918, March 1920, February 1922, and June 1924.

Hopkins, 1926. pp. 360–361. (Figure)

3

A 15-year rhythmic cycle in Dressed Beef Prices, U.S.A., 1880–1942, is alleged.

"...the cycle in the price of (dressed) beef is about 15 years in length."

Paarlberg, 1947. (Figure)

BUILDING MATERIAL PRICES

4

An 18 – 20-year rhythmic cycle in Building Material Prices, Berlin, Germany, 1810–1936, is alleged.

The purchasing power of building materials have shown a fairly close relationship to the building cycle. A crest in the ideal pattern in this 18–20-year cycle occurred in 1928.

Warren and Pearson, 1939. pp. 124–125. (Figure)

BUTTER PRICES

5

A 4 – 5-year rhythmic cycle in Butter Prices, U.S.A., 1880–1942, is alleged.

In small degree, the price of butter is related to the price of pork which has an irregular 4 – 5-year cycle.

Paarlberg, 1947. (Figure)

6

A 7-year rhythmic cycle in Butter Prices, U.S.A., 1890–1929, is alleged.

In addition to the long fluctuations in butter prices (13–19 years), shorter savings of about seven years between low points were noted.

U.S.D.A. Yearbook of Agriculture, 1930. p. 588. (Figure)

7

A 13 – 19-year cycle in Butter Prices, U.S.A., 1890–1929, is alleged.

Using a 12-month moving average of the prices of 92-score butter at New York (adjusted for changes in the commodity price level), the Department of Agriculture noted a 13–19-year cycle. Highs were recorded in 1893, 1912, and 1927; lows in 1904, and 1917.

U.S.D.A. Yearbook of Agriculture, 1930. p. 588. (Figure)

8

A 15-year rhythmic cycle in Butter Prices, U.S.A., 1880–1942, is alleged.

The price of butter has tended to fluctuate with the 15-year cycle in the price of beef.

Paarlberg, 1947. (Figure)

CATTLE PRICES
(BEEF CATTLE, DAIRY CATTLE, CATTLE)
(also see BEEF PRICES)

9

A 2 – 3-year rhythmic cycle in Beef Cattle Prices, U.S.A., 1850–1924, is alleged.

Hopkins postulated a series of minor cycles in addition to the major cycle (7–18 years) in beef cattle prices. From 1866 to 1924, five waves stood out as of greater amplitude than the others. Measured from trough to trough, the first, lasting from 1868 to 1871, reached its high point in 1870. It was followed by a series of three short waves between two and three years long with the high point in these waves having been reached in 1875 and the low point having been reached in 1876.

Hopkins, 1926. p. 349. (Figure)

10

A 5-year rhythmic cycle in Cattle Prices, Netherlands, no dates given, is alleged.

Tinbergen and Polak, 1950. p. 93.

11

A 5 – 7-year rhythmic cycle in Cattle Prices, U.S.A., no dates given, is alleged.

Using the cobweb theory as a tool, Ezekiel noted that a 5–7-year rhythmic pattern was present in cattle prices in the United States.

Ezekiel, 1938.

12

A 7–18-year rhythmic cycle in Beef Cattle Prices, U.S.A., 1850–1924, is alleged.

The major waves in the 7–18-year beef cattle cycle have varied in length from less than 7 to more than 17 years if measured from peak to peak; from 13 to 18 years if measured from trough to trough. Highs occurred in June 1870, May 1882, December 1899, November 1912, and in February 1919. Lows were recorded in July 1876, March 1889, November 1903, and November 1921.

Hopkins, 1926. (Figure)

13

A 10 – 12-year rhythmic cycle in Cattle Prices, U.S.A., 1910–1958, is alleged.

Ensminger, 1960. p. 692. (Figure)

14

A 10–19-year rhythmic cycle in Cattle Prices, U.S.A., is alleged.

Regular cycles of from 10 to 19 years in length have been noted in the price
of cattle, 1880–1947 (farm value per head at January 1). Peaks were reached
in 1884, 1900, 1919, and 1929; lows, in 1891 or 1895, 1905, 1922, and 1934.
Intervals between peaks varied from 10 to 19 years while intervals between
lows ranged from 10 to 17 years and averaged 13.75 years.

Hadorn, 1947. (Figure)

15

Using cattle values on Illinois farms at January 1 from 1866 through 1930,
Norton and Wilson found a clearly noticeable 10–19-year cycle. Peaks
appeared in 1869, 1884–1885, 1900–1901, 1919–1920, and apparently 1929–
1930; the intervals, therefore, having come at 15, 15, 19, and 10 years.

Norton and Wilson, 1930. p. 537. (Figure; data)

16

A 12 – 17-year rhythmic cycle in Beef Cattle Prices, U.S.A., 1890–1939, is
alleged.

Beef cattle prices have shown a marked cyclic type of movement during the
period under observation. Three prominent peaks, approximately 15 years
apart, appeared when the farm value per head of cattle (other than milk
cows) was divided each year by the corresponding Bureau of Labor Statistics Wholesale Price Index of All Commodities. Cyclic highs occurred in
1900, 1915, and 1930. Lows were recorded in 1905, 1922, and 1934.

Shepherd, 1941. (Figure)

17

A 14–16-year rhythmic cycle in Beef Cattle Prices, U.S.A., is alleged.

A study of beef cattle prices from 1880 through 1928 revealed that prices
have tended to move up and down in well-defined cycles of 14 to 16 years
when measured from peak to peak or from trough to trough.

Hodges, 1928. (Figure)

18

"Periods between peaks of purchasing power of beef cattle have averaged
14 to 16 years in length . . . . Both beef cattle (at farm prices) and all cattle
slaughtered (at market prices) were high in purchasing power in 1898 and
1899, again in 1914 and 1915, and again in 1929 and 1930 . . . . During each
of the past cycles, there was a long period of low prices, 1890–1895, 1904–
1910, and 1920–1925."

Hughes, 1940-A. (Figure)

19

Studying the value of beef cattle on farms from January 1, 1880 through
January 1, 1939, Lorie found a 14—16-year cycle and recorded highs in
1885, 1899, 1915, and 1929. He also stated that the series "was marked
by irregular short-term fluctuations of minor amplitude."

Lorie, 1947. (Figure)

20

Nance noted that beef cattle prices have tended to peak (and to trough) at
14- to 16-year intervals. Peaks (in dollar values) came in 1885, 1899, 1915,
and 1929; lows, in 1891, 1905, 1925, and 1934.

Nance, 1953.

21

The beef cattle cycle (purchasing power of beef cattle calculated in terms
of the 30 basic commodities from 1880 to 1938) has varied in length from 14
to 16 years and has been largely independent of fluctuations in commodity
prices.

Warren and Pearson, 1938. (Figure)

22

A 14 – 16-year rhythmic cycle in Dairy Cattle Prices, U.S.A., is alleged.

Dairy cattle prices from 1875 through 1936 have moved in 14—16-year waves
which correspond to those found in beer cattle prices.

Thomsen, 1936. (Figure)

23

Warren and Pearson found that the dairy cattle price cycle from 1873 to
1937 was almost a facsimile of the beef cattle cycle: wave lengths have
varied from 14 to 16 years and the cycles have been largely independent
of fluctuations in commodity prices.

Warren and Pearson, 1937. (Figure)

24

A 14 – 16-year rhythmic cycle in Cattle Prices, U.S.A., is alleged.

Beef cattle prices and dairy cattle prices have tended to exhibit the same
cyclical fluctuations and normally have moved in cycles of 14 to 16 years
in length during the period from 1890 through 1942.

Pearson, Myers, and Curtiss, 1942. (Figure)

25

Hadorn noted that the price of cattle and the purchasing power of cattle (value adjusted for prices received for other farm products) have moved in similar cycles approximately 14–16 years in length. Normally, purchasing power and prices in the data for the period from 1880 through 1947 moved up and down together, with exceptions occurring during World Wars I and II.

Hadorn, 1947. (Figure)

26

A 14.8-year rhythmic cycle in Beef Cattle Prices, U.S.A., 1880–1937, is alleged.

There has been a tendency for the purchasing power of beef cattle prices to move in cyclical swings averaging about 14.8 years in length.

Dewey and Dakin, 1947. p. 137. (Figure)

27

A 15-year rhythmic cycle in Cattle Prices, U.S.A., 1890–1944, is alleged.

The farm value per head of cattle other than milk cows in the United States for the period from 1890 through 1944 appeared to fluctuate in waves which measured approximately 15 years.

Shepherd, 1947. pp. 42–43. (Figure)

28

A 15-year rhythmic cycle in Beef Cattle Prices, U.S.A., no dates given, is alleged.

Ross, 1951.

29

A 15-year rhythmic cycle in the Purchasing Power of Cattle, New York City and U.S.A., 1870–1945, is alleged.

There has been a tendency for the purchasing power of cattle (both beef and dairy) in the New York area and in the United States (as a whole) to move in a cycle approximately 15 years in length.

Bond, 1946. (Figure)

30

A 16-year rhythmic cycle in Beef Cattle Prices, U.S.A., 1890–1929, is alleged.

Although this study shows only one complete cycle (1893–1920), it appears to support a 16-year cycle in beef cattle prices.

U.S.D.A. Yearbook of Agriculture, 1930. p. 586. (Figure)

31

Morse asserted that the cattle cycle averages 16 years in length.

Morse, 1948.

32

A 17-year rhythmic cycle in Cattle Prices, U.S.A., no dates given, is alleged.

Tinbergen and Polak, 1950. p. 93.

COCOA BEAN PRICES

33

A 3.48-year (41.7-month) rhythmic cycle in Cocoa Bean Prices, New York City, January 1923—August 1959, is alleged.

An analysis of the period from 1923 to 1959, excluding the war period of controlled prices, has revealed a rhythmic cycle with an average length of 41.7 months. In the 1947 to 1959 period, six times out of six, the ideal cycle and the actual cycle moved in the same direction. Over the entire period, from 1923 to 1959, the cycle and the price moved in the same direction 75% of the time. The average strength of the cycle has been 24.2% above trend at ideal crest and 19.5% below trend at ideal trough. A trough in the ideal pattern occurred in January 1960.

Shirk, 1960-O. (Figure)
Shirk, 1961-K. (Figure)

34

The 41.7-month repetitive wave, first discovered in June 1960, in cocoa bean prices (Accra at New York) appeared to fade out after the ideal 1960 low through 1962.

Shirk, 1962-N. pp. 132—133. (Figure)

35

A 5 1/2-year rhythmic cycle in Cocoa Bean Prices, U.S.A., 1946—1961, is alleged.

Shirk noted that there is a strong hint of a 5 1/2-year cycle in cocoa bean prices in the United States during the period under observation. This cycle showed a crest in the ideal pattern at about 1958—1959.

Shirk, 1963-A.

COFFEE PRICES

36

A 12—18-year rhythmic cycle in Coffee Prices, U.S.A., 1850—1930, is

alleged.

Graphs presented by Gilboy showed that distinct cycles have existed in the price of coffee (when computed in terms of the variable weight index of wholesale prices of Warren and Pearson) which ranged from 12 to 18 years in length. Peaks were recorded in 1860, 1876–1877, 1893–1894, 1912–1913, and 1927; lows, in 1854, 1865, 1884, 1901, and 1918.

Gilboy, 1934. (Figure; data)

37

A 16-year rhythmic cycle in Coffee Prices, New York City, 1854–1954, is alleged.

Coffee cycles, as measured by prices (Purchasing Power of New York Wholesale Prices), have averaged 16 years in length with the exception of the period during and following World War II. Peaks occurred in 1863, 1877, 1894, 1912, and 1928. Lows were recorded in 1855, 1869, 1882, 1903, 1918, and 1940. For the first 80 years of data, the length of the actual cyclical fluctuations closely approximated the 16-year theoretical cycle. During the last 20 years studied, however, the actual cycle did not follow the theoretical one.

Pearson, 1954. (Figure)

38

A 16-year rhythmic cycle in Coffee Prices, no locale cited, 1850–1912, is alleged.

A figure taken from *Nederlandsche Conjunctuur* dated June 1930 (p. 26) revealed the presence of a 16-year rhythmic pattern in coffee prices for the years from 1850 through 1912.

Tinbergen and Polak, 1950. p. 93.

39

A 16 2/3-year rhythmic cycle in Coffee Prices, U.S.A., 1854–1954, is alleged.

In conjunction with the 16-year cycle in coffee prices as recorded by Pearson, Dewey noted that the slightly longer length of 16 2/3 years would provide a better fit if all turning points and all intermediate values were taken into account.

Dewey, 1955-P. p. 183.

COPPER PRICES

40

A 29.2-month (2.43-year) rhythmic cycle in Copper Prices, U.S.A., 1784–1953, is noted.

There appears to be a cycle of this length in copper prices.

Dewey, 1953-E. p. 104.

41

A 32.36-month (2.70-year) rhythmic cycle in Copper Prices, U.S.A., 1784–1956, is alleged.

The 32.36-month cycle in copper prices has exhibited an amplitude of 2.33% above trend at ideal crest and 2.27% below trend at ideal trough with a crest in the ideal pattern occurring in the second quarter of 1958. Dewey uses a chart to plot the synthesis of this cycle and four others (8.60-year, 9.28-year, 12.53-year, and 14.8-year).

Dewey, 1957-J. (Figure)

42

A 5.91-year (70.9-month) rhythmic cycle in Copper Prices, U.S.A., 1784–1953, is alleged.

A crest in the ideal pattern occurred at 1959.89 in this 5.91-year cycle in copper prices. Typical amplitude has been approximately 5.6% above trend at ideal crest and 5.3% below trend at ideal trough.

Dewey, 1957-F.

43

An 8-year rhythmic cycle in Copper Prices, New York, 1860–1937, is alleged.

A number of short-time oscillations appeared in a study of copper prices by Barbour but a definite wave length of 8 years persisted throughout the entire period.

Barbour, 1937. (Figure)

44

An 8.60-year rhythmic cycle in Copper Prices, U.S.A., 1784–1953, is alleged.

The length of this cycle in copper prices is 8.60 years from crest to crest or trough to trough. Typical amplitude of the ideal cycle has averaged 11.9% above trend at crest and 10.7% below trend at trough. A crest in the ideal pattern occurred in the fourth quarter of 1950.

Dewey, 1954-K. (Figure)

45

According to Shirk, the 8.6-year rhythmic cycle continued as one of the four dominant cycles present in the price of copper in the United States during the period beginning 1784 and ending 1961.

Shirk, 1962-A.

46

A 9.28-year rhythmic cycle in Copper Prices, U.S.A., 1784–1953, is alleged.

A regular, persistent cycle of 9.28 years has been evident in copper prices from the earliest figures available (1784) through 1953. Percentage deviations of a 17-quarter moving average from a 41-quarter moving average of the actual prices during this 170-year period and the ideal cycle are noted on a chart.

Dewey, 1954-N. (Figure)

47

Later work showed that typical amplitude of the ideal 9.28-year cycle has been 14.3% above trend at crest and 12.5% below trend at trough.

Dewey, 1954-K. (Figure)

48

One of the four important cycles in the price of copper in the United States during the period from 1784 through 1961 was a 9.3-year cycle.

Shirk, 1962-A.

49

A 10-year rhythmic cycle in Copper Prices, U.S.A., no dates given, is alleged.

Szatrowski cited that copper prices in the United States have shown a definite tendency to be dominated by a 10-year cycle.

Szatrowski, 1949-A.

50

A 12.53-year rhythmic cycle in Copper Prices, U.S.A., 1784—1956, is alleged.

This cycle has displayed a typical amplitude of 8.4% above trend at time of ideal crest and 7.7% below trend at time of ideal trough. A crest in the ideal pattern occurred in the fourth quarter of 1952.

Dewey, 1957-J. (Figure)

51

A 12.53-year wave continued to be present, along with an 8.6-, a 9.3-, and a 14.8-year wave, in copper prices in the United States during the period from 1784 through 1961.

Shirk, 1962-A.

52

A 14.8-year rhythmic cycle in Copper Prices, U.S.A., 1784—1956, is alleged.

A crest in the ideal pattern occurred during the second quarter of 1959 in this 14.8-year cycle in copper prices. Typical amplitude has been 5.6% above trend at time of ideal crest and 5.4% below trend at time of ideal trough.

Dewey, 1957-J. (Figure)

53

An additional article carried the synthesis of five cycles in copper prices
(32.36-month, 8.60-year, 9.28-year, 12.53-year, and 14.8-year) into the third
quarter of 1959. The combination of these cycles tended to peak in the
first quarter of 1956; the actual peak, however, came one quarter later.

Shirk, 1959-L. (Figure)

54

One of the component cycles used in the combined cycle chart of copper
prices in the United States during the period under observation was the
14.8-year cycle.

Shirk, 1962-A.

55

A 54-year rhythmic cycle in Copper Prices, U.S.A., 1784—1956, is alleged.

This 54-year cycle in copper prices has displayed three prominent waves in
the study of data available. Typical amplitude averaged 39% above trend at
ideal crest and 28% below trend at ideal trough.

Dewey, 1957-C. (Figure)

CORN PRICES

56

A 3—11-year rhythmic cycle in Corn Prices, U.S.A., 1866—1929, is alleged.

Irregular cycles have been observed in the price of corn (average annual
Illinois farm prices, corrected for changes in general price level). High
prices were recorded in 1864, 1867—1868, 1870, 1874—1875, 1882, 1888,
1891, 1902, 1908—1909, 1912, 1917—1920, and 1924—1925. Intervals between the price peaks were noted at 3 years (three times), 4 years (once),
5 years (twice), 6 years (twice), 7 years (once), and 11 years (once).

Norton and Wilson, 1930. pp. 494—499. (Figure; data)

57

A 3 1/2—3 2/3-year rhythmic cycle in Corn Prices, U.S.A., 1720—1954, is
alleged.

Although there was no one cycle length which dominated throughout the
data employed, several cycles were manifest for long periods; e.g., a cycle
of about 3 2/3 years continued for 92 years from 1734 to 1826 and another
of about 3 1/2 years was evident in the 95-year period from 1860 to 1955.

Dewey, 1955-S. (Figure)

58

A 3.49-year (41.9-month) rhythmic cycle in Corn Prices, U.S.A., 1760–1954, is alleged.

The length of the 3 1/2-year cycle in corn prices was refined to 3.49 years by Dewey who stated that this cycle was present as a hidden component prior to 1860 as well as being the visible cycle after 1860. A crest in the ideal pattern occurred at the end of the 1953–1954 crop year.

Dewey, 1955-R. (Figure)

59

A 5–10-year rhythmic cycle in Corn Prices, U.S.A., 1850–1924, is alleged.

Intervals in the cyclical fluctuations in corn prices, calculated in terms of the size of the corn crop and the general condition of business activity, have ranged from 5 to 10 years in length. High prices were reported in June 1870, December 1874, July 1882, April 1891, December 1901, September 1908, April 1912, November 1917, and January 1925; lows, in November 1872, December 1878, May 1886, September 1896, February 1906, March 1911, January 1913, and October 1921.

Hopkins, 1926, as quoted by Hadorn, 1949. (Figure)

60

A 5 1/2-year rhythmic cycle in Annual Corn Prices, U.S.A., 1862–1875, is alleged.

A 5 1/2-year cycle (an 11-year pattern comprised of alternating 5-year and 6-year waves) in the price of corn displayed crests in 1864, 1869, and 1875. Benner recorded his observation of a W-shaped 11-year cycle (or two 5 1/2-year cycles every 11 years) which he called a 5-year–6-year cycle.

Benner, 1875. (Figure; data)

61

Dewey provided additional information regarding the Benner cycle in corn prices in 1955. The strength of the cycle, after allowance for excessive values during the Civil War, averaged 11.1% above trend at ideal crest and 10.0% below trend at ideal trough. He also stated that the cycle had continued to assert itself through the year 1955.

Dewey, 1955-C. (Figure)

62

A 5.61-year (67 1/3-month) rhythmic cycle in Monthly Corn Prices, U.S.A., January 1900–December 1954, is alleged.

By employing monthly figures which offered opportunity for exact measurement, Dewey refined the length of the 5 1/2-year cycle in corn prices to

5.61 years for the period from January 1900 through December 1954.

Dewey, 1955-C. (Figure)

63

Additional work extended data from the crop year 1858–1859 through 1955–1956. Typical amplitude was 30% above trend at time of ideal crest and 23% below trend at time of ideal trough. A trough in the ideal pattern occurred in July 1955.

Dewey, 1957-M. (Figure)

64

The 5.61-year cycle in corn prices continued through 1961 and was found to dominate 73% of the time.

Shirk, 1961-M. (Figure)

65

A 6–12-year rhythmic cycle in Corn Prices, U.S.A., 1866–1947, is alleged.

Corn prices have exhibited a definite tendency to follow a 9-year rhythm in the general level of all-commodity prices. Computing percentage deviations of a three-year moving average from a nine-year moving average, Hadorn found peaks in 1874, 1882, 1891, (or 1893), 1902, 1908, 1918, 1928, and 1935. Lows occurred in 1871, 1877, 1885, 1897, 1905, 1914, 1921, 1932, and 1938. Intervals between peaks ranged from 6 to 11 years (8.7-year average). Intervals between troughs also ranged from 6 to 11 years (8.4-year average).

Hadorn, 1948. (Figure; data)

COTTON PRICES

66

A 2-year rhythmic cycle in Cotton Prices, U.S.A., 1903-04–1911-12, is alleged.

Tinbergen and Polak, 1950. pp. 93–94. (Figure)

67

A 3-year rhythmic cycle in Cotton Prices, U.S.A., 1890–1915, is alleged.

"Between 1890 and 1915, cotton prices reached low points approximately every three years...."

Smith, 1928. (Figure; data)

68

A 5.575-year (66.9-month) rhythmic cycle in Cotton Prices, U.S.A., 1731–1732–1950-1951, is alleged.

This 5.575-year cycle appears to be one of the four overlapping repetitive elements which comprise the 6-year cycle sometimes visible in cotton prices (average annual spot price).

Dewey, 1952-U. p. 40.

69

A 5.91-year (70.9-month) rhythmic cycle in Cotton Prices, U.S.A., 1731-1732—1950-1951, is alleged.

When present, this 5.91-year cycle appears to be one of the four components of the 6-year cycle in cotton prices (average annual spot price) as well as a submultiple of a longer wave of about 17.75 years.

Dewey, 1952-U. p. 40. (Figure)

70

Additional work in 1959 indicated that government control of cotton prices had obstructed the 5.91-year cycle and Shirk asserted that the cycle "cannot be expected to resume until the laws of supply and demand are again permitted to operate."

Shirk, 1959-D. (Figure)

71

A 6-year rhythmic cycle in Cotton Prices, U.S.A., 1900—1944, is alleged.

The data pertaining to cotton prices (average annual spot price for the crop year beginning August) were expressed as percentages of a six-year moving average. This 6-year cycle exhibited an average wave amplitude of 13% above trend at time of ideal crest.

Dewey, 1950-G. p. 7. (Figure)

72

Employing data for the period from 1731—1732 through 1949—1950, Dewey has found that the 6-year cycle, when present, seems to be a complex composed of four overlapping repetitive cycles of about 6 years in length: these cycles being 5.575 years, 5.91 years, 6.11 years, and 6.45 years long.

Dewey, 1952-U. p. 40. (Figure)

73

A 6.11-year (73.3-month) average cycle in Cotton Prices, U.S.A., 1731-1732—1950-1951, is alleged.

The 6.11-year cycle in cotton prices (average annual spot price) appears as one of the four components which create the 6-year cycle sometimes present in cotton prices.

Dewey, 1952-U. p. 40.

74

A 6.45-year (77.4-month) average cycle in Cotton Prices, U.S.A., 1731-

1732—1950-1951, is alleged.

It appears that this 6.45-year cycle is one of the four overlapping repetitive forces which create the 6-year cycle sometimes present in cotton prices (average annual spot price).

Dewey, 1952-U. p. 40.

75

A 7.8-year (93.6-month) average cycle in Cotton Prices, U.S.A., 1731-1732—1939-1940, is alleged.

A multiple harmonic analysis of over 200 years of data revealed the possibility of a 7.8-year cycle in cotton prices.

Dewey, 1952-C. p. 5.
Dewey, 1953-G. p. 142.

76

A 7.95-year (95.4-month) average cycle in Cotton Prices, U.S.A., 1735—1945, is alleged.

Using a multiple harmonic analysis of over 200 years of data, Dewey found that a 7.95-year cycle displayed great strength above trend at time of crest.

Dewey, 1953-G. pp. 142—143.
Dewey, 1956-I. pp. 272—273.

77

An 8.5-year average cycle in Cotton Prices, U.S.A., 1731-1732—1939-1940, is alleged.

A strong 8.5-year cycle in cotton prices was revealed by means of a multiple harmonic analysis.

Dewey, 1952-C. p. 5.

78

Various average cycles (shortest length: 8.9 years) in Cotton Prices, U.S.A., 1731-1732—1940-1941, are suggested.

A multiple harmonic analysis of cotton prices reported in 1954 suggested cycles with lengths of approximately 8.9, 9.1, 9.3, and 9.6 years.

Dewey, 1954-N. p. 37.

79

A multiple harmonic analysis of cotton prices published in 1951 revealed the possibility of cycles measuring approximately 21 3/4 years, 27 3/4 years, and 33 3/4 years. These cycles showed a relative strength of 1.56, 2.41, and 1.82, respectively.

Dewey, 1951-J. (Figure)
Dewey, 1951-K.

80

A multiple harmonic analysis of wholesale cotton prices reported upon in 1950 gave a hint of the following cycles: 36 3/4-year, 41-year, 52 1/2-year, 57-year, 66 1/2-year, and 90-year. These possible cycles displayed the following relative strengths: 2.8, 3.85, 3.99, 4.35, 4.9, and 4.5, respectively.

Dewey, 1950-E. (Figure)
Dewey, 1950-F.

81

An 11-year rhythmic cycle in Cotton Prices, U.S.A., 1821–1875, is alleged.

Benner noted that an 11-year cycle was evident in the price of cotton. Ignoring the Civil War peaks in prices of cotton, he recorded highs in 1825, 1836, 1847, 1858, and 1869.

Benner, 1875. (Figure; data)

82

Andrews suggested a correlation between sunspot activity and the price of cotton.

Andrews, 1936.

83

A 12.8-year average cycle in Cotton Prices, U.S.A., 1731-1732–1954-1955, is alleged.

A tendency has been noted for cotton prices to move in cyclical swings averaging 12.8 years. Typical amplitude was recorded to be 2.3% above trend at ideal crest and 2.3% below trend at ideal trough. A crest in the ideal pattern occurred at 1955.6.

Dewey, 1957-G.

84

A 17 3/4-year rhythmic cycle in Cotton Prices, U.S.A., 1731-1732–1953-1954, is alleged.

Cotton prices have been characterized by a 17 3/4-year cycle for more than 200 years. The ideal cycle has a typical strength of 19% above trend at ideal crest and 16% below trend at ideal trough.

Dewey, 1955-H. (Figure)

85

A 37-year rhythmic cycle in Cotton Prices, U.S.A., 1731-1732–1950-1951, is alleged.

A 37-year cycle, found to exist in various phenomena, has been evident in cotton prices since the crop year 1731–1732.

Dewey, 1951-S.

86

A 54-year rhythmic cycle in Cotton Prices, U.S.A., 1731–1944, is alleged.

Huntington reported that Dewey had discovered a 54-year cycle in cotton prices in the United States as well as cycles of similar length in U.S. wholesale commodity prices, wheat prices in England, and wars.

Dewey, as reported by Huntington, 1945. (Figure)

EGG PRICES
(also see POULTRY AND POULTRY PRODUCT PRICES)

87

An 18 1/6-month (1.51-year) rhythmic cycle in Egg Prices, U.S.A., 1920–1962, is alleged.

The prices of "fresh firsts" eggs in the United States during the 1920's and 1930's appeared to be characterized by an 18 1/6-month repetitive pattern which disappeared during World War II and has failed to reappear.

Shirk, 1963-B. p. 66.

88

A 26.5-month (2.21-year) rhythmic cycle in Egg Prices, U.S.A., 1947–1957, is alleged.

There has been a tendency for the price of eggs to move in cyclical swings of approximately 26.5 months in addition to a seasonal fluctuation. Typical amplitude of the 26.5-month cycle has been 17.2% above trend at ideal time of crest and 14.7% below trend at ideal time of trough. February 1958 dates a crest in the ideal pattern.

Shirk, 1958-F. (Figure)

89

The 26.5-month repetitive cycle in the wholesale prices of eggs (extras, large, at Chicago) continued to move in the ideal pattern through May of 1962. This cycle had an ideal top (in relation to trend) at April 1960.

Shirk, 1962-Q. (Figure)

90

A 26.5–28-month rhythmic cycle in Egg Prices, U.S.A., 1949–1962, is alleged.

Following up the study of 1958, Shirk brought the data on the 26.5-year cycle in average monthly wholesale prices of eggs (extras, large) at Chicago through 1962. It was noted that although the cycle has continued it may be slightly longer – perhaps 28 months in length. The timing then would be changed to January 1963 for an ideal crest, not June 1962 as previously stated. Typical amplitude at time of an ideal peak measured 17.2% above trend; at time of an ideal low, 14.7% below trend.

Shirk, 1963-B. (Figure)

91

A 2 1/2-year rhythmic cycle in Egg Prices, U.S.A., 1910—1929, is alleged.

Regular and pronounced cycles have been noted in the purchasing power of eggs. The average length of these cycles, eliminating the period during and following World War I, was 30 months.

Funk, 1931. (Figure; data)

92

A 5-year rhythmic cycle in Egg Prices, U.S.A., 1880—1949, is alleged.

Benjamin, Pierce, and Termohlen, 1949. p. 308.

93

A 6—11-year rhythmic cycle in Egg Prices, U.S.A., 1867—1948, is alleged.

Yearly farm prices of eggs have exhibited a definite tendency to follow a 9-year rhythm present in the general level of all-commodity prices. Computing percentage deviations of a three-year moving average from a nine-year moving average, Hadorn noted peaks in 1874, 1882, 1892, 1903, 1909, 1919, 1929, and in 1936. Troughs were evident in 1872, 1879, 1886, 1897, 1906, 1915, 1922, 1932, and in 1939. Intervals between peaks ranged from 6 to 11 years and averaged 8.9 years, while intervals between troughs ranged from 7 to 11 years for an 8.4-year average.

Hadorn, 1948. (Figure; data)

94

A 6—17-year rhythmic cycle in Egg Prices, U.S.A., is alleged.

Study of price data for a period of 100 years indicated that swings in the purchasing power of eggs, measured from high point to high point, have varied in length from 6 to 17 years, averaging nearly 10 years.

Card, 1928. (Figure)

95

An 8-year rhythmic cycle in the Purchasing Power of Eggs, U.S.A., 1873—1936, is alleged.

The poultry cycle (in terms of the purchasing power of eggs) has exhibited a length of approximately 8 years and has been largely independent of fluctuations of commodity prices.

Warren and Pearson, 1937. p. 171. (Figure)

FOOD PRICES

96

A 10-year rhythmic cycle in Prices of the Most Necessary Articles of Food, London, no dates given, is alleged.

Williams reported that a paper was read by J. T. Danson in February 1848 before the Statistical Society of London which attempted to correlate the decennial periodic changes in the condition of the people and the variations occurring in the same decennial periods in the prices of the most necessary articles of food.

Williams, 1959. p. 40.

GENERAL AGRICULTURAL ACTIVITY

97

A 2-year rhythmic cycle in the Prices of Agricultural Produce, no locale cited, no dates given, is alleged.

Tinbergen and Polak, 1950. p. 239.

98

An 8-year rhythmic cycle in Prices of Agricultural Commodities, U.S.A., no dates given, is alleged.

According to Johnson, the purchasing power exerted by agriculture varies in cycles that are identical with the rainfall cycles of 8 and 33 years.

Johnson, 1915.

99

A 33-year rhythmic cycle in Prices of Agricultural Commodities, U.S.A., no dates given, is alleged.

The purchasing power exerted by agriculture, according to Johnson, varies in fluctuations that appear to be identical with the rainfall cycles which measure 8 and 33 years.

Johnson, 1915.

GRAIN PRICES

100

An 11-year rhythmic cycle in Grain Prices, U.S.A., no dates given, is alleged.

The price of grain appears to fluctuate with the sunspot cycle.

Andrews, 1936.

101

An 11.11-year average cycle in Grain Prices, England, 1259–1793, is alleged.

It was reported by Williams that Professor W. Stanley Jevons, in a paper read before the Bristol Meeting of the British Association in 1875, derived a cycle of 11.11 years in the prices of wheat, barley, oats, beans, peas, vetches, and rye.

Jevons, 1875, as reported by Williams, 1959. p. 46.

102

A 36–38-year rhythmic cycle in Grain Prices, England, 1265–1957, is alleged.

Dewey wrote that the cycle in grain prices, first discovered by Clough in 1905, has continued to move in the ideal fashion since discovery. He noted that from 1265 to 1600 or 1650 moves in waves which measured 38 years in length; from 1600 or 1650 through 1957, the waves averaged 36 years in length.

Dewey, 1962-D.

HOG PRICES

103

A 2–9 1/2-year rhythmic cycle in Hog Prices, U.S.A., 1850–1924, is alleged.

When corrected for seasonal variation, the price of hogs has exhibited a well-defined cyclical fluctuation. Highs were reported in December 1869, September 1874, June 1882, September 1888, February 1893, July 1902, February 1907, March 1910, July 1913, July 1919, and May 1922. Lows occurred in July 1867, June 1872, January 1879, October 1885, February 1891, September 1896, May 1904, February 1908, May 1911, March 1915, September 1921, and June 1923.

Hopkins, 1926. pp. 380, 384. (Figure)

104

A 3-year rhythmic cycle in Hog Prices, U.S.A., 1900–1925, is alleged.

There has been a definite tendency for the price of hogs to move in a 3-year cycle. Hog prices have been prone to swing downward for a period of from 18 to 24 months and then reverse themselves for a similar period.

Elliott, 1927. (Figure)

105

A 3–4-year rhythmic cycle in Hog Prices, no locale cited, no dates given,

is alleged.

A 3—4-year rhythmic pattern has been evident in hog prices in many countries over long periods of time, according to Tinbergen and Polak.

Tinbergen and Polak, 1950. p. 92.

106

A 3—4-year rhythmic cycle in Hog Prices, Germany, 1900—1913, is alleged.

A 3—4-year cycle in hog prices which Wagemann said was "amazingly regular" was noted for the period from 1900 through 1913.

Wagemann, 1930. p. 141. (Figure)

107

Hanau is reported to have found a 3—4-year cycle in hog prices in Germany
during the period from 1900 through 1913.

Hanau, 1927, as reported by Tinbergen and Polak, 1950. p. 92. (Figure)

108

A 3—4-year rhythmic cycle in Hog Prices, U.S.A., is alleged.

A 3—4-year cycle in hog prices, 1861—1935, has been observed which ex-
hibits a pattern wherein major cycles have been alternately followed by
minor cycles.

Wallace and Bressman, 1947. (Figure)

109

"During the period of 1904 to 1915, hog prices had a steady upward trend....
The general tendency of the price was to swing first above the trend and
then below, each complete swing taking about three to four years."

Haas and Ezekiel, 1926. (Figure; data)

110

A 3—5-year rhythmic cycle in Hog Prices, U.S.A., 1910—1958, is alleged.

Ensminger, 1960. p. 692. (Figure)

111

A 3—6-year rhythmic cycle in Hog Prices, U.S.A., is alleged.

From 1861 through 1940, hog prices have tended to follow a regular 3—6-year
cyclic pattern, averaging approximately four years in length. An alternate

major and minor cycle pattern was evident throughout the study. The length
of major cycles was 4 to 6 years while the length of minor cycles was 3 to
4 years.

Shepherd, 1941. (Figure)

112

Heavy hog prices at Chicago from 1890 through 1929 (adjusted for changes
in the general price level) moved in cycles varying in length from 3 to 6
years. A definite tendency was noted for the prices to move in an alternate
major and minor cycle pattern. Peaks were reported in 1893, 1902, 1910,
1919, and 1926; troughs, in 1896, 1904—1905, 1911, 1921, and 1927—1928.
Minor peaks were evident in 1898, 1906, 1914, and 1922; minor troughs, in
1899, 1907—1908, 1915, and 1923—1924.

U.S.D.A. Yearbook of Agriculture, 1930. p. 586. (Figure)

113

A 3—9 1/2-year rhythmic cycle in Hog Prices, U.S.A., 1878—1914, is alleged.

Bjorka affirmed that major and minor cycles in hog prices alternate with
each other. Crests of the major cycles were registered in the summer of
1882, the early part of 1893, the summer of 1902, and the winter of 1910.
Crests of the minor cycles were noted in the summer of 1888, the winter
of 1906—1907, and the fall of 1912.

Bjorka, 1927. (Figure; data)

114

A 3.18-year (38.2-month) rhythmic cycle in Hog Prices, Chicago, 1860—1959,
is alleged.

In addition to a 12-month seasonal cycle, the price of hogs has shown a
definite tendency to move in a 38.2-month cycle. This 38.2-month cycle
displayed an average strength of 15.6% above trend at time of ideal crest.
A trough in the ideal pattern occurred in February 1959.

Shirk, 1959-I. (Figure)

115

The 38.2-month cycle in hog prices, first reported upon in October 1959,
continued to follow in the ideal pattern through August 1962.

Shirk, 1962-B and 1962-U. (Figure)

116

A 3.2-year (38.4-month) rhythmic cycle in Hog Prices, U.S.A., 1890—1925,
is alleged.

Shirk reported that F. C. Mills had found a 38.4-month cycle in the prices
of light hogs.

Shirk, 1959-I. p. 225.

117

A 3.25-year (39-month) rhythmic cycle in Hog Prices, U.S.A., 1890—1928, is alleged.

In addition to longer (5-year) fluctuations in hog prices, Bean recorded shorter swings of approximately 3.25 years.

Bean, 1928. (Figure)

118

A 4-year rhythmic cycle in Hog Prices, U.S.A., is alleged.

Cochrane noted that the hog price cycle (spring pig crop) for the period from 1910 through 1956 appeared to move in a pattern which measured 4 years in length. He went on to say that this cycle may actually measure 4, 5, 6, or even 7 years in duration.

Cochrane, 1958. p. 73.

119

Heavy hog prices at Chicago from 1879 through 1952 appeared to fluctuate in waves which measured approximately 4 years in length.

Fruechte, 1953.

120

A 4-year wave in the price of hogs in the United States for the period from 1910 through 1926 was noted by Jordan.

Jordan, 1927. pp. 161—162.

121

Hog prices have shown a general tendency to move in swings approximately 4 years long.

Morse, 1948.

122

For the period from 1861 through 1919, Ross found a 4-year cycle in hog prices in the United States.

Ross, 1951.

123

Heavy hog prices at Chicago for the period from 1861 through 1945 appeared to move in waves which measured approximately 4 years in length.

Shepherd, 1947. pp. 29—30. (Figure)

124

A 4 1/2-year rhythmic cycle in Hog Prices, U.S.A., 1860—1940, is alleged.

"The hog cycle (purchasing power of the price of heavy hogs at Chicago in terms of 30 Basic Commodities, 1860—1940) averages 4 1/2 years from peak to peak...."

Pearson, 1940. (Figure)

125

A 5-year rhythmic cycle in Hog Prices, U.S.A., is alleged.

Alternate major and minor cycles in the price of hogs, 1890–1928, were recorded by Bean. The average duration of the major cycles was 60 months (rise of 36 months and fall of 24 months) while the average duration of the minor cycles was 39 months (rise of 24 months and fall of 15 months).

Bean, 1928. (Figure)

126

Although individual waves have varied greatly in length, a definite 5-year cycle in the price of hogs was evident during the period from 1901 to 1935.

Thomsen, 1936. (Figure)

127

A 5--7-year rhythmic cycle in the Purchasing Power of Heavy Hogs, Chicago, 1860–1930, is alleged.

Zimmerman, 1951. p. 310.

128

A 5–9-year rhythmic cycle in Hog Prices, U.S.A., 1866–1929, is alleged.

Before 1890, peaks in the average annual Illinois farm price of hogs formed a regular 5–6-year pattern. The pattern then lengthened to 7–9 years. The cyclic pattern was further altered by the addition of intermediate minor peaks.

Norton and Wilson, 1930. pp. 531–534. (Figure; data)

129

A 5–11-year rhythmic cycle in Hog Prices, U.S.A., 1867–1949, is alleged.

Hog prices (farm value, January 1) have exhibited a definite tendency to follow a 5- to 11-year (average 9-year) rhythm in the general level of all-commodity prices, with intervals appearing in 1870, 1876, 1883, 1888, 1894, 1902, 1912, 1919, 1926, 1937, and 1945. Troughs occurred in 1873, 1880, 1886, 1891, 1897, 1905, 1916, 1923, 1933, and 1940.

Hadorn, 1949-B. (Figure)

130

A 5 1/2-year average cycle in Purchasing Power of Hogs, U.S.A., is alleged.

There has been a tendency for the purchasing power of hogs to move in waves varying from 3 to 9 1/2 years in length (average cycle length has been 5 1/2 years or 67 months). During the period studied, 1862 to 1924, this cycle repeated itself 11 times.

Green and Howe, 1926.

131

Benner asserted that, during the years from 1847 to 1874, a 5 1/2-year cycle
(an 11-year pattern composed of a 5-year and a 6-year cycle) was evident in
high prices for hogs. Peaks in the prices were noted in 1847, 1853, 1858,
1864, 1869, and 1875; lows, in 1850, 1855, 1861, 1866, and 1872.

Benner, 1875. (Figure)

132

A 5.58-year (67.0-month) rhythmic cycle in Heavy Hog Prices, Chicago,
1879—1952, is alleged.

Fruechte, 1953.

133

A 6-year rhythmic cycle in Heavy Hog Prices, Chicago, 1879—1952, is
alleged.

The annual average prices of heavy hogs at Chicago for the period from
1879 through 1952 appeared to move in a 6-year repetitive cycle. Ideal
highs occurred at 1882 and each 6 years thereafter; ideal lows, at 1879
and each 6 years thereafter. Over-all amplitude was measured as 43 1/2%.

Fruechte, 1953.

134

An 8.9-year rhythmic cycle in Heavy Hog Prices, Chicago, 1879—1952, is
alleged.

Fruechte, 1953.

HORSE PRICES

135

A 13—35-year rhythmic cycle in Horse Prices, U.S.A., 1867—1949, is
alleged.

In the past, horse prices have moved in a cycle approximately a quarter-
century in length. Peaks occurred in 1871, 1884, 1911, and 1937; lows,
in 1879, 1897, and 1932. Hadorn asserted that with the increasing mecha-
nization of agriculture, cyclical fluctuations have become erratic.

Hadorn, 1949-B. (Figure)

136

A 19—26-year rhythmic cycle in Horse Prices, U.S.A., 1866—1929, is
alleged.

During the period studied, two complete cycles of 19 and 26 years duration emerged. Highs were noted in 1889 and in 1910; lows, in 1879, 1896, and 1922. The authors felt that the cycle had been adversely influenced by the substitution of motor for horse power.

Norton and Wilson, 1930. pp. 545—546. (Figure; data)

137

A 22.5-year rhythmic cycle in Horse Prices, U.S.A., 1880—1937, is alleged.

King reproduced a diagram, "Prices of Horses Relative to Those of All-Commodities at Wholesale," which demonstrated a 22.5-year cycle with peaks emerging in 1888 and 1909.

King, Willford I., 1938. p. 230. (Figure)

138

A 25-year rhythmic cycle in Horse Prices, U.S.A., 1873—1937, is alleged.

There has been a tendency for the horse price cycle to average 25 years in length. Fluctuations have been largely independent of variations in the general level of commodity prices.

Warren and Pearson, 1937. pp. 163—164, 167—168. (Figure)

IRON PRICES
(also see STEEL PRICES)

139

A 29.2-month (2.43-year) rhythmic cycle in Pig Iron Prices, U.S.A., is alleged.

A cycle very close to this length appears to be present in pig iron prices.

Dewey, 1953-E. p. 104.

140

A 3.33-year (40-month) rhythmic cycle in Pig Iron Prices, U.S.A., 1902—1921, is alleged.

Nineteen months prior to the publication of this article, an analysis of pig iron prices was made and a definite date on which the trend would turn downward was forecast. This article graphically verified that prediction and stated that the 40-month cycle was accepted as authentic by leading men in the iron and steel industry.

Industrial Digest, 1924. (Figure)

141

Various average cycles (shortest length: 4.1 years) in Pig Iron Prices,

U.S.A., 1784—1951, are suggested.

A multiple harmonic analysis of pig iron prices gives a hint of the following cycles and their relative strength:

Cycle Length	Relative Strength	Cycle Length	Relative Strength	Cycle Length	Relative Strength
4.1-year	1.8	5.8-year	3.1	7.9-year	4.8
4.2-year	1.6	5.9-year	3.1	9.1-year	11.0
4.3-year	1.8	6.1-year	3.9	9.2-year	11.1
4.5-year	2.8	6.3-year	1.9	10.4-year	5.8
4.6-year	1.5	6.4-year	2.3	11.1-year	2.2
4.7-year	2.0	6.5-year	2.2	12.2-year	2.5
4.8-year	2.0	6.6-year	2.1	13.8-year	9.6
5.0-year	2.7	6.8-year	4.6	15.2-year	8.5
5.1-year	1.2	6.9-year	4.2	17.8-year	16.4
5.3-year	4.4	7.2-year	2.7	27.8-year	11.8
5.4-year	4.3	7.4-year	2.8	52.2-year	21.4
5.5-year	3.4	7.6-year	2.8	151.8-year	41.2

Dewey, 1952-H. (Figure)

142

A 5.91-year (70.9-month) rhythmic cycle in Pig Iron Prices, U.S.A., 1784—1953, is alleged.

The 5.91-year cycle has displayed typical strength of 5.5% above trend at ideal crest and 5.1% below trend at ideal trough.

Dewey, 1957-F.

143

A 7.9-year (94.8-month) rhythmic cycle in Pig Iron Prices, U.S.A., 1784—1961, is alleged.

One of the component cycles which appear to produce the 8 1/6-year wave in pig iron prices in the United States during the period under observation is the 7.9-year cycle. The 7.9-year wave displayed an ideal crest in 1957. Typical amplitude measured 3% above and below trend at time of ideal crests and troughs.

Dewey, 1962-B. pp. 152—153.

144

An 8-, 9-, 10-year and repeat (average 9-year) rhythmic cycle in Pig Iron Prices, U.S.A., 1835—1875, is alleged.

Benner stated that changes in the length of the intervals between periods of highs and lows in pig iron prices have been periodical and not haphazard. These intervals have varied only to follow a pattern of gradual and natural order: crests occur at 8-, 9-, and 10-year intervals (1837, 1845, 1854, 1864) and repeat: lows fall at 9-, 7-, and 11-year intervals (1834, 1843, 1850, and

1861) and repeat.

Benner, 1875. (Figure; data)

145

Articles showing the fulfillment of Benner's forecast were published.

Dewey, 1952-A. (Figure)
Dewey, 1952-V. (Figure)
Dewey, 1954-O. (Figure)

146

Extending Benner's pattern back to 1784 and forward to 1960, Shirk found that the actual cycle matched the ideal cycle 75% of the time; furthermore, she found that, from 1784 until the early 1940's, the forecast was almost perfect.

Shirk, 1961-C. (Figure)

147

An 8 1/6-year rhythmic cycle in Pig Iron Prices, U.S.A., 1784–1961, is alleged.

According to Dewey, an 8 1/6-year rhythmic cycle was present in pig iron prices in the United States during the period from 1784 through 1961. This cycle, he stated, was a compound cycle composed of component cycles which measure approximately 7.9 and 8.5 years. The strength of the 8 1/6-year cycle was approximately 5% above and below trend at time of ideal turnings.

Dewey, 1962-B. (Figure)

148

An 8.5-year rhythmic cycle in Pig Iron Prices, U.S.A., 1784–1961, is alleged.

The 8.5-year repetitive wave in pig iron prices in the United States was, according to Dewey, one of the cycles which produced the 8 1/6-year cycle. Typical average amplitude of this cycle was 3% above trend at time of an ideal crest and 3% below trend at time of an ideal trough.

Dewey, 1962-B. pp. 152–153.

149

An 8.53-year rhythmic cycle in Pig Iron Prices, U.S.A., 1784–1953, is alleged.

The 8.53-year cycle in pig iron prices appeared in the residual after adjustment for the 9.20-year cycle. A crest falls ideally at the end of the first quarter of 1788 and every 8.53 years thereafter; troughs fall ideally 4.26 years after crests. Typical amplitude averaged 6.4% above trend at ideal crest and 6% below trend at ideal trough.

Dewey, 1953-L. (Figure)
Dewey, 1954-L. (Figure)

150

A 9.20-year rhythmic cycle in Pig Iron Prices, U.S.A., 1784–1953, is
alleged.

Pig iron prices have fitted into a 9.20-year cycle pattern with crests falling
every 9.20 years since 1790 and with troughs falling every 4.6 years after
crests. Typical amplitude averaged 12.2% above trend at ideal crest and
10.9% below trend at ideal trough.

Dewey, 1953-L. (Figure)
Dewey, 1954-L. (Figure)

151

A figure, showing prices of pig iron, January 1951 through February 1956,
verified the continuance of the 9.2-year cycle.

Dewey, 1956-H. p. 146. (Figure)

152

A 16 2/3-year rhythmic cycle in Wrought Iron Prices, England, 1277–1918,
is alleged.

During the 642-year period under review, it was observed that the 16 2/3-
year cycle in wrought iron prices in England tended to conform to a perfectly regular pattern which repeated 38 times. Typical amplitude was recorded at 11% above trend at crest and 9.1% below trend at trough.

Dewey, 1955-A. p. 138.
Dewey, 1955-Q. (Figure)

153

A 17 3/4-year rhythmic cycle in Pig Iron Prices, U.S.A., 1784–1951, is
alleged.

Examination of pig iron prices revealed a series of waves which averaged
17 3/4 years in length. Typical timing placed a crest between 1814 and
1815 and every 17 3/4 years thereafter. Troughs followed the crests at
intervals of 8.9 years. Amplitude of this cycle has averaged 20.2% of trend
at ideal time of crest and 16.9% of trend at ideal time of trough.

Dewey, 1952-J. (Figure)

154

An 18-year rhythmic cycle in Pig Iron Prices, U.S.A., no dates given, is
alleged.

It was noted by Szatrowski that cyclical studies indicate that pig iron
prices tend to follow an 18-year pattern.

Szatrowski, 1949-A.

155

An 18 1/3-year rhythmic cycle in Pig Iron Prices, U.S.A., no dates given, is alleged.

An 18 1/3-year rhythm, for a period dating back to the latter part of the 18th Century, has been reflected to notable extent in the price of pig iron.

Klemme, 1950.

156

A 23-year rhythmic cycle in Pig Iron Prices, U.S.A., 1854–1924, is alleged.

Kuznets, 1930. p. 94.

LAMB PRICES

157

An 8–9-year rhythmic cycle in Lamb Prices, U.S.A., 1901–1929, is alleged.

"Lamb prices at Chicago adjusted for changes in the general price level tend to move in cycles. The first cycle shown extended over a period of eight years and the second one over a period of nine years...."

U.S.D.A. Yearbook of Agriculture, 1930. p. 587. (Figure)

LARD PRICES

158

A 6-year rhythmic cycle in Lard Prices, U.S.A., no dates given, is alleged.

Hoskins, 1939.

LEAD PRICES

159

A 4.43-year (53.16-month) rhythmic cycle in the Price of Lead, New York City, 1832–1960, is alleged.

The price of lead has been characterized by a 4.43-year cycle. This cycle has been overwhelmed by random forces from time to time, but of the 61 turning points since 1823, 40 have come within a year of ideal timing. Typical strength of the 4.43-year cycle has been 7.2% above trend at ideal time of crest and 6.7% below trend at ideal time of trough.

Shirk, 1960-I. (Figure)

LEATHER PRICES

160

A 15–18-month rhythmic cycle in Leather Prices, U.S.A., no dates given, is alleged.

Mack, 1958.

LEMON PRICES

161

A 25–30-year rhythmic cycle in Lemon Prices, California, 1924-25–1961-62, is alleged.

French and Bressler, 1962. p. 1035.

METAL PRICES
(also see individual metals by name)

162

A 15–18-month rhythmic cycle in Ferrous and Nonferrous Metal Prices, U.S.A., no dates given, is alleged.

Mack, 1958.

MILK PRICES

163

A 6-month rhythmic cycle in Milk Prices, U.S.A., no dates given, is alleged.

Cochrane, 1958. p. 76.

164

A 15-year rhythmic cycle in Milk Prices, U.S.A., 1880–1942, is alleged.

The price of milk has tended to move with the price of butter in an irregular cycle approximately 15 years long. This cycle has fluctuated about 10% above and below trend. Paarlberg also asserted that cyclical movements in the price of milk moved inversely to the number of cattle in the United States.

Paarlberg, 1947. (Figure)

MISCELLANEOUS PRICES

165

A 22.7-month (1.89-year) rhythmic cycle in the Price of an Unnamed Commodity, U.S.A., 1892–1941, is alleged.

The 22.7-month cycle in the price of a commodity (the company concerned would not permit the naming of the product) displayed great strength, but

it was mingled with waves of varying intervals so that the exact length or
significance could not be determined.

Dewey, 1951-W.

166

A 7.5-year average cycle in External Raw Materials Prices, United Kingdom, 1870—1914, is suggested.

Tinbergen, 1951. pp. 123—124.

167

A 60-year rhythmic cycle in Certain Industrial Prices, no locale cited, no
dates given, is alleged.

According to Chambers, certain significant industrial prices in industrial
nations have followed a long wave which spans up to 60 years.

Chambers, 1961. p. 50.

OAT PRICES
(also see GRAIN PRICES)

168

A 26.64-month (2.22-year) rhythmic cycle in Oat Prices, U.S.A., January
1923—May 1958, is alleged.

When the seasonal cycle was removed from the data studied, a 26.64-month
cycle in oat prices was uncovered. Typical amplitude of this cycle has
been 7.9% above trend at crest and 7.3% below trend at trough.

Shirk, 1958-G. (Figure)

169

In a subsequent article, it was noted that the price of oats followed the
ideal 26.64-month pattern 75% of the time from January 1923 through June
1960.

Shirk, 1960-Q. (Figure)

170

A graph exhibited the 26.64-month cycle in oat prices in combination with a
seasonal cycle. Data were extended through May 1961.

Shirk, 1961-J. (Figure)

171

A 4—11-year rhythmic cycle in Oat Prices, U.S.A., 1866—1929, is alleged.

Well-marked, although irregular, cycles have been observed in the price of
oats (average Illinois farm price). Peaks occurred in 1868, 1875, 1883,
1891, 1902, 1908, 1918—1920, and 1924. The intervals from peak to peak
were 7, 8, 8, 11, 6, 10, and 4, in order. The authors noted that there has

been a clearly marked tendency for the fluctuations in the price of oats to correspond to those of corn prices.

Norton and Wilson, 1930. pp. 499–502. (Figure; data)

PEA PRICES
(see GRAIN PRICES)

PEPPER PRICES

172

A 12–17-year rhythmic cycle in Pepper Prices, U.S.A., 1860–1940, is alleged.

An important characteristic of pepper prices is the tendency for alternate periods of high and low prices to succeed each other. The purchasing power of pepper (in terms of the 30 basic commodities) reached peaks in 1873, 1886, 1901, 1916, and 1928; lows were noted in 1880, 1896, 1909, 1922, and 1939. The cycle length has varied from 12 to 17 years, averaging about 14 years.

Pearson, Cassetta, and Bennett, 1941. p. 16. (Figure; data)

173

A 14.8-year rhythmic cycle in Black Pepper Prices, U.S.A., 1860–1945, is alleged.

There has been a tendency for the price of black pepper to follow a regular 14.8-year cycle.

Dewey and Dakin, 1947. p. 138. (Figure)

174

A 15 1/7-year rhythmic cycle in the Wholesale Prices of Black Pepper, New York City, 1818–1953, is alleged.

The length of the so-called 14.8-year cycle in black pepper prices, based on 43 additional years of data, was found to be, on the average, slightly longer than 14.8 years, namely 15 1/7 years.

Dewey, 1955-B. (Figure)

PIG IRON PRICES
(see IRON PRICES)

PIPE FITTINGS PRICES

175

Various rhythmic cycles (shortest length: 21 months) in Malleable Iron Pipe

Fittings Prices, March 1923—June 1951, are alleged.

An analysis of the price of malleable iron pipe fittings disclosed the possibility of four distinct cycles.

Cycle Length	Date of an Ideal Crest	Amplitude Above Trend
21-month	June 1925	5.2%
30-month	November 1924	7.2%
41-month	September 1924	7.2%
44-month	August 1926	6.4%

Dewey, 1951-B. and 1951-N. (Figure)
Dewey, 1953-V. (Figure)

PORK PRICES

176

A 4-year rhythmic cycle in Pork Prices, Germany, 1896—1930, is alleged.

With the exception of war and post-war years (1914—1924), the price of
pork in Germany showed a tendency to move in a cycle averaging 4 years
in length. Peaks were noted in 1898, 1902, 1906, 1910, 1914, ..., 1926,
and 1930; lows; in 1896, 1900, 1904, 1908, 1912, ..., 1924, and 1928.

Hanan, as quoted by Hrase, 1938.

177

A 4—5-year rhythmic cycle in Pork Prices, U.S.A., 1875—1940, is alleged.

An irregular 4—5-year cycle in the price of pork has been noted.

Paarlberg, 1947.

POTATO PRICES

178

A 2–3–4-year rhythmic cycle in Potato Prices, U.S.A., 1910—1956, is
alleged.

According to Cochrane, a "beautifully clear" 2-, 3-, or even 4-year cycle
was found in potato prices through 1940. It disappeared somewhat in the
1940's but re-emerged in the 1950's.

Cochrane, 1958. pp. 61, 69.

179

A 3-year average cycle in Potato Prices, U.S.A., 1913—1953, is alleged.

Although potato prices have been characterized by violent fluctuations, the
most repetitive pattern observed was a 3-year cycle with prices showing a

one-year rise and a two-year decline or a two-year rise and a one-year decline.

Pearson and Myers, 1955. p. 5215. (Figure)

POULTRY AND POULTRY PRODUCT PRICES
(also see EGG PRICES)

180

A 1–3-year rhythmic cycle in the Purchasing Power of Poultry, U.S.A., 1909–1943, is alleged.

The purchasing power of poultry in the United States has shown a tendency to move in cycles approximately 1–3 years in length. Poultry price cycles and hog price cycles move in the same direction almost 75% of the time, although poultry price cycles have been reported to change with 50% less violence than hog cycles.

Pearson and Myers, 1944.

181

A 3-year rhythmic cycle in Poultry Prices, U.S.A., no dates given, is alleged.

There has been a tendency for the price of chickens to move in cyclical swings averaging 3 years in length.

Morse, 1948.

182

A 6–18-year rhythmic cycle in Poultry Prices, U.S.A., no dates given, is alleged.

When measured from peak to peak, swings in the purchasing power of poultry have varied in length from 6 to 18 years.

Card, 1928.

183

An 8-year rhythmic cycle in Poultry and Poultry Product Prices, U.S.A., 1846–1935, is alleged.

The 8-year cycle in the purchasing power of poultry and poultry products has appeared as a secondary cycle in a 17-year rhythmic pattern.

Ronk. (Figure; data)

184

A 17-year rhythmic cycle in Poultry and Poultry Product Prices, U.S.A., 1846–1935, is alleged.

There has been a tendency for the cycle in the purchasing power of poultry and poultry products to average about 17 years in length.

Ronk. (Figure; data)

PURCHASING POWER

185

A 3–5-year rhythmic cycle in Purchasing Power per Capita, U.S.A., 1859–1930, is alleged.

Vial, in noting the year-to-year fluctuations of the purchasing power per capita in relation to the building cycle, suggested that there has been a shorter cycle (shorter than the 18-year average cycle) of 3 to 5 years duration superimposed on the longer cycle.

Vial, 1937.

186

An 18-year rhythmic cycle in Purchasing Power per Capita, U.S.A., 1859–1930, is alleged.

Vial noted that major changes in the purchasing power per capita have tended to fluctuate with, but not so violently as, the building cycle. Peaks in the 18-year cycle in the per capita purchasing power occurred during the periods 1868–1873, 1883–1893, 1905–1910, and 1923–1929.

Vial, 1937.

RICE PRICES

187

A 6-year rhythmic cycle in Rice Prices, U.S.A., 1910–1930, is alleged.

Campbell reported that the price of rice (farm price on December 1) has followed a definite cyclical trend, rising three years and falling three years.

Campbell, 1932. (Figure; data)

RYE PRICES
(see GRAIN PRICES)

SHEEP PRICES
(also see WOOL PRICES)

188

A 6–10-year rhythmic cycle in Sheep Prices, U.S.A., 1867–1929, is alleged.

Well-marked cycles which averaged 6 to 10 years in length became evident in this study of sheep prices. Peaks were reported in 1867, 1873, 1881–1883, 1893, 1901, 1907–1911, 1919, and, apparently, 1926–1929.

Norton and Wilson, 1930. pp. 543–544. (Figure; data)

189

A 6—11-year rhythmic cycle in Sheep Prices, U.S.A., 1868—1947, is alleged.

Hadorn stated that periods of rising prices in the price of sheep have regularly alternated with periods of falling prices. Peaks in the price of sheep (farm value on January 1) occurred in 1873, 1883, 1893, 1900, 1910, 1918, 1929, 1936, and 1943; lows, in 1869, 1879, 1886, 1895, 1904, 1912, 1922, 1933, 1939, and 1945. Intervals between peaks (and also between troughs) ranged from 6 to 11 years and averaged 8.4 years.

Hadorn, 1947. (Figure)

190

A 7—8-year rhythmic cycle in Sheep Prices, U.S.A., 1885—1940, is alleged.

Prior to World War I, the purchasing power of sheep fluctuated in a fairly regular 7—8-year cycle. From 1885 to 1912, three complete cycles occurred with peaks having been reached in 1892, 1899, and 1908. Since World War I, the cycle has become more erratic.

Hughes, 1940. (Figure)

191

A 7—10-year rhythmic cycle in Sheep Prices, U.S.A., no dates given, is alleged.

There has been a tendency for the price of sheep to move in a cyclical pattern approximately 7—10 years in length.

Morse, 1948.

192

A 7—12-year rhythmic cycle in Sheep Prices, U.S.A., no dates given, is alleged.

Ross, 1951.

193

An 8—10-year rhythmic cycle in Sheep Prices, U.S.A., 1885—1941, is alleged.

An 8—10-year cycle in the purchasing power of sheep (farm value on January 1) has been suggested by Pearson and Myers.

Pearson and Myers, 1941. (Figure)

194

A 9-year rhythmic cycle in Sheep Prices, U.S.A., 1880—1937, is alleged.

Largely independent of fluctuations in commodity prices, the price of sheep has displayed a tendency to move in waves 7 to 11 years (average 9 years) long.

Warren and Pearson, 1937. pp. 163—164, 170. (Figure)

195

A 9–10-year rhythmic cycle in Sheep Prices, U.S.A., 1910–1958, is alleged.

Ensminger, 1960. p. 692. (Figure)

196

An 11-year rhythmic cycle in Sheep Prices, U.S.A., 1867–1946, is alleged.

After eliminating price level fluctuations, Bond observed an average 11-year cycle in purchasing power of sheep. During the period from 1900 to 1946, peaks were recorded in 1908, 1918, 1929, and 1943. Lows were noted in 1903, 1912, 1922, and 1933.

Bond, 1946. p. 12. (Figure)

STEEL PRICES

197

A 7.5-year (90-month) rhythmic cycle in the Price of Steel (Finished Products), Belgium, 1880–1915, is alleged.

In francs per ton, the pre-war (World War I) price of finished steel products in Belgium evidenced a wave length of 7.5 years.

Kuznets, 1930. p. 144. (Figure)

STRAWBERRY PRICES

198

A 4–6-year rhythmic cycle in Strawberry Prices, U.S.A., 1918–1934, is alleged.

Thomsen uncovered a 4–6-year cycle in the price of strawberries during the period under observation. A chart revealed peaks occurring in 1920, 1926, and 1930–1931; lows, in 1924 and 1928.

Thomsen, 1936. p. 264. (Figure)

SUGAR PRICES

199

A 34-market-day rhythmic cycle in Raw Sugar Prices, U.S.A., year of 1934, is alleged.

A 34-market-day rhythm in raw sugar prices was reported by Dewey and Dakin who noted that this tendency persisted before and after 1934. This cycle also showed a tendency for every third wave to be of greater amplitude than the two which directly precede or follow.

Dewey and Dakin, 1947. p. 137. (Figure)

TEA PRICES

200

A 6–10-year rhythmic cycle in Tea Prices, U.S.A., 1850–1930, is alleged.

Using the method of successive elimination of waves, two cycles were evident in the price of tea. The first cycle varied from 6 to 10 years in length.

Gilboy, 1934. (Figure)

201

A 12–22-year rhythmic cycle in Tea Prices, U.S.A., 1850–1930, is alleged.

The 12–22-year cycle in the price of tea was the second rhythmic pattern found by Gilboy.

Gilboy, 1934. (Figure)

TEXTILE PRICES

202

A 15–18-month rhythmic cycle in Cotton Textile Prices, U.S.A., no dates given, is alleged.

Mack, 1958.

VETCH PRICES
(see GRAIN PRICES)

WHEAT PRICES
(also see GRAIN PRICES)

203

Various average cycles (shortest length: 2.735 years) in Wheat Prices, Europe, 1500–1869, are alleged.

Beveridge's periodogram analysis suggested 18 different cycles in the price of wheat. Those cycles have been listed below; the cycles to which he attributed special significance have been starred.

Cycle Length	Cycle Length	Cycle Length	Cycle Length
2.735 year	5.667 year*	11.000 year*	17.333 year*
3.417 year	5.933 year	12.000 year	20.000 year*
4.417 year	7.417 year	12.800 year*	36.000 year*
5.100 year*	9.750 year*	15.250 year*	54.000 year*
5.400 year*			68.000 year*

Beveridge, 1922. (Figure; data)

204

A 4—8-rhythmic cycle in Wheat Prices, U.S.A., 1866—1929, is alleged.

Irregular cycles have been evident in the price of wheat (average Illinois farm price adjusted for changes in the general price level). Intervals between peaks ranged from 4 to 8 years in length and peaks were reported in 1867—1868, 1873, 1877, 1881—1883, 1891, 1897, 1904, 1909, 1917—1920, and 1925.

Norton and Wilson, 1930. (Figure; data)

205

A 4.7-year (56.4-month) rhythmic cycle in Wheat Prices, U.S.A., 1858-59— 1952-53, is alleged.

A 4.7-year cycle has been found in wheat prices. This cycle crested ideally at January 1, 1896 and every 4.7 years forward and backward from that date. Typical amplitude of this cycle has been 14.3% above trend at time of ideal crest.

Dewey, 1953-U. (Figure)

206

A 5 1/2-year cycle in Wheat Prices, Great Britain, no dates given, is alleged.

DeLury reported that the price of wheat in the British Isles appeared to show the "double pulse" type of response to the sunspot cycle.

DeLury, 1938. pp. 47—48.

207

A 7.5-year (90-month) rhythmic cycle in Wheat Prices, U.S.A., 1858-59— 1951-52, is alleged.

The 7.5-year cycle in wheat prices has appeared to influence, but not to dominate, the stronger 9.3-year cycle. This cycle has shown an average amplitude of 9.9% above trend at time of ideal crest and 8.9% below trend at time of ideal trough.

Dewey, 1953-T. (Figure)

208

An 8-year rhythmic cycle in Wheat Prices, U.S.A., 1884—1930, is alleged.

Working found a cycle of approximately 8 years in length in the price of wheat. (Data for the war-time crop years from 1917—1918 to 1920—1921 were omitted.) Peaks were reported in 1890—1891, 1897—1898, 1904—1905, 1908—1909, and 1925—1926; lows, in 1886—1887, 1894—1895, 1901—1902, 1906—1907, 1912—1913, and 1922—1923.

Working, 1931. (Figure; data)

209

A 9.31-year rhythmic cycle in Wheat Prices, U.S.A., 1866-67—1951-52, is alleged.

There has been a tendency for the average annual price of wheat, during the 86-year period studied, to move in a cycle with a length of 9.31 years. A trough in the ideal pattern occurred in the crop year 1875—1876. Typical amplitude of the ideal cycle has been 17.5% above and below trend.

> Dewey, 1953-K. (Figure)
> Dewey, 1953-T.

210

Data were carried through June 1957. The actual behavior continued to follow the ideal cycle.

> Dewey, 1957-P. (Figure)

211

Follow-up articles on the 9.31-year cycle illustrated its continuance in the ideal pattern through 1960 and 1961 and 1962, a total period of 96 years. The 1960 article revealed that the actual low in wheat prices matched the ideal low in February 1960.

> Shirk, 1960-A. (Figure)
> Shirk, 1961-I.   (Figure)

212

Shirk noted in 1962 that the 9.3-year cycle was the most important of the three cycles (the others measuring 7.5 years and 4.7 years) so far isolated in wheat prices.

> Shirk, 1962-P. (Figure)

213

An 11-year rhythmic cycle in Wheat Prices, U.S.A., no dates given, is alleged.

A correlation between sunspot activity and the price of wheat was noted by Andrews.

> Andrews, 1936.

214

A 37-year rhythmic cycle in Wheat Prices, Western Europe, 1265—1700, is alleged.

Wheat prices in western Europe have appeared to vary directly with the amount of rainfall in a pattern often referred to as the Bruckner (or 37-year) cycle. Its waves range in length from 30 to 45 years.

> Clough, 1939. pp. 399—400.

215

A 54-year rhythmic cycle in Wheat Prices, England, 1260—1940, is alleged.

From 10-year averages of 680 years of data, the authors reported a strong
54-year cycle which repeated itself 13 1/2 times. To compensate for the
fact that, at the beginning of the period studied, the variation in actual
cents was very small, the price of wheat was charted graphically in percentages of trend.

Dewey and Dakin, 1947. pp. 70—73. (Figure)

216

Anent the 54-year cycle in European wheat prices, Dewey maintained that
the true length of this cycle may be 53 1/2 years. He noted that although
typical amplitude at time of an ideal crest averaged only 5%, that the wave
is very clear and definitized.

Dewey, 1962-E. (Figure)

217

An 84-year rhythmic cycle in Wheat Prices, England, 1259—1949, is alleged.

A persistent 84-year pattern in the price of wheat in England has been reported by Appel.

Appel, 1950.

218

A 106-year rhythmic cycle in Wheat Prices, England, 1259—1949, is alleged.

A major 106-year cycle in English wheat prices for a period of almost 700
years has been noted.

Appel, 1950.

WHOLESALE COMMODITY PRICES

219

A 1.92-year (23-month) rhythmic cycle in Wholesale Commodity Prices,
U.S.A., 1866—1914, is alleged.

Based on information furnished by the United States Department of Labor,
Frickey reported that wholesale prices in the United States moved in a
1.92-year cycle.

Frickey, 1935.

220

A 3—7-year rhythmic cycle in Wholesale Commodity Prices, U.S.A., 1790—
1957, is alleged.

Babson, 1959. pp. 194—195.

221

A 3.20-year (38.4-month) rhythmic cycle in Wholesale Commodity Prices, U.S.A., 1866–1914, is alleged.

From data presented in the *Review of Economic Statistics*, Frickey computed that wholesale prices have shown a tendency to move in cycles approximately 3.20 years in length.

Frickey, 1935.

222

A 3.33-year (40-month) rhythmic cycle in Wholesale Commodity Prices, U.S.A., and Great Britain, 1890–1922, is alleged.

Kitchin maintained that movements of wholesale prices, as well as general economic phenomena, are composed of (1) minor cycles averaging 3.33 years (40 months); (2) major cycles which are merely aggregates of two or three minor cycles; and (3) fundamental movements or trends.

Kitchin, 1923. (Figure)

223

A 4–5-year rhythmic cycle in Wholesale Commodity Prices, Portugal, 1750–1850, is alleged.

Godinho, 1955.

224

A 6-year average cycle in Wholesale Commodity Prices, Great Britain, 1870–1914, is suggested.

Tinbergen, 1951. p. 123.

225

A 6–10-year rhythmic cycle in Wholesale Commodity Prices, London, 1793–1893, is alleged.

According to Commons, the "credit cycle" which affected wholesale commodity prices, measured in gold, "made its rounds in 6 to 10 years."

Commons, 1893.

226

An 8-year rhythmic cycle in Wholesale Commodity Prices, Great Britain, 1850–1914, is alleged.

Wholesale commodity prices in Great Britain from 1850 through 1914 appeared to fluctuate in "long waves" which averaged approximately 8 years in length. The authors noted that the periods from 1850 through 1873 and 1896 through 1914 indicated six years of prosperity and two years of depression while the period from 1873 through 1896 indicated two years of prosperity and six years of depression.

Clough and Cole, 1952.

227

An 8-year rhythmic cycle in Wholesale Commodity Prices, England, 1818–
1921, is alleged.

Moore maintained that the origin of the 8-year cycle in wholesale prices in
England was caused by a lapse of 8 years between the return to "the maximum approach to a straight line" in the periodic conjunctions of the earth
and Venus with the sun.

Moore, 1923. p. 97.

228

An 8–9-year rhythmic cycle in Wholesale Commodity Prices, no locale
cited, 1830–1916, is alleged.

Mitchell quoted *Teknisk Tidskrift* (Veckoupplagen, 1916) as having found
an 8–9-year rhythmic cycle in wholesale commodity prices and several
other series of economic data.

Mitchell, 1927.

229

A 9-year rhythmic cycle in Wholesale Commodity Prices, U.S.A., England,
is alleged.

A strong 9-year cycle has been prominent in wholesale prices for the period
1830 through 1945.

Dewey and Dakin, 1947. pp. 92–94. (Figure)

230

Dewey stated that the 9-year cycle in wholesale prices has been distorted
since 1945 because of price controls during World War II and of the presence
of concurrent cycles with lengths close to that of 9 years. He illustrated,
using data from 1912 through 1953, that it makes little difference whether or
not the values of wholesale prices are adjusted to a gold basis when the cycles have short durations.

Dewey, 1954-N. p. 38. (Figure)

231

Davis felt that the 9-year cycle in wholesale commodity prices, uncovered
by means of a periodogram analysis, which exhibited considerable energy,
was real and influenced price changes.

Davis, 1941. p. 305.

232

Moore observed from Sauerbeck's Index of English wholesale commodity
prices that a minor cycle of approximately 9 years (or perhaps 8.7 years)
appeared to influence price fluctuations in England during the period
from 1818 through 1913.

Moore, 1923. p. 66.

233

George McCormack, according to Williams, noted a correlation between the 9-year cycle of the moon's maximum declination and the 9-year cycle in wholesale commodity prices in the United States.

McCormack, 1947, as reported by Williams, 1947.

234

A 9.2-year rhythmic cycle in Wholesale Commodity Prices, composite data for U.S.A., Great Britain, and Germany, 1818–1910, is alleged.

Employing data compiled by Schumpeter, Huntington reported that the wholesale commodity price cycle for three countries (U.S.A., Great Britain, and Germany) moved in waves approximately 9.2 years in length. Figures after 1910 were not employed because of World War I distortion.

Huntington, 1945. pp. 485–486. (Figure)

235

Various rhythmic cycles (shortest length: 10 years) in Wholesale Commodity Prices, U.S.A., 1790–1920, are alleged.

A graph illustrated the possibility of three cycles (10-, 22-, and 50-year) in wholesale prices in the United States.

Schumpeter, 1939. p. 469. (Figure)

236

An 11-year rhythmic cycle in Commodity Prices, United States, Great Britain and Ireland, is alleged.

An 11-year cycle in wholesale commodity prices in the United States (no dates given) was suggested by Andrews who correlated this cycle with the cycle dominating sunspot activity.

Andrews, 1936.

237

Commodity prices in Great Britain and Ireland, 1784–1869, have exhibited a response to the sunspot cycle in inverse phase with a lag of a year.

DeLury, 1938. p. 47.

238

A 13-year rhythmic cycle in Wholesale Commodity Prices, Portugal, 1750–1850, is alleged.

Godinho, 1955.

239

A 13-year rhythmic cycle in Wholesale Commodity Prices, U.S.A., 1831–1930, is alleged.

By means of a periodogram analysis, Davis found a hint of a 13-year (minor) cycle in wholesale commodity prices in the United States.

Davis, 1941. p. 304.

240

An 18–22-year rhythmic cycle in Wholesale Commodity Prices, Cincinnati, 1816–1861, is alleged.

Berry, 1943. (Figure; data)

241

A 19-year rhythmic cycle in Wholesale Commodity Prices, England, 1818–1913, is alleged.

A periodogram of Sauerbeck's Index numbers of English wholesale prices over the period from 1818 through 1918 indicated the presence of a minor cycle approximately 19 years in length.

Moore, 1923. p. 66.

242

A 40–50-year rhythmic cycle in Wholesale Commodity Prices, Germany, 1825–1920, is alleged.

Trough years in price movements in Germany for the period under observation appeared in 1826, 1873, and 1913 while peak years were dated at 1850 and 1895 by DeWolff.

DeWolff, 1924. As quoted by Wagemann, 1930.

243

A 50-year rhythmic cycle in Wholesale Commodity Prices, Great Britain, 1818–1913, is alleged.

Moore, using a periodogram analysis of Sauerbeck's Index, noted an "obvious" 50-year cycle in wholesale commodity prices in Great Britain. Moore also observed minor cycles of 9 years and 19 years duration.

Moore, 1923. p. 66. (Figure; data)

244

A 50-year rhythmic cycle in Wholesale Commodity Prices, U.S.A., is alleged.

Wholesale commodity prices in the United States from the Napoleonic Wars to 1932 have displayed a tendency to move in cycles averaging approximately

50 years. Babson noted that such prices generally rise for about 30 years, then fall for 20 years.

Babson, 1932. pp. 143—144.

245

Peaks in a 50-year pattern which seemed to be present in commodity prices in the United States occurred at 1815, 1865, and 1920; troughs, at 1849 and 1896.

Bratt, 1937. p. 94.

246

Wholesale commodity prices in the United States for the period 1797—1940 have appeared to follow a 50-year cyclical pattern. Although only three such cycles have been observed in modern data (peaks occurring at November 1814, August 1864, and May 1920), Davis noted that it appears that the pattern could be traced as far back as the Punic Wars in international wholesale commodity prices. Minor cycles appeared at 9- and 13-year intervals.

Davis, 1941. pp. 13, 304—305, 468—469. (Figure)

247

Prices in the United States moved in 40—70-year waves, according to Hamberg. The average duration of the cyclic pattern was 50 years.

Hamberg, 1951. p. 9.

248

According to Kirkbride, waves approximately "half a century" in length have dominated wholesale commodity prices in the United States for the period from 1776 through 1939. Peaks occurred in 1814, 1864, and 1920. Kirkbride correlates this cycle with the pattern followed by his "Great War Cycle."

Kirkbride, 1939. (Figure)

249

Wallace asserted that a 50-year cycle (a "cycle of the generations") was present in wholesale commodity prices in the United States.

Wallace, 1934. p. 228.

250

A 50—60-year rhythmic cycle in Wholesale Commodity Prices, England, France, and U.S.A., varying dates, is alleged.

Kondratieff, 1926. pp. 105—107. (Figure)

251

A 50—60-year rhythmic cycle in Wholesale Commodity Prices, U.S.A.,

1790—1957, is alleged.

In addition to the short term movements of 3—7 years in wholesale commodity prices in the United States from 1790 through 1957, a long term movement of between 50 and 60 years was noted. Lows, according to Babson, occurred in 1783, 1848, 1898, and 1933; peaks, in 1809, 1865, 1920, and 1950.

Babson, 1959. pp. 194—195.

252

A 50—60-year rhythmic cycle in Wholesale Commodity Prices, U.S.A. and Great Britain, 1790—1930, is alleged.

Estey, 1941. p. 18.

253

A 50—60-year rhythmic cycle in Wholesale Commodity Prices, Germany, no dates given, is alleged.

Wagemann, 1940. p. 70. As cited by Bernstein, 1940. p.534.

254

A 54-year rhythmic cycle in Wholesale Commodity Prices, worldwide, 1260—1938, is alleged.

International wholesale commodity prices have shown the tendency to "closely follow a 54-year cycle since the year 1260, but, during the past 150 years, this has varied from 51 to 55 years."

Davies, 1938.

255

A 54-year rhythmic cycle in Wholesale Commodity Prices, U.S.A., 1790—1945, is alleged.

Wholesale commodity prices have shown a tendency to follow a 54-year cyclical pattern. This cycle becomes more evident when war periods are omitted. Ideal crests were recorded in 1817, 1871, and 1925; ideal lows, in 1790, 1844, 1898, and 1952.

Dewey and Dakin, 1947. pp. 70—71. (Figure)

256

Klemme noted a 54-year rhythmic cycle in wholesale commodity prices in the United States.

Klemme, 1950.

257

A 54-year rhythmic cycle in Wholesale Commodity Prices, England, 13th Century—1950, is alleged.

For over 7 centuries, wholesale commodity prices in England have tended to follow a 54-year pattern.

Klemme, 1950.

258

A 56-year rhythmic cycle in Wholesale Commodity Prices, U.S.A., is alleged.

Wholesale commodity prices, during the period from 1890 through 1935, have been dominated by a 56-year cycle. Peaks occurred in 1812, 1864, and 1920.

McGrath, 1936.

259

Williams reported that wholesale commodity prices in the United States from 1761 through 1948 have shown a tendency to move in cycles averaging 56 years in length. Peaks were noted in 1779, 1864, 1920, and 1948.

Williams, 1947. (1948 postscript added.) p. 3.

260

An 84-year rhythmic cycle in Wholesale Commodity Prices, U.S.A., 1749–1949, is alleged.

According to Appel, the 84-year cycle is one of two rhythms which account for the major movements in wholesale commodity prices in the United States. Peaks of this cycle occurred in 1780, 1864, and 1948.

Appel, 1950. (Figure)

261

A 106-year rhythmic cycle in Wholesale Commodity Prices, U.S.A., 1749–1949, is alleged.

The 106-year cycle along with the 84-year cycle join together to form the major wholesale commodity price pattern in the United States. Peaks of this 106-year cycle occurred in 1814 and 1920.

Appel, 1950. (Figure)

WOOL PRICES
(also see SHEEP PRICES)

262

A 2–6-year rhythmic cycle in Wool Prices, U.S.A., 1900–1929, is alleged.

Domestic wool prices (adjusted for changes in the all-commodity price level at Boston) displayed a tendency to follow a 2–6-year pattern. Peaks were recorded in 1905, 1909, 1912, 1915, 1917–1918, 1924, and 1928; lows, in 1901–1902, 1908, 1911, 1913, 1916, 1920–1921, and 1926–1927.

U.S.D.A. Yearbook of Agriculture, 1930. p. 587. (Figure)

263

A 9-year rhythmic cycle in Wool Prices, U.S.A., 1870—1935, is alleged.

Wool prices have appeared to experience cyclical fluctuations that inversely correspond with the apparent sheep production cycle. This cycle in wool prices averaged 9 years in length and Thomsen noted peaks occurring in 1872, 1880, 1892, 1900, 1907, 1918, 1924, and 1933.

Thomsen, 1936. p. 384.

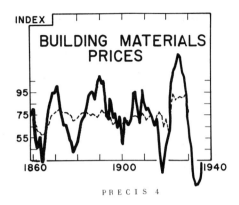

PRECIS 4

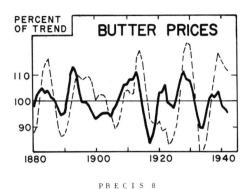

PRECIS 8

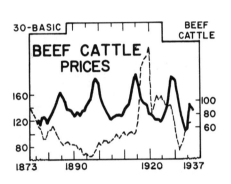

PRECIS 23

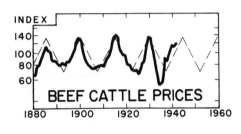

PRECIS 26

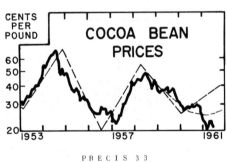

PRECIS 33

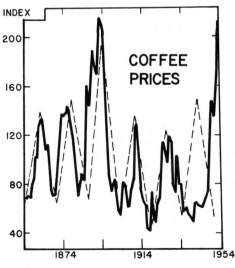

PRECIS 37

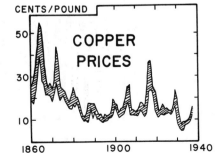

PRECIS 43

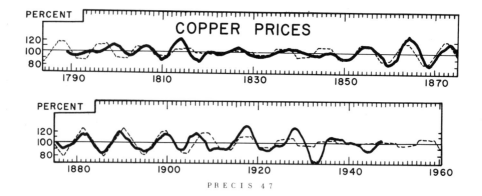

PRECIS 47

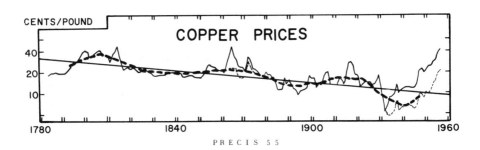

PRECIS 55

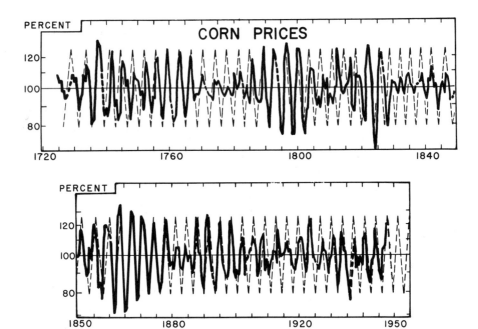

PRECIS 57

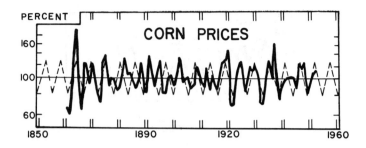

PRECIS 61

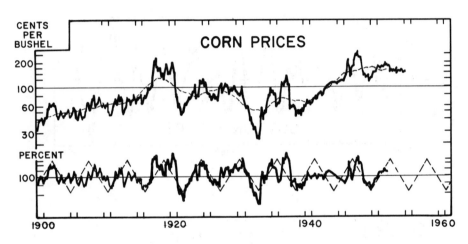

PRECIS 62

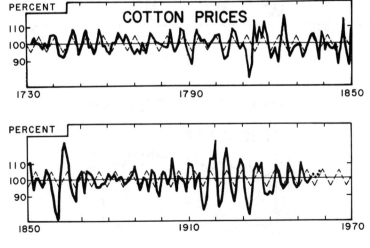

PRECIS 70

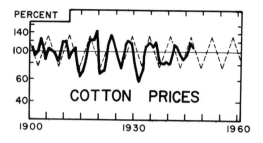

PRECIS 71

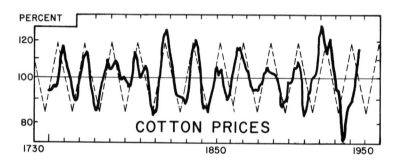

PRECIS 84

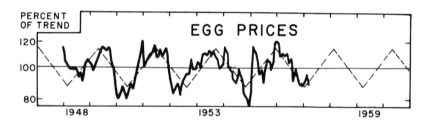

PRECIS 88

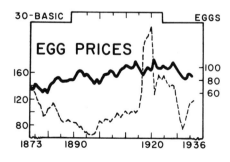

PRECIS 95

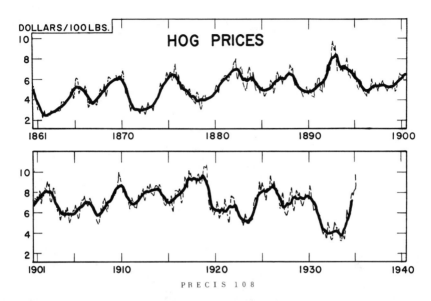

HOG PRICES

DOLLARS/100 LBS.

PRECIS 108

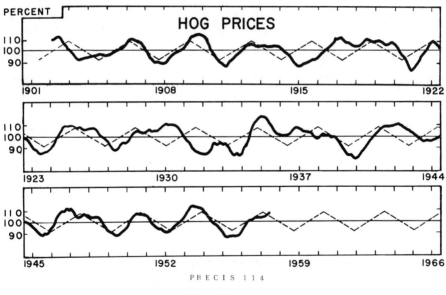

HOG PRICES

PERCENT

PRECIS 114

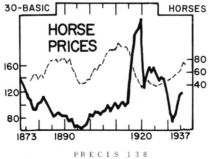

30-BASIC

HORSES

HORSE PRICES

PRECIS 138

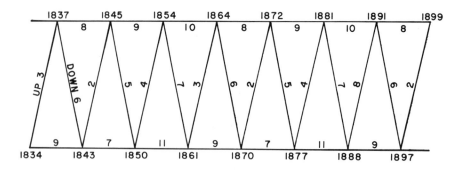

PRECIS 144

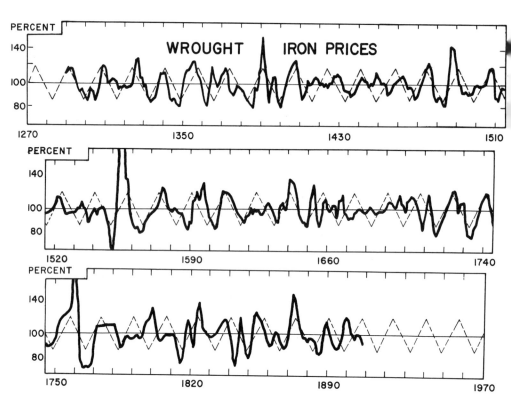

PRECIS 152

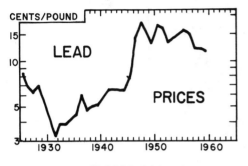

PRECIS 159

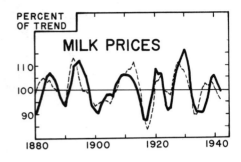

PRECIS 164

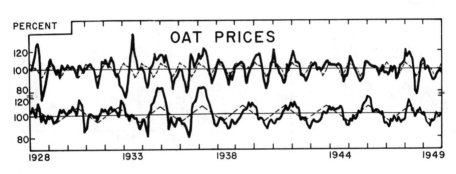

PRECIS 168

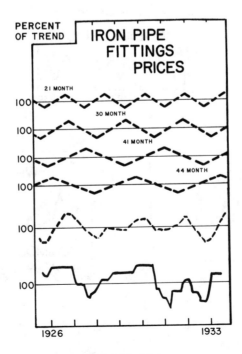

PRECIS 175

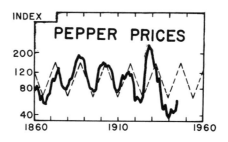

PRECIS 173

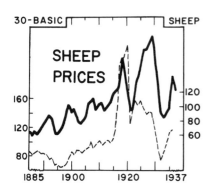

PRECIS 194

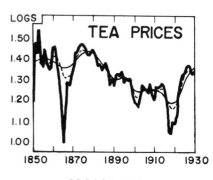

PRECIS 200

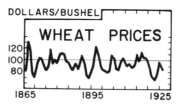

PRECIS 204

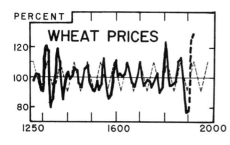

PRECIS 215

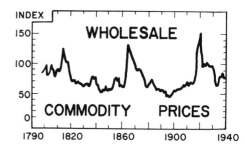

PRECIS 246

STOCK PRICES

STOCK PRICES

264

A 20-hour rhythmic cycle in Stock Prices, U.S.A., no dates given, is alleged.

According to Seager, the 20-hour cycle in American stock prices is the old 21-hour cycle, the length of which has varied because of the changes in trading hours.

Seager, 1962.

265

A 17-market-day rhythmic cycle in Combined Stock Prices, U.S.A., October 5, 1957—December 28, 1957, is alleged.

This short stock market cycle (New York Times Daily Averages of 50 Combined Stocks) appears to be about 17 market sessions in length.

Seager, 1958. (Figure)

266

Various rhythmic cycles (shortest length: 28 days) in Stock Prices, U.S.A., no dates given, are suggested.

Rhythmic waves which measure 28 days, 13 weeks, 26 weeks, 39 weeks, and 200 days were suggested by Seager as being possible influences in American stock prices.

Seager, 1962.

267

A 6.55-week (45.86-day) rhythmic cycle in Consorcio Stock Prices, Bogota, Columbia, April 1951—February 1953, is alleged.

Fifteen dominant and regular repetitions of a 45 6/7-day cycle appeared in this study of the price of Consorcio stock. A crest in the ideal pattern fell on February 6, 1953.

Grand, as reported by Dewey, 1953-I. (Figure)
Dewey, 1953-W. p. 230.

268

A 6.8—7.1-week rhythmic cycle in Stock Prices, U.S.A., 1919—1924, is alleged.

The 6.8—7.1-week cycle in common stock prices (Standard Statistics Index) was discovered by Blackett and Wilson by means of their "Bracket Analysis" system. This cycle was one of three sinusoidal components within the series and was the shortest of the waves uncovered.

Blackett and Wilson, 1936–1938. (Figure)

269

Various rhythmic cycles (shortest length: 2.975 months) in Industrial Stock Prices, U.S.A., are alleged.

A study of the Cowles Commission Index figures for the years 1871–1943 and the Clement Burgess Index for the years 1854–1870 suggested waves of many different lengths. Some of the more important have been listed below.

Cycle Length	Cycle Length	Cycle Length	Cycle Length
2.975-month	18.17-month	4.89-year	11.0-year
8.00 -month	24.25-month	5.50-year	12.0-year
8.80 -month	29.28-month	6.07-year	14.5-year
10.95 -month	31.00-month	6.86-year	21.0-year
14.40 -month	3.40-year	8.17-year	
17.17 -month	3.79-year	9.2 -year	

Dewey, 1951-E. pp. 85–88.

270

Overall amplitude of the ideal pattern and ideal timing for the 10 longer (over 4 1/2 years) cycles listed above was published.

Cycle Length	Overall Amplitude	Timing of Ideal Crest
4.89-year	7.0%	1949
5.50-year	14.0%	1946–1947
6.07-year	12.0%	1947–1948
6.86-year	16.6%	1950
8.17-year	16.4%	1945–1946
9.2 -year	34.4%	1946
11.0 -year	7.6%	1952
12.0 -year	30.2%	1951
14.5 -year	24.5%	1957
21.0 -year	34.0%	1950

Dewey, 1951-V. (Figure)
Dewey, 1951-R. (Figure)

271

A 12.31-week (2.83-month) rhythmic cycle in General Motors Common Stock, U.S.A., January 1948–February 1962, is alleged.

Shirk discovered a "small but fairly regular and persistent cycle" in the price of General Motors common stock during the period under observation. This cycle displayed an amplitude of 1% above trend at time of an ideal crest. A crest in the ideal pattern was dated at the middle of the week of February 16, 1962 and every 12.31 weeks before and after that date.

Shirk, 1962-L. (Figure)

272

A 12.9–14.4-week rhythmic cycle in Stock Prices, U.S.A., 1919–1924, is alleged.

The 12.9–14.4-week cycle in common stock prices (Standard Statistics Index) was one of the three sinusoidal components discovered by Blackett and Wilson through their "Bracket Analysis" system. This cycle was the least stable of the three — the cycle would show marked prominence for a period of approximately three years and then completely disappear for a period of time.

Blackett and Wilson, 1936–1938. (Figure)

273

Various average cycles (shortest length: 13.04 weeks) in Industrial Stock Prices, U.S.A., October 1945–June 1951, are alleged.

Various cycles and their amplitudes and timings derived from a quarterly average of the Dow-Jones Industrials were published in Predix Plate II. The study refined original published work by adding the following cycles to the synthesis:

Cycle Length	Cycle Length	Cycle Length
13.04-week (0.25-year)	34.96-week (0.67-year)	57.40-week (1.10-year)
24.21-week (0.464-year)	39.13-week (0.75-year)	63.14-week (1.21-year)
26.09-week (0.50-year)	49.57-week (0.95-year)	74.09-week (1.42-year)
32.25-week (0.62-year)		

Predix Plate II, 1951. (Figure)

274

A 16.39-week (3.77-month) rhythmic cycle in Industrial Stock Prices, U.S.A., 1928–1937, is suggested.

The varying length of the so-called 17-week cycle in industrial stock prices may be due to the presence of one or more cycles of closely related wave length. A 16.39-week cycle appears to be one of the cycles that may be causing the distortion.

Dewey, 1958-C. p. 263.

275

A 17-week (3.91-month) rhythmic cycle in Combined Stock Prices, U.S.A., January 1956–December 1957, is alleged.

There has been a tendency for stock prices (New York Times Daily Averages

of 50 Combined Stocks) to move in a cycle about 17 weeks long. "Old-
timers," according to Seager, call this "the cycle of 84-day tops."

Seager, 1958. (Figure)

276

A 17-week (3.91-month) rhythmic cycle in Industrial Stock Prices, U.S.A.,
1938—1947, 1947—1958, is alleged.

The 17-week cycle in industrial stock prices (Standard and Poor's Corporation Industrial Stock Price Index), although not dominant and often irregular, persisted throughout the two ten-year periods studied. This cycle displayed an amplitude of 1.2% of trend at time of ideal crest and 1.1% of
trend at time of ideal trough. A crest in the ideal pattern occurred March
19, 1958.

Shirk, 1958-C. (Figure)
Shirk, 1958-D. (Figure)

277

A 17.1-week (3.93-month) rhythmic cycle in Industrial Stock Prices, U.S.A.,
1873—1961, is alleged.

Industrial stock prices in the United States for the 87 years under observation appeared to move in a 17.1-week cycle which, according to Seager,
was checked and verified to have a record of consistent performance.

Seager, 1962.

278

A 17.12-week (3.94-month) rhythmic cycle in Industrial Stock Prices, U.S.A.,
is alleged.

Further study, using 10 additional years on data, of the 17-week cycle in
industrial stock prices (Standard and Poor's Corporation Industrial Stock
Price Index, 1928—1957), indicated that this cycle averaged a little longer
than 17 weeks, namely 17.12 weeks. The strength of the 17.12-week cycle
was 1.4% above trend at time of ideal crest. Its varying length appeared
to be due to the presence of one or more cycles of closely related wave
length.

Dewey, 1958-C. (Figure)

279

Dewey reported that several independent researchers had found a cycle of
about this length in industrial stock prices and that Alex von Reuter had
traced one such cycle back to 1890.

Dewey, 1959-D.

280

A *Cycles* reader, D. S. Castle, suggested that the 17.12-week cycle might
be a member of the 17.75-year complex.

Castle, 1959.

281

A 17.17-week (3.95-month) rhythmic cycle in Industrial Stock Prices, U.S.A., 1897–1959, is alleged.

By using weekly figures of Dow-Jones Industrial Stock Price Averages from January 8, 1879, Dewey refined the length of the 17.2-week cycle in industrial stock prices to a quarter-of-a-day longer, or 17.17 weeks. From 1897 to 1959, there were 192 repetitions of this cycle, and of the actual highs noted, 138 came within five weeks of the ideal timing. This wave length appears to be somewhat irregular; it has consistently shown a tendency to be alternately longer or shorter than 17 1/6 weeks. Other variations of wave length and amplitude were noted but not studied.

Dewey, 1960-D. (Figure)
Dewey, 1960-E. (Figure)
Shirk, 1960-K. (Figure)

282

Data were carried through July 1961.

Shirk, 1961-S. (Figure)

283

A 17.63-week (4.05-month) rhythmic cycle in Westinghouse Electric Stock Prices, U.S.A., 1952–1960, is alleged.

A 17.63-week cycle in Westinghouse common stock prices was isolated. Typical amplitude of this cycle was recorded as 1.4% above trend at time of ideal crest and 1.4% below trend at time of ideal trough. The 17.63-week cycle operated in addition to, or in combination with, a 32-week cycle.

Shirk, 1961-D. (Figure)

284

The 17.63-week and the 32-week cycles along with the trend in the average weekly price of Westinghouse stock were plotted through January of 1962. They appeared to be closely following the ideal pattern.

Shirk, 1962-G. (Figure)

285

Various average cycles (shortest length: 5.1 months) in Industrial Stock Prices, U.S.A., 1871–1950, are suggested.

Six multiple harmonic analyses of industrial common stock prices (Standard and Poor's Corporation Industrial Stock Price Index) were made which included one analysis of the series as a whole, three analyses of the series by thirds, and two analyses of the last third of the series by sixths. From this information, periodograms were constructed. The 110 possible wave lengths which were suggested by this method were published which also included, for comparison, wave lengths of railroad stock prices suggested by an earlier periodogram. No allegations of statistical significance were made concerning any of the suggested lengths.

Entire Series Mo.	1st Third Mo.	2nd Third Mo.	3rd Third Mo.	5th Sixth Mo.	6th Sixth Mo.	Entire Series Mo.	1st Third Mo.	2nd Third Mo.	3rd Third Mo.	5th Sixth Mo.	6th Sixth Mo.
				5.1	5.1		35.6		36.2		
				5.3	5.3				39.0		
				5.6	5.6		41.6	41.6			
					5.8				43.0		
				6.0	5.9	46.6			46.7		
				6.4	6.3	48.6					
				6.5							
				6.8	6.7						
				7.5	7.6						
				7.8		Yrs.	Yrs.	Yrs.	Yrs.	Yrs.	Yrs.
				8.0	8.1	4.2	4.2		4.2		
				8.5	8.3	4.3					
				9.2	9.2	4.4					
					9.3	4.5					
					9.9						
	10.6		10.5	10.3	10.2	4.8		4.8			
	10.8	10.9	10.7			4.9					
	11.1		11.1	11.2							
	11.5	11.5		11.4	11.6	5.3					
	12.0	12.1	11.9		11.9	5.4					
	12.5	12.6									
		12.9	12.8						5.7		
	13.1	13.2	13.6	13.1	13.3						
	13.7	13.9	13.8			6.0	6.1				
	14.4	14.5	14.5								
	14.6	14.9	14.7								
	15.3		15.5			7.0					
	16.4	16.8									
	17.3		17.8								
	18.3	18.7	18.7			7.9					
	19.6	19.6					8.5	8.2	8.5		
	21.6					9.3					
		22.2	22.7			10.8			10.7		
	23.7	23.2	23.7			11.3					
			24.3				12.7				
		24.9	23.9			13.1					
	25.8					13.6					
		27.8									
	28.6		29.1			17.8					
		30.5	30.2			19.1					
	31.2							24.2	24.2		
		34.2	34.2			25.8					

Malinowski, as reported by Dewey, 1952-G. (Figure)

286

A 26.6–32.4-week rhythmic cycle in Stock Prices, U.S.A., 1919–1924, is
alleged.

The 26.6–32.4-week cycle in common stock prices (Standard Statistics Index) was the longest, most persistent, and strongest of the three sinusoidal
components revealed through the "Bracket Analysis" system by Blackett
and Wilson.

Blackett and Wilson, 1936–1938. (Figure)

287

A 27.41-week (6.33-month) average cycle in Industrial Stock Prices, U.S.A.,
1871–1953, is alleged.

One of the short-term cycles that has seemingly been present in industrial
common stock prices (Standard and Poor's Corporation Industrial Stock
Price Index) has been a 6.33-month cycle. A trough in the ideal pattern
was dated at mid-May 1871. The over-all amplitude of the 6.33-month cycle
is about 1.1% of trend from time of ideal trough to time of ideal crest or
from time of ideal crest to time of ideal trough.

Dewey, 1953-S.

288

A 27.84-week (6.41-month) average cycle in Industrial Common Stock Prices,
U.S.A., 1871–1953, is alleged.

A survey of stock market prices (Standard and Poor's Corporation Industrial
Stock Price Index) revealed that the 6.41-month cycle in industrial common
stock prices appeared to be the most important of those in the general area
of 6 months. The 6.41-month cycle crested ideally in May 1871 and every
6.41 months thereafter.

Dewey, 1953-R.

289

A 32-week (7.36-month) rhythmic cycle in Westinghouse Electric Common
Stock Prices, U.S.A., 1951–1960, is alleged.

A 32-week cycle in the price of Westinghouse Electric common stock has
appeared to persist with regularity for the period 1951 through 1960. Typical amplitude of this cycle has been 3.5% of trend at time of ideal crest
and 3.4% of trend at time of ideal trough. The week that ended November
11, 1960 dated a trough in the ideal pattern.

Shirk, 1961-G. (Figure; data)

290

A 34-week (7.82-month) rhythmic cycle in Industrial Stock Prices, U.S.A.,
1927–1959, is alleged.

A possible 34-week cycle in industrial stock prices was uncovered by

Dewey in a preliminary examination of Standard and Poor's Weekly Index of Industrial Stock Prices. Shirk reported that several readers of *Cycles* had also found a cycle of this length in the prices of individual issues and in the Dow-Jones Industrial Stock Price Averages. The 34-week designation was purely an average as the length varied. Data examined seemed to suggest a length of about 33.87 weeks. Shirk asserted that additional work was needed for an exact determination of length, strength, and timing.

Shirk, 1960-J. (Figure)

291

An 8-month (34.78-week) rhythmic cycle in Industrial Stock Prices, U.S.A., 1941–1948, is alleged.

During the period under observation, 1941–1948, industrial stock prices appeared to be influenced by an 8-month cycle.

Tripp, 1948.

292

An 8-month (34.78-week) average cycle in Air Transportation Stock Prices, U.S.A., January 7, 1939–September 29, 1961, is suggested.

Power spectrum analysis revealed the possibility of an 8-month cycle in air transportation stock prices for the period from January 7, 1939 through September 29, 1961.

Granger and Morgenstern, 1963. p. 21.

293

An 8-month (34.78-week) average cycle in the Stock Prices of American Can Company, U.S.A., January 1946–December 1960, is suggested.

Using power spectrum analysis, Granger and Morgenstern found the possibility of an 8-month average cycle in the stock prices of American Can Company from January 1946 through December 1960.

Granger and Morgenstern, 1963. p. 22.

294

An 8-month (34.78-week) average cycle in Stock Prices of Durable Goods Manufactured, U.S.A., January 7, 1939–September 29, 1961, is suggested.

Power spectrum analysis of the stock prices of durable goods manufactured in the United States from January 7, 1939 through September 29, 1961 revealed the possibility of an 8-month cycle.

Granger and Morgenstern, 1963. p. 21.

295

An 8-month (34.78-week) average cycle in the Stock Prices of Chrysler

Corporation, U.S.A., January 1946—December 1960, is suggested.

Power spectrum analysis of the stock prices of Chrysler Corporation from January 1946 through December 1960 revealed the possibility of an 8-month cycle.

Granger and Morgenstern, 1963. p. 22.

296

An 8-month (34.78-week) average cycle in General Transportation Stock Prices, U.S.A., January 7, 1939—September 29, 1961, is suggested.

The possibility of an 8-month cycle in general transportation stock prices in the United States for the period under observation was suggested by Granger and Morgenstern, using power spectrum analysis as a tool.

Granger and Morgenstern, 1963. p. 21.

297

An 8-month (34.78-week) average cycle in Railroad Stock Prices, U.S.A., January 7, 1939—September 29, 1961, is suggested.

The possibility of an 8-month cycle in railroad stock prices in the United States for the period under observation was revealed by means of power spectrum analysis.

Granger and Morgenstern, 1963. p. 21.

298

An 8-month (34.78-week) average cycle in Stock Prices of General Manufactures, U.S.A., January 7, 1939—September 29, 1961, is suggested.

Using power spectrum analysis as a tool, Granger and Morgenstern found a suggestion of an 8-month average cycle in the stock prices of general manufactures in the United States from January 7, 1939 through September 29, 1961.

Granger and Morgenstern, 1963. p. 21.

299

An 8-month (34.78-week) average cycle in Industrial Stock Prices, U.S.A., January 1915—January 1958, is suggested.

Power spectrum analysis of the Dow-Jones Industrial Stock Price Index, January 1915 through January 1958, revealed a possible 8-month cycle.

Granger and Morgenstern, 1963. p. 23.

300

An 8-month (34.78-week) average cycle in Industrial Stock Prices, U.S.A.,

January 7, 1939—September 29, 1961, is suggested.

Composite stock prices as recorded by the Securities and Exchange Commission Index (300 stocks in 32 industrial groups) when analyzed by power
spectrum analysis indicated the presence of an 8-month cycle.

Granger and Morgenstern, 1963. p. 21.

301

An 8-month (34.78-week) average cycle in Mining Stock Prices, U.S.A., January 7, 1939—September 29, 1961, is suggested.

Power spectrum analysis revealed the possibility of an 8-month cycle in
mining stock prices in the United States for the period under observation.

Granger and Morgenstern, 1963. p. 21.

302

An 8-month (34.78-week) average cycle in Non-Durable Goods Stock Prices,
U.S.A., January 7, 1939—September 29, 1961, is suggested.

Using power spectrum analysis as a tool, Granger and Morgenstern found
the possibility of an 8-month average cycle in stock prices for non-durable
manufactured goods for the period under observation.

Granger and Morgenstern, 1963. p. 21.

303

An 8-month (34.78-week) average cycle in Radio, Television, and Communications Stock Prices, U.S.A., January 7, 1939—September 29, 1961, is suggested.

Power spectrum analysis of radio, television and communications stock
prices in the United States from January 7, 1939 through September 29, 1961
revealed the possibility of an 8-month cyclic pattern.

Granger and Morgenstern, 1963. p. 21.

304

An 8-month (34.78-week) average cycle in Stock Prices, U.S.A., 1875—1952,
is suggested.

Power spectrum analysis of Standard and Poor Series, 1875—1952, revealed
an 8-month component which the authors felt "was invariably of some importance."

Granger and Morgenstern, 1963. pp. 13, 23.

305

An 8-month (34.78-week) average cycle in the Stock Prices of United States
Steel Corporation, U.S.A., January 1946—December 1960, is suggested.

The possibility of an 8-month cycle in the stock prices of United States
Steel Corporation for the period under observation was revealed by means
of power spectrum analysis.

Granger and Morgenstern, 1963. p. 22.

306

Various rhythmic cycles (shortest length: 8.2 months) in Railroad Stock
Prices, U.S.A., 1900—1955, are alleged.

In 1912, a forecast of railroad stock prices was made on the basis of four
periodicities (8.2-month, 14.45-month, 41-month, and 20-year). This material was projected by Dewey using Standard and Poor's Corporation Index
of Railroad Stock Prices. The conformation of the actual cycle to a projection of the ideal cycle was quite accurate. Typical timing and amplitude of
those cycles are listed below.

Cycle Length	Time of an Ideal Crest	Typical Amplitude
8.2-month	Mid-March 1909	7
14.45-month	September 1902	11
20.0-month	July 1908	45
41.0-month	July 1909	27

Dewey, 1952-O. (Figure)

307

A 9-month-and-longer rhythmic cycle in Stock Prices, U.S.A., 1937—1949,
is alleged.

Using Standard and Poor's Corporation Common Stock Price Index, Szatrowski found that a 9-month-and-longer cycle has been one of the "three dominant" cycles in common stock prices. He noted a 3-year and a 9-year cycle
as the other dominant cycles.

Szatrowski, 1949.

308

A 9.20-month (40-week) rhythmic cycle in Stock Prices, U.S.A., no dates
given, is alleged.

Davis, 1936.

309

An 11.35-month (49.33-week) rhythmic cycle in General Motors Common
Stock Prices, U.S.A., 1951—1961, is alleged.

The price of General Motors common stock has tended to move in a cycle
which averaged 49.33 weeks in length. This cycle displayed a typical

amplitude of 24% of trend at time of an ideal crest. A crest in the ideal pattern occurred the week ending July 7, 1961. This wave has followed the ideal pattern about 78% of the time.

Shirk, 1961-B. (Figure)

310

A 15 1/3-month (1.28-year) rhythmic cycle in Industrial Stock Prices, U.S.A., 1871—1950, is alleged.

It was observed through data from Standard and Poor's Corporation Industrial Stock Price Index and the Cowles Commission Index that a cycle approximately 15 1/3 months in duration was present. This cycle may contribute to the peculiar shape of the 45.5-month cycle, since this cycle is approximately one-third the length of the longer cycle.

Dewey, 1952-W. p. 270.

311

Various cycles (shortest length: 16.95 months) in Copper Share Prices, U.S.A., 1918—1960, are alleged.

The figures used in this analysis of Standard and Poor's Index of Copper Share Prices were quarterly averages of the monthly indices. The author isolated 21 cycles in the figures and combined those 21 cycles with a trend to obtain a synthesis.

Cycle Length		Date of	Amplitude	
Months	Years	Typical Crest	Plus	Minus
16.95	1.413	1960.874	3.5	3.4
17.79	1.483	1959.600	3.0	2.95
20.01	1.668	1959.874	3.0	2.95
22.44	1.870	1959.511	3.5	3.4
23.61	1.968	1959.224	3.5	3.4
25.65	2.138	1959.187	5.4	5.16
27.60	2.300	1959.272	4.5	4.28
28.38	2.365	1957.965	5.0	4.72
30.60	2.550	1959.370	7.6	7.10
33.3	2.775	1959.224	5.2	4.94
35.49	2.958	1957.579	11.4	10.26
39.99	3.333	1959.705	12.0	10.67
42.38	3.531	1958.465	11.7	10.46
45.75	3.813	1956.685	10.7	9.64
52.95	4.413	1955.824	18.3	15.47
60.99	5.083	1955.665	10.7	9.64
70.92	5.91	1959.088	20.0	16.63
85.2	7.10	1958.126	29.2	22.59
103.2	8.60	1957.773	7.2	6.68
111.0	9.25	1956.101	57.0	36.32
150.36	12.53	1952.514	41.3	29.21

Anonymous, 1960. (Figure)

312

A favorable comparison of the actual price of copper shares through the second quarter of 1961 and the 21 cycles and trend listed in Precis 311 was noted.

Shirk, 1961-R. (Figure)

313

Various average cycles (shortest length: 18.7 months) in Industrial Stock Prices, U.S.A., 1908–1951, are alleged.

Predix Plate I and Predix Plate I-A suggested 29 cycles of varying lengths in industrial common stock prices (quarterly averages of the Dow-Jones Industrials).

Cycle Length	Over-all Amplitude	Cycle Length	Over-all Amplitude
1.56-year (18.7-month)	5.3%	7.40-year	31.8%
1.83-year (22.0-month)	9.2%	7.70-year	13.4%
1.92-year (23.0-month)	8.5%	8.50-year	10.4%
2.02-year (24.2-month)	8.5%	9.20-year	35.0%
2.25-year (27.0-month) or	17.8%	10.00-year	13.4%
2.50-year (30.0-month)	17.8%	10.65-year	10.8%
2.56-year (30.7-month)	11.4%	12.00-year	24.4%
2.82-year (33.8-month)	14.8%	13.50-year	10.8%
3.06-year (36.7-month)	6.1%	16.00-year	32.2%
3.38-year (40.6-month)	11.4%	18.30-year	51.8%
3.94-year (47.3-month)	7.1%	19.50-year	24.4%
4.88-year (58.6-month)	17.4%	23.25-year	17.8%
5.56-year (66.7-month)	10.8%	30.00-year	19.2%
6.00-year	21.8%	37.50-year	14.8%
7.22-year	11.4%	51.50-year	29.6%

Predix Plate I, 1951.
Predix Plate I-A, 1951.

314

A 22.7-month (1.89-year) rhythmic cycle in Stock Prices, U.S.A., 1882–1950, is alleged.

The 22.7-month cycle in common stock prices was isolated from data supplied by the Cowles Commission Index. Although this cycle was prominent from May of 1882 forward, it was badly distorted prior to that date. Typical amplitude of the 22.7-month cycle was 3.7% above trend at time of ideal crest. December 1942 dated a crest in the ideal pattern; October 1943, a trough in the ideal pattern.

Dewey, 1951-W. p. 11.

315

A 23-month (1.92-year) rhythmic cycle in Industrial Stock Prices, U.S.A.,

1871–1950, is alleged.

A 23-month cycle was observed from a study of Standard and Poor's Corporation Industrial Stock Price Index and the Cowles Commission Index. This cycle may contribute to the peculiar shape of the 45.5-month cycle, since it is about one-half the length of the longer cycle.

Dewey, 1952-W. p. 270.

316

A 114-week (26.22-month) rhythmic cycle in Chrysler Stock Prices, U.S.A., October 1951–February 1962, is alleged.

According to Shirk, the 114-week cycle which was present in Chrysler stock prices in the United States during the period under observation displayed great strength and repeated itself 4 1/2 times. A trough in the ideal pattern occurred in 1951 and every 114 weeks thereafter. Although the swings are well defined, the significance of this cycle is questionable.

Shirk, 1962-M. (Figure)

317

A 27-month (2.25-year) average cycle in Canadian Gold Mining Stock Prices, Canada, January 1932–May 1950, is alleged.

A periodogram constructed by Coppock, which analyzed six groups of common stock, indicated that an average cycle of 27 months duration may be present in Canadian gold mining stock prices.

Coppock, as reported by Dewey, 1951-E. pp. 83, 84. (Figure)

318

A 27.5-month (2.29-year) rhythmic cycle in Stock Prices, U.S.A., 1854–1954, is alleged.

A minor cycle of 27.5 months duration which repeated itself 43 times was found in data from the Clement-Burgess Index (1854–1870) and the Standard and Poor's Corporation Industrial Stock Price Index (1871–1954). The 27.5-month cycle had an over-all amplitude of 4.2% and crested ideally in July 1952 and every 27.5 months forward and backward from that time.

Dewey, 1954-R. (Figure)

319

A 29-month (2.42-year) average cycle in Farm Equipment Stock Prices, U.S.A., January 1932–May 1950, is alleged.

In a periodogram analysis, Coppock uncovered a strong average cycle of 29 months duration in the prices of farm equipment stock.

Coppock, as reported by Dewey, 1951-E. pp. 83, 85. (Figure)

320

A 29.2-month (2.43-year) rhythmic cycle in Stock Prices, U.S.A., 1854–
1954, is alleged.

Research into data provided by the Clement-Burgess Index (1854–1870) and
Standard and Poor's Corporation Industrial Stock Price Index (1871–1954)
indicated that an important minor cycle in common stock prices was that of
29.2 months. Over-all amplitude of this cycle which repeated itself 41
times in the data studied was 7.1%. It crested ideally at the end of 1952
and every 29.2 months forward and backward from that time.

Dewey, 1954-R. (Figure)

321

A 30-month (2.5-year) average cycle in Leveraged Investment Company
Stock Prices, U.S.A., January 1932—May 1950, is alleged.

A periodogram analysis by Coppock indicated that stocks in the Leveraged
Investment Company tended to peak at an interval of, or very close to, 30
months.

Coppock, as reported by Dewey, 1951-E. pp. 83, 84. (Figure)

322

A 31-month (2.58-year) rhythmic cycle in Stock Prices, U.S.A., 1854–1954,
is alleged.

A 31.0-month cycle in stock prices in the United States, although a minor
one, was very regular and repeated itself 38 times in the data studied
(Clement Burgess Index for the years 1854 through 1870 and Standard and
Poor's Corporation Industrial Stock Price Index for the years 1871 through
1954). Over-all amplitude of the average cycle was 7.2%. A crest in the
ideal pattern occurred in mid-June 1951.

Dewey, 1954-R. (Figure)

323

A 35.4-month (2.95-year) rhythmic cycle in Industrial Common Stock Prices,
U.S.A., 1871–1951, is alleged.

Reinforcing the theory of a 3-year cycle in industrial common stock prices
alleged by Dewey in 1940, Malinowski reported that a cycle of 35.4 months
duration was isolated by freeing it from the dominant 41-month cycle by a
series of moving averages. Typical over-all amplitude of this 35.4-month
cycle was 8% of trend. Standard and Poor's Corporation Industrial Stock
Price Index (adjusted for trend) was used in the determination of the cycle
length.

Malinowski, 1952. (Figure)

324

An audit of the 35.4-month cycle extending data back to the year 1789 and
forward through 1960 indicated that this cycle showed only a 59% match

between the actual and the ideal cycle.

Shirk, 1961-F. (Figure)

325

A 3-year average cycle in Leveraged Investment Company Stock Prices,
U.S.A., January 1932—May 1950, is alleged.

A periodogram analysis by Coppock indicated that the price of stocks of the
Leveraged Investment Company moved in waves approximately 36 months in
length.

Coppock, as reported by Dewey, 1951-E. pp. 83, 84. (Figure)

326

A 3-year-and-longer rhythmic cycle in Industrial Stock Prices, U.S.A., 1931—
1948, is alleged.

According to Szatrowski, who used Standard and Poor's Corporation Industrial Stock Price Index (quarterly) as basic data, a 3-year-and-longer cycle
is one of the "three dominant" cycles in industrial stock prices. A 9-month
and a 9-year cycle were also noted as dominant.

Szatrowski, 1949.

327

Tripp stated that the 3-year cycle in industrial stock prices (average 3 1/2-
year cycle before 1920) was "one of the most consistent in common stock
prices."

Tripp, 1948. (Figure)

328

A 3—5-year rhythmic cycle in Industrial Stock Prices, U.S.A., 1872—1936,
is alleged.

Using data from the Federal Reserve Bank of New York Index of Industrial
Common Stock Prices (1872—1896) and the Dow-Jones Index of Industrial
Common Stock Prices (1897—1936) adjusted for comparability, Wheldon
noted a cycle of 3 to 5 years duration (in addition to a longer cycle, 8—11-
year) in industrial common stock prices.

Wheldon, 1937. (Figure)

329

Various average cycles (shortest length: 37 months) in Railroad Stock
Prices, U.S.A., are alleged.

Burns and Mitchell reported that railroad stock prices have moved in varying cyclical patterns according to data compiled by the National Bureau of
Economic Research. The average cycle displayed a length of 63 months
from 1857 to 1889; a length of 37 months from 1889 to 1907; and a length of
49 months from 1907 to 1932.

Burns and Mitchell, 1946. pp. 355, 385. (Figure; data)

330

A 3.19-year (38.3-month) rhythmic cycle in Stock Prices, U.S.A., February
1878—August 1913, is alleged.

Stock prices in the United States during the period under observation moved
in 8 full cycles which averaged 38.3 months in duration.

                                                    Morgenstern, 1959.

331

A 3.30-year (39.56-month) rhythmic cycle in Railroad Stock Prices, U.S.A.,
1866—1914, is alleged.

Railroad stock prices (Harvard Economic Society's Series, shifted to the
level of the Dow-Jones averages, monthly) appeared to be influenced by a
3.30-year cycle during the period under observation.

                                                    Frickey, 1935. p. 140.

332

A 3.33-year (40-month) rhythmic cycle in Composite Stock Prices, U.S.A.,
is alleged.

In each of the two decades observed (1901—1911 and 1911—1920), three
cycles, each approximately 3 1/3 years in length, emerged from the data
supplied by Standard and Poor's Composite Index, Monthly Average for
June and December.

                                                    Smith, 1954. pp. 15—16. (Figure)

333

Ayres noted a 40-month rhythmic cycle in stock market prices for the period
1831—1939, along with corresponding 40-month cycles in bond prices, interest rates, capital issues, and general business activity. An interrelationship
of these 40-month cycles is indicated. The stock price cycle showed a
tendency for the upswing to be 67% longer than the downswing.

                                                    Ayres, 1939. (Figure)

334

A 3.33-year (40-month) average cycle in Stock Prices, U.S.A., 1875—1952,
is suggested.

In addition to an 8-month average cycle (which Granger and Morgenstern
noted was an harmonic of the business cycle), a slight 40-month tendency
was also revealed in the power spectrum analysis of Standard and Poor
Series, 1875—1952.

                                                    Granger and Morgenstern, 1963. pp. 13, 23.

335

A 3.33-year (40-month) rhythmic cycle in Rate of Change of Industrial Stock

Prices, U.S.A., no dates given, is alleged.

Newbury, 1952. pp. 182—183.

336

A 3.39-year (40.68-month) rhythmic cycle in Industrial Stock Prices, U.S.A., 1871—1951, is alleged.

Data from Standard and Poor's Corporation Industrial Index (monthly averages) revealed a 40.68-month wave in the price of industrial common stocks. This cycle, first observed in 1912, displays an average amplitude of 23.3% above trend at time of ideal crest. It appeared that the 3.39-year cycle might be a combination of two cycles of very nearly the same length since it consistently showed a tendency to become stronger in the middle of the 80-year period under consideration.

Dewey, 1951-H. pp. 327—335. (Figure)
Dewey, 1951-I. pp. 371—377.

337

A 3.395-year (40 3/4-month) rhythmic cycle in Industrial Stock Prices, U.S.A., 1871—1950, is alleged.

Dewey suggested that a 40 3/4-month cycle in industrial common stock prices would be one of two perfectly regular cycles which intermingle and cause a reversing tendency to occur in the 46-month cycle. Time charts were used to confirm the presence of a 40 3/4-month cycle as well as one of a 51 1/4 months duration.

Dewey, 1952-F. (Figure)

338

A 3.4-year (40.8-month) rhythmic cycle in Industrial Stock Prices, U.S.A., 1897—1946, is alleged.

From the Dow-Jones Industrial Stock Price Index, Collins uncovered a 3.4-year rhythmic cycle which displayed an average rising phase of 20.2 months and an average declining phase of about 20.6 months.

Collins, 1947. (Figure)

339

During the period under observation, 1872—1936, industrial stock prices (Federal Reserve Bank of New York Index, 1872—1896, and Dow-Jones Index, 1897—1936, adjusted for comparability) tended to move in a cyclical pattern approximately 3.4 years long.

King, 1938.

340

Macaulay reported that a typical trough in Collins' 40.8-month cycle would fall at May 1897 and every 3.4 years thereafter.

Macaulay, 1947.

341*

A 3.42-year (41-month) rhythmic cycle in Industrial Stock Prices, U.S.A., is alleged.

A 41-month cycle in industrial stock prices (Dow-Jones Industrial Averages) for the period January 1901 through March 1946 became evident when charted as rate of change in industrial stock prices.

Hoskins, 1938, as reported by Dewey and Dakin, 1947. (Figure)

342

Industrial stock prices, as measured by the Dow-Jones Index of Industrial Common Stock Prices, 1898–1941, have tended to fluctuate persistently in a 41-month cycle. Huntington suggests a correlation between the 41-month cycle in industrial stocks and the cyclical pattern of atmospheric electricity.

Huntington, 1941. pp. 6–7. (Figure)
Huntington, 1945. pp. 468–469. (Figure)

343

There has been a tendency for industrial stock prices (Dow-Jones Industrials, 1897–1950) to move in a cycle approximately 41 months long.

Financial Reports, 1951. p. 7.

344

Further inspection of the data in the Dow-Jones Industrial Averages indicated that the 41-month cycle had almost, if not entirely, disappeared. Dewey suggested that the 41-month length may have been the result of the interplay of several (probably four) cyclic forces of that general order of magnitude.

Dewey, 1954-M. (Figure)

345

After isolating the 41-month cycle in the Dow-Jones Industrial Averages (1897–1953), Lane suggested that this cycle had not disappeared, but had, instead, reversed.

Lane, as reported by Dewey, 1954-I. (Figure)

346

A 3 1/2-year rhythmic cycle in Stock Prices, U.S.A., 1883–1930, is alleged.

Haney, 1931. pp. 313–314.

---

*Although each separate precis under each individual allegation has been placed in alphabetical order throughout this catalogue, an exception has been made in this instance wherein, for the sake of clarity, chronological order has been employed.

347

A 3 1/2-year rhythmic cycle in Stock Prices, New York, 1853–1952, is alleged.

A 3 1/2-year cycle in stock prices in the New York Market was noted by Langham.

Langham, 1954.

348

A 3 1/2-year rhythmic cycle in United States Steel Corporation Earnings per Share of Common Stock, U.S.A., 1900–1948, is alleged.

Earnings per share of United States Steel Corporation common stock has been influenced by three long cycles, one of which was 3 1/2 years in duration (the others were 6 and 11 years long).

Szatrowski, 1949.

349

A 3.59-year (43.08-month) rhythmic cycle in Stock Prices, U.S.A., 1872–1926, is alleged.

Wardwell observed a minor cycle in stock market averages approximately 3.59 years in length.

Wardwell, 1927. p. 74. (Data)

350

A 3.83-year (46-month) rhythmic cycle in Industrial Stock Prices, U.S.A., 1834–1952, is alleged.

The 46-month cycle in the movement of industrial stock prices was observed in a study based on the Axe-Houghton Index of Industrial Stock Prices for the years 1883 to 1952 supplemented by the Clement Burgess Index from 1854 to 1883 and an index of stock prices beginning in 1834 to 1954 published in the *Review of Economic Statistics*. This cycle displayed 97% accuracy in the 119-year period studied. The 46-month cycles were observed to occur at 3-4-4-4-4-year intervals and then repeat with the six cycles recurring each 23 years.

Dunbar, 1952. pp. 11–12. (Data)

351

Dewey corroborated Dunbar's work on the 3.83-year cycle in industrial stock prices. This cycle displays M-shaped waves wherein the second peak is higher than the first. Dewey stated that the M-shape may be explained by the presence of cycles about half the length of the 46-month cycle and others about 1/3 that length (15 1/3 months) in a series along with the basic 46-month pattern. Dewey noted that his periodogram analysis of industrial stock prices suggested the possibility of the above mentioned cycle lengths.

Dewey, 1952-F. pp. 297–299. (Figure)
Dewey, 1952-W. pp. 267–270.

352

Additional information revealed that the 3.83-year cycle continued to display 97% accuracy.

Dewey, 1956-D. pp. 221—227. (Figure)

353

The correspondence between the Axe-Houghton Index of Industrial Stock Prices used by Dunbar in his analysis of the 46-month cycle and the more popular Dow-Jones Averages Index was charted.

Dewey, 1956-A. pp. 314—315. (Figure)

354

Adding to the performance record of Dunbar's 46-month cycle in industrial stock prices, Shirk noted that the actual performance continued to match the ideal performance. The cycle, therefore, displayed 98% accuracy in the 127-year period studied.

Shirk, 1960-C. pp. 78—79. (Figure)

355

Various average cycles (shortest length: 3.9 years) in Railroad Stock Prices, U.S.A., 1831—1950, are suggested.

A multiple harmonic analysis of railroad stock prices suggested a multitude of possible cycles. A star indicates the possibility of multiple cycles.

Cycle Length in Years	Cycle Length in Years	Cycle Length in Years
100.0	*10.2	5.3
92.3—60.0	9.2	5.3
54.4	*8.3	*5.1
48.0—40.0	*7.9	*5.0
32.4	*7.8	*4.9
26.1	*7.2	*4.8
*20.0	*7.0	4.6
*19.0	*6.6	*4.5
*16.4	*6.5	*4.4
*15.6	*6.2	*4.3
13.3 & 12.8	*6.1	*4.2
or 13.3—12.8	*5.9	*4.1
11.4—10.9	*5.6	*4.1
*10.7	*5.5	3.9
*10.3	*5.4	

Dewey, 1952-I. (Figure)

356

A 4.02-year (48.2-month) rhythmic cycle in Industrial Stock Prices, U.S.A.,

1866—1914, is alleged.

A 4.02-year cycle appears to influence industrial stock prices (Clement-Burgess Monthly Index, 1866—1882, and Axe-Houghton Monthly Index, 1883—1914).

Frickey, 1935. p. 139.

357

A 4.15-year (49.8-month) average cycle in Railroad Stock Prices, U.S.A., 1857—1932, is alleged.

Burns and Mitchell, 1946. (Figure)

358

A 4.25-year (51-month) rhythmic cycle in Stock Market Activity, U.S.A., 1932—1962, is alleged.

"...every four years and three months something significant happens in the stock market."

Doane, 1962.

359

A 4.25-year (plus few days) rhythmic cycle in Stock Prices, U.S.A., no dates given, is alleged.

"Every 4 years, three months, and a few days, the stock market falls out of bed," said Blau. Troughs were dated at June 18, 1949; September 21, 1953; and December 23, 1957.

Blau, 1962.

360

A 4.31-year (51.25-month) rhythmic cycle in Industrial Stock Prices, U.S.A., 1871—1950, is alleged.

A time chart analysis suggested a possible 51 1/4-month cycle in industrial stock prices.

Dewey, 1952-F. pp. 297—299. (Figure)

361

A 4.8-year (57.6-month) rhythmic cycle in Cigarette Stock Prices, U.S.A., 1912—1961, is alleged.

Wilson, 1962-A. p. 159.

362

Various rhythmic cycles (shortest length: 4.89 year) in Stock Prices, U.S.A., 1855—1943, are alleged.

A preliminary analysis of data from the Clement Burgess Index for the period from 1855 through 1870 and Standard and Poor's Corporation Combined Index for the period from 1871 through 1953 revealed the possibility of ten cycles which measured over 4 1/2 years in length in stock prices in the U.S.A.

These waves and their ideal crests and their amplitudes are shown below.

Preliminary Cycle Length in Years	Preliminary Date of Crest	Preliminary Amplitude Above Trend
4.89	1861	3.5%
5.50	1864	7.0%
6.07	1905	6.0%
6.86	1854	8.3%
8.17	1872	8.2%
9.2	1854	17.2%
11.0	1864	3.8%
12.0	1855	15.1%
14.5	1870	12.25%
21.0	1866	17.0%

Dewey, 1954-J. (Figure)

363

A 5 1/2-year rhythmic cycle in Bituminous Coal Stock Prices, U.S.A., 1918–1961, is alleged.

A 5 1/2-year repetitive pattern in soft coal stock prices in the United States during the period from 1918 through 1961 was evident. This cyclic wave averaged 12% above trend at time of an ideal crest and 11% below trend at time of an ideal trough. An ideal low occurred at July 1926 and every 5 1/2 years thereafter.

Dorland, 1962-A. (Figure)

364

A 5.91-year (70.9-month) rhythmic cycle in Combined Stock Prices, U.S.A., 1871–1956, is alleged.

Combined annual stock prices (Standard and Poor's Corporation Combined Stock Price Index) have shown a tendency to move in waves approximately 5.91 years long. Typical amplitude is displayed at about 6.4% above trend at time of ideal crest and 6.0% below trend at time of ideal trough. 1958.69 dated a crest in the ideal pattern. This cycle was originally (1944) measured at 6.07 years; refined study, however, placed the length at 5.91 years.

Dewey, 1957-A. p. 176. (Figure)
Dewey, 1957-D. pp. 93–98. (Figure)

365

Castle reported that the lows in the 5.91-year cycle occur at 1932.6, 1938.5, 1944.4, 1950.3, and 1956.2. It was noted that the 5.91-year cycle may be part of the 17.75-year complex in combined stock prices.

Castle, 1959.

366

A 5.91-year (70.9-month) rhythmic cycle in Coal Stock Prices, U.S.A.,

1871–1940, is alleged.

Combined soft and hard coal stock prices in the United States during the period from 1871 through 1940 appeared to fluctuate in a cycle which measured approximately 5.91 years in length. An ideal peak occurred at February of 1876 and every 5.91 years thereafter. Typical amplitude at time of an ideal crest averaged 23% above trend; typical amplitude at time of an ideal crest measured about 19% below trend.

Dorland, 1962-B. (Figure; data)

367

A 5.92-year (71-month) rhythmic cycle in Railroad Stock Prices, U.S.A., 1831–1956, is alleged.

A study of railroad stock prices shows a cycle of approximately 5.92 years has been present in the 126 years of available figures. Typical amplitude of this cycle is 8.6% above trend at time of ideal crest and 8.0% below trend at time of ideal trough. A crest in the ideal pattern occurred at 1958.68. Dewey pointed out that this length fits into one of the well-established families of cycles; it is almost exactly one-third of 17.75 years.

Dewey, 1957-D. pp. 93–98. (Figure)
Dewey, 1957-E. pp. 16–24. (Figure)
Dewey, 1957-F. p. 20.

368

A 6-year rhythmic cycle in Industrial Stock Prices, U.S.A., 1900–1945, is alleged.

Data (Standard and Poor's Corporation Industrial Stock Price Index) adjusted for a 9-year rhythm show highs and lows relative to trend. The average wave amplitude of this 6-year cycle is about 12% above trend at time of ideal crest. A crest in the ideal pattern occurred in 1947.

Dewey, 1950-G. pp. 4–5. (Figure)

369

Tripp noted that a 6-year cycle may be present in industrial stock prices for the period from 1871 through 1947.

Tripp, 1948.

370

A 6-year rhythmic cycle in United States Steel Corporation Earnings per Share of Common Stock, U.S.A., 1900–1948, is alleged.

Szatrowski stated that the earnings per share of United States Steel Common Stock was influenced by three long cycles, one of which was a 6-year cycle (the others being 3 1/2 and 11 years long).

Szatrowski, 1949-A. (Figure)

371

A 6-year rhythmic cycle in United States Steel Corporation Common Stock Prices, U.S.A.,1900–1948, is alleged.

Preliminary work by Szatrowski suggested a 6-year cycle in the price of United States Steel Common Stock which did not appear to have any relationship to the 6-year cycle in earnings of United States Steel Corporation Common Stock.

Szatrowski, 1949-A.

372

A 6.16-year (73.9-month) rhythmic cycle in Cigarette Stock Prices, U.S.A., 1912–1961, is alleged.

Wilson, 1962-A. p. 159.

373

A 7-year rhythmic cycle in Industrial Stock Prices, U.S.A., 1897–1947, is alleged.

Weigel contended that industrial stock prices have tended to follow a 7-year rhythmic pattern.

Weigel, 1948.

374

A 7-year rhythmic cycle in Combined Stock Prices, U.S.A., 1871–1957, is alleged.

Using fifteen years of additional data, Shirk reported that the 6.86-year cycle in stock prices (Standard and Poor's Corporation Combined Stock Price Index) alleged by Dewey in 1954 (see Precis 362) was actually an even 7-year cycle. Typical strength of this 7-year cycle was measured as 6.9% above trend at time of ideal crest. 1957.9 dated a crest in the ideal pattern.

Shirk, 1958-C. (Figure)

375

A 7.1-year (85.2-month) rhythmic cycle in Railroad Stock Prices, U.S.A., 1831–1957, is alleged.

Railroad stock prices (Cleveland Trust Company Index of Rail Stock Prices from 1831 through 1872, adjusted, and Standard and Poor's Corporation Index of Railroad Stock Prices from 1873 through 1957) have shown a tendency to move in a cyclical pattern approximately 7.1 years in length. Typical strength of this cycle, which favorably compares with the 7-year cycle in combined stocks, is 4.2% above trend at time of ideal crest. A crest in the ideal pattern occurred at 1958.45.

Shirk, 1958-B. (Figure)

376

A 7.42-year (89.0-month) rhythmic cycle in Stock Prices, Great Britain,

February 1878—August 1913, is alleged.

The four full waves present in stock prices in Great Britain during the period under observation averaged about 89.0 months in duration.

Morgenstern, 1959.

377

A 7.56-year (90.7-month) rhythmic cycle in Stock Prices, Germany, February 1878—August 1913, is alleged.

During the period from February 1878 through August 1913, stock prices in Germany moved in 3 full cycles which averaged approximately 90.7 months long.

Morgenstern, 1959.

378

A 7.94-year (95.3-month) rhythmic cycle in Railroad Stock Prices, U.S.A., 1831—1955, is alleged.

Railroad stock prices (Cleveland Trust Company Index of Rail Stock Prices from 1831 through 1872, adjusted, and Standard and Poor's Corporation Index, of Railroad Stock Prices from 1873 through 1955) appear to have been influenced by a cycle approximately 7.94 years in length. Typical amplitude of this 7.94-year cycle is 4.2% above trend at time of ideal crest; 4.1% below trend at time of ideal trough. A crest in the ideal pattern occurred at 1953.09.

Dewey, 1956-J. (Figure)
Dewey, 1957-E. (Figure)

379

A 7.95-year (95.4-month) rhythmic cycle in Railroad Stock Prices, U.S.A., 1831—1955, is alleged.

An analysis of the 7.95-year cycle in railroad stock prices which covered a period of 125 years showed a strength of 2% above trend at time of ideal crest.

Dewey, 1956-I.

380

An 8—9-year rhythmic cycle in Ordinary Shares, England, 1870—1957, is alleged.

This study of ordinary shares in England was compiled from data from the London & Cambridge Economic Service Index of Industrial Shares for those periods during which it was compiled, from the Kitchin Index from 1915 to 1924, and from Moody's Share Index from 1950 to 1958, linking the indices where necessary. McDougall reported that the cyclic pattern followed by ordinary shares appeared to display an average duration of 8—9 years.

McDougall, 1958-B.

381

An 8-, 9-, 10-year and repeat rhythmic cycle in Stock Prices, U.S.A., 1884–
1955, is alleged.

A *Cycles* reader, C. R. Ringer, asserted that stock prices in the United
States followed a modified version of Benner's pig iron price pattern.

Ringer, 1955. (Figure)

382

An 8–10-year rhythmic cycle in Security Prices, U.S.A., 1912–1941, is
alleged.

The cycle that dominated security prices, 1912–1941, appeared to have
varied alternately between 8 and 10 years in length. Eaton reported the
following cycles: an 8-year cycle from 1912–1920; a 10-year cycle from
1920–1930; an 8-year cycle from 1930–1938; and a probable 10-year cycle from 1938.

Eaton, 1941, as reported by King, 1958. (Figure)

383

An 8–11-year rhythmic cycle in Industrial Stock Prices, U.S.A., 1872–
1936, is alleged.

Using data from the Federal Reserve Bank of New York Index of Industrial
Common Stock Prices (1872–1896) and the Dow-Jones Index of Industrial
Common Stock Prices (1897–1936), adjusted for comparability, Wheldon
noted a cycle of 8–11 years duration in industrial stock prices in addition
to a shorter one 3–5 years long.

Wheldon, 1937, as reported by King, 1958. (Figure)

384

An 8.17-(8 1/6) year rhythmic cycle in Industrial Stock Prices, U.S.A.,
1871–1951, is alleged.

Industrial stock prices from 1871 through 1951 appeared to have been influenced by a cycle approximately 8.17-(8 1/6) years in length. Dewey noted
that it is possible that the 8.17-year cycle is a compound cycle comprised
of two cycles approximately 7.7 years and 8.5 years in length.

Dewey, 1952-C. (Figure)
Dewey, 1953-G.

385

An 8.17-(8 1/6) year rhythmic cycle in Stock Prices, U.S.A., 1871–1956, is
alleged.

An audit of the 8.17-year cycle (first discovered in 1944) in stock prices in the United States revealed no change in length. Typical amplitude, however, was reduced from 8.2% to 4.7%. A crest in the ideal pattern was dated at 1954.1.

Dewey, 1957-K. (Figure)

386

An 8.39-year rhythmic cycle in Railroad Stock Prices, U.S.A., 1831–1955, is alleged.

An analysis of railroad stock prices from 1831 through 1955 (Standard and Poor's Corporation Railroad Stock Price Index, 1873–1956, combined with the Cleveland Trust Company Index of Railroad Stock Prices, 1831–1872) suggests that this series has been characterized in part by an 8.39-year cycle. Typical amplitude of this cycle is 4% above trend at time of ideal crest and 3.8% below trend at time of ideal trough. A crest in the ideal pattern occurred at 1954.59.

Dewey, 1956-J. (Figure)
Dewey, 1957-E. (Figure; data)

387

A 9-year rhythmic cycle in Industrial Stock Prices, U.S.A., is alleged.

There has been a tendency for industrial stock prices (Dow-Jones Industrial Stock Price Index), 1900–1950, to move in a 9-year cyclical pattern. Highs were recorded in 1901, 1910, 1919, 1928, 1937, and 1946.

Financial Reports, 1951. pp. 6–7.

388

The 9-year cycle has been manifest for a great number of years in industrial stock prices in the United States (Dow-Jones daily averages of prices on 30 industrial stocks).

Klemme, 1950.

389

Industrial stock prices in the United States (Standard and Poor's Corporation Index of Industrials) appear to be dominated by three important cycles: a 9-year, a 3-year, and a 9-month.

Szatrowski, 1949-B.

390

Tripp alleged that the 9-year cycle in industrial stock prices in the United States (Standard and Poor's Index of Industrial Stock Prices, 1870–1947) is "the important long cycle."

Tripp, 1948. (Figure)

391

A 9-year rhythmic cycle in Railroad Stock Prices, U.S.A., is alleged.

Davis reported that a periodogram analysis of data (Cleveland Trust Company Index of Railroad Stock Prices, 1831–1930) showed a concentration of energy in a harmonic component with a period of 9 years.

Davis, 1941. p. 551.

392

There appears to be a recurring cycle of about 9 years in length in railroad stock prices in the United States (Cleveland Trust Company Index of Railroad Stock Prices, 1831–1870, and Standard and Poor's Corporation Railroad Stock Price Index, 1871–1950).

Dewey, 1951-H.

393

A 9-year rhythmic cycle in Stock Prices, U.S.A., is alleged.

A 9-year cycle appears to be one of the dominating forces in stock prices in the United States for the period 1875 through 1946 (Leonard Ayres Index, 1831–1871, and Standard and Poor's Composite Stock Price Index, 1871–1946).

Smith, 1948.

394

Smith studied the 9-year cyclic pattern that was evident in the 12-month percent of change in stock market prices in conjunction with a 36-year cyclic pattern.

Smith, 1959. pp. 160–161. (Figure)

395

A 9-year rhythmic cycle in Stock Prices, London, 1857–1957, is alleged.

Peak years of prices on the London Stock Exchange from 1857 through 1957 occurred at 1857, 1866, 1873, 1882, 1890, 1900, 1907, 1913, 1920, 1928, 1937, 1946, and 1955, for an average rhythm of approximately 9 years.

Sprake, 1959. p. 21.

396

A 9.18-year rhythmic cycle in Railroad Stock Prices, U.S.A., 1831–1955, is alleged.

An audit of a study made in 1944 revealed that the so-called 9-year cycle in railroad stock prices was actually 9.18 years in length. Data (Cleveland Trust Company Railroad Stock Price Index, 1831–1940, spliced to Standard and Poor's Corporation Railroad Stock Price Index, 1871–1955) showed the average amplitude to be 17.4% above trend at time of ideal crest and 15.8% below trend at time of ideal trough. 1955.36 dated a crest in the ideal pattern.

Dewey, 1956-E. (Figure)

397

A study of railroad stock prices, 1831–1955, refined the so-called 9 1/5-year cycle to a length of 9.18 years. The amplitude of the 9.18-year cycle

(calculated from data provided by the Cleveland Trust Company Railroad
Stock Price Index, 1831–1940, spliced to Standard and Poor's Corporation
Railroad Stock Price Index, 1871–1955) was typically 16.9% above trend at
time of ideal crest and 14.6% below trend at time of ideal trough. The 9.18-
year cycle crested, ideally, at 1955.56.

Dewey, 1956-F. (Figure)

398

A 9.18-year rhythmic cycle in Industrial Stock Prices, U.S.A., 1871–1955,
is alleged.

Dewey reported that the length of the so-called 9-year cycle in industrial
stock prices appeared to be slightly longer or 9.18 years. A study of the
data (Standard and Poor's Corporation Industrial Stock Price Index) placed
a crest in the ideal pattern at 1955.62. Typical amplitude of this cycle was
19.0% above trend at time of an ideal crest and 16.2% below trend at time of
an ideal trough.

Dewey, 1956-E. (Figure)

399

A 9.18-year rhythmic cycle in Combined Stock Prices, U.S.A., 1871–1955,
is alleged.

An additional study of the so-called 9-year cycle in combined stock prices
(Standard and Poor's Corporation Combined Index, 1871–1956) revised the
length to 9.18 years. The typical amplitude of this cycle was 17.1% above
trend at time of an ideal crest and 14.8% below trend at time of an ideal
trough. A crest in the ideal pattern was dated at 1955.62.

Dewey, 1956-E. (Figure)

400

Although it appeared that the 9.18-year cycle in stock prices in the United
States had ceased to operate during the period from 1956 to 1960, Dewey
reported that the rate of price increase in stocks had followed the cyclic
pattern.

Dewey, 1960-A. (Figure)

401

A 9.20-year rhythmic cycle in Stock Prices, U.S.A., is alleged.

During the period under observation, 1854–1945, data from the Axe-
Houghton Index appeared to indicate that stock market prices in the United
States fitted more closely to a 9.20-year cycle than a 9-year cycle.

Dewey and Dakin, 1947. pp. 88, 90. (Figure)

402

A 9.20-year rhythmic cycle in Industrial Stock Prices, U.S.A., is alleged.

Collins reported that, during the period from 1897 through 1946, industrial stock prices were influenced by a 9.20-year cycle as well as a shorter (40.8-month) cycle. The Dow-Jones Industrial Stock Price Index was used for this calculation.

Collins, 1947. (Figure)

403

Dewey reported that the so-called 9-year cycle in industrial stock prices fit more closely into a 9.20-year pattern. During the period under observation, 1854–1951, typical over-all amplitude of this cycle was about 42% of trend. (This length was further refined in 1956 to 9.18 years.)

Dewey, 1951-L. (Figure)
Dewey, 1951-O.

404

A 9.25-year rhythmic cycle in Industrial Stock Prices, U.S.A., 1921–1949, is alleged.

Harvey reported that a basic cycle influencing industrial stock prices (Dow-Jones Industrial Stock Price Index) measured 9.25 years in length.

Harvey, 1958.

405

A 9.5–10.0-year rhythmic cycle in Industrial Stock Prices, U.S.A., 1854–1949, is alleged.

Using autocorrelation as a tool, Daniels "upheld Smith's and Erdley's findings" of a cycle in industrial stock prices the duration of which was between 9.5 and 10.0 years.

Daniels, 1955.

406*

A 10-year rhythmic cycle in Industrial Stock Prices, U.S.A., is alleged.

A recurrent 10-year cycle, which Smith calls a Decennial Pattern, is evident in the behavior of industrial stock prices during the period from 1881 through 1936. This Decennial Pattern, calculated from the Investment Managers Company Index (an index compiled by Smith with behavior parallel to that of the Standard Statistics Index of Industrials, although its base differs), "shows quite clearly that something is at work on these stock prices, not once every ten years but throughout each ten year period, so that each such period has a wave-like motion tending to resemble similar wave-like movements occurring at approximately the same relative time or position in a majority of other decades."

Smith, 1939. pp. 7–9. (Figure)

---

*Although each separate precis under each individual allegation has been placed in alphabetical order throughout this catalogue, an exception has been made in this instance wherein, for the sake of clarity, chronological order has been employed.

407

Comparison of the summary description of Smith's Decennial Pattern and the actual behavior of the Dow-Jones Industrial Stock Price Index for the period 1953–1959 was published.

Shirk, 1960-B. (Figure)
Shirk, 1960-M. (Figure)

408

Gaubis augmented the Decennial Pattern theory in industrial stock prices by stating that prices were influenced by "three overlapping ten-year cycles."

Gaubis, 1961. (Figure)
Gaubis, 1962-A.

409

Gaubis reaffirmed his belief in the decennial pattern and stated that in its entire history (1897–1962) of the Dow-Jones Industrial Averages, this pattern has worked in the ideal fashion, with only one technical exception.

Gaubis, 1962-B.

410

A 10-year rhythmic cycle in Stock Prices, U.S.A., is alleged.

Daniels reported that Smith and Erdley, using an electronic analog of Kalecki's model of an economic system, had found a 10-year cycle in stock prices in the United States (Axe-Houghton Index, 1854–1910, and New York Times Index, 1911–1952). An additional study was made using the Axe-Houghton Index, 1854–1949, which confirmed the 10-year cycle.

Daniels, 1955.

411

Stock market prices in the United States from 1870 through 1949 have tended to follow a Decennial Pattern in the 12-month percent of change (December).

Smith, 1949.

412

The Decennial Pattern in stock prices (Standard and Poor's Composite Index of Stock Prices — monthly average figures) was re-emphasized by Smith. During the first two decades of this century (1901–1910 and 1911–1920), it was evident that not single 10-year cycles influenced prices, but, instead, three cycles to each decade — each measuring about 3 1/3 years in length.

Smith, 1954. pp. 15–17. (Figure)

413

A 10.32-year rhythmic cycle in Stock Prices, U.S.A., 1872–1926, is alleged.

Wardwell observed a major cycle in United States stock market averages approximately 10.32 years in length.

Wardwell, 1927. p. 74. (Data)

414

A 10.83-year rhythmic cycle in Combined Stock Prices, U.S.A., 1878–1956, is alleged.

An audit of the so-called 11-year stock market cycle, originally discovered by Dewey in 1944, refined the length to 10.83 years. The refined length was based on a longer series of prices (Standard and Poor's Corporation Combined Index) plus 15 years of additional figures. Typical amplitude of the 10.83-year cycle at time of an ideal crest was 5.9% above trend. A crest in the ideal pattern was dated at 1949.45.

Shirk, 1959-E. (Figure)

415

An 11-year rhythmic cycle in Industrial Stock Prices, U.S.A., 1915–1946, is alleged.

Stetson alleged a correlation of sunspot activity with industrial stock prices (Dow-Jones Industrial Averages, yearly).

Stetson, 1946. p. 19. (Figure)

416

An 11-year rhythmic cycle in Stock Prices, U.S.A., no dates given, is alleged.

A correlation of sunspot activity with stock market transactions was reported by Andrews.

Andrews, 1936. p. 934.

417

An extremely high degree of correlation between sunspot activity and New York stock prices (Barron's Averages) was reported by Garcia-Mata and Shaffner. The authors later used Dow-Jones Industrial Averages of New York stock prices to substantiate the correlation.

Garcia-Mata and Shaffner, 1934. pp. 45–51. (Figure)

418

An 11-year rhythmic cycle in Stock Prices, London, no dates given, is alleged.

Garcia-Mata and Shaffner reported that there was a correlation between sunspot activity and stock prices in London (Banker's Magazine Index).

Garcia-Mata and Shaffner, 1934. pp. 45–51. (Figure)

419

An 11-year rhythmic cycle in United States Steel Corporation Earnings per

Share of Common Stock, U.S.A., 1900–1948, is alleged.

Szatrowski reported that the earnings per share of common stock of the
United States Steel Corporation were influenced by three long cyclical fluctuations, one of which was an 11-year cycle (the others measuring 3 1/2
years and 6 years).

Szatrowski, 1949.

420

A 12-year rhythmic cycle in Stock Prices, U.S.A., 1931–1948, is alleged.

A 12-year cycle in common stock prices (Standard and Poor's Corporation
Common Stock Price Index) was detected by Szatrowski by means of his
"Dynamic Cycle Analysis."

Szatrowski, 1948, as reported by King, 1958. p. 33.

421

A 12-year rhythmic cycle in Cigarette Stock Prices, U.S.A., 1912–1961, is
alleged.

A 12-year wave-like pattern appeared to influence cigarette stock prices in
the United States during the period from 1912 through 1961. This cycle displayed a crest in the ideal pattern at 1913 and every 12 years thereafter.
Typical amplitude above trend at time of an ideal crest averaged 25%; typical amplitude below trend at time of an ideal trough, 24%.

Wilson, 1962-A. (Figure; data)

422

A 12.8-year rhythmic cycle in Combined Stock Prices, U.S.A., 1871–1956,
is alleged.

Additional work on the so-called 12.0-year cycle in common stock prices,
discovered in 1944, revised the length to 12.8 years. Standard and Poor's
Corporation Combined Stock Price Index was used in this audit which revealed that typical amplitude of the waves averaged 10.9% above trend at
time of ideal crest and 9.8% below trend at time of ideal trough. 1953.9
dated a crest in the ideal pattern.

Dewey, 1957-G. (Figure)
Dewey, 1957-A.

423

A 12.8-year rhythmic cycle in Railroad Stock Prices, U.S.A., 1831–1956, is
alleged.

Railroad Stock Prices have appeared to be influenced by a 12.8-year cycle
which displays a typical amplitude of 7.2% above trend at time of ideal
crest and 6.7% below trend at time of ideal trough. A crest in the ideal
pattern of this 12.8-year cycle occurred at 1953.9.

Dewey, 1957-G. (Figure)

424

A 14-year rhythmic cycle in Industrial Stock Prices, U.S.A., is alleged.

A minor 14-year cycle was reported by Woods as one of the factors influencing trends in the common stock market in the United States (Dow-Jones Corporation Industrial Averages) from 1897 through 1946.

Woods, 1946.

425

A 13–15-year (average 14-year) cycle in industrial stock prices (E. W. Axe and Company Industrial Averages) was reported by Westendorf.

Westendorf, 1948. (Figure)

426

A 16 1/2–18-year rhythmic cycle in Combined Stock Prices, U.S.A., 1831–1954, is alleged.

Stock prices in the United States (Standard and Poor's Corporation Combined Index, 1871–1954, plus the Clement Burgess Index, 1854–1870, adjusted for comparability, plus the Cleveland Trust Company Railroad Stock Price Index, 1831–1954, adjusted for comparability) appeared to have been dominated by 16 1/2–18-year cycle during the period from 1831 through 1905. After 1905, however, a cycle of this length was not evident.

Dewey, 1955-G. (Figure)

427

A 17.0-year rhythmic cycle in Cigarette Stock Prices, U.S.A., 1912–1961, is alleged.

Wilson, 1962-A. p. 159.

428

A 17–22-year rhythmic cycle in Railroad Stock Prices, U.S.A., 1831–1950, is alleged.

A study of railroad stock prices (Cleveland Trust Company Index, 1831–1870, adjusted for comparability to Standard and Poor's Corporation Railroad Stock Price Index, 1871–1950) showed a perfectly regular 17-year cycle until 1885. After 1885, a 22-year cycle appeared to dominate railroad stock prices.

Dewey, 1951-M. (Figure)

429

A 17.2-year rhythmic cycle in Stock Prices, U.S.A., 1831–1954, is alleged.

An audit of the 16 1/2–18-year cycle in stock prices refined the length of the cycle to approximately 17.2 years. Typical amplitude of the cycle averaged 17.5% above trend at time of ideal crest and 13% below trend at time of ideal trough. 1955.4 dated a crest in the ideal pattern.

Dewey, 1955-A and 1955-I. (Figure)

430

A 17.33-year rhythmic cycle in Industrial Stock Prices, U.S.A., 1896–1951, is alleged.

Stokes observed a tendency for industrial stock prices (Dow-Jones Averages) to repeat their behavior pattern at 17.33-year intervals.

Stokes, 1952.

431

A 17 3/4-year rhythmic cycle in Stock Prices, U.S.A., 1831–1958, is alleged.

The so-called 16 1/2–18-year cycle in stock prices appears to measure approximately 17 3/4 years. Although its behavior after 1905 failed to conform to an ideal cyclic pattern, it appears to respond after 1945 and Dewey stated that this cycle may be reasserting itself.

Dewey, 1959-C. (Figure)

432

An 18-year rhythmic cycle in Industrial Stock Prices, U.S.A., is alleged.

A long 18-year cycle appeared to influence industrial stock prices (Standard and Poor's Index of Industrials) from the period from 1871 through 1947.

Tripp, 1948. (Figure)

433

Industrial stock prices, as calculated from the Warren-Pearson—Dow-Jones Index of Industrial Stocks for the period 1880–1897 and the Dow-Jones Index of Industrial Stocks from 1898–1936, have appeared to follow the same pattern as the building cycle.

Warren and Pearson, 1937. p. 145. (Figure)

434

An 18-year rhythmic cycle in Railroad Stock Prices, U.S.A., 1831–1936, is alleged.

The major swings in railroad stock prices (Cleveland Trust Company Index of Railroad Stock Prices) have shown a tendency to move with the building cycle.

Warren and Pearson, 1937. p. 145. (Figure)

435

An 18-year rhythmic cycle in Stock Prices, U.S.A., is alleged.

An autocorrelation of the Axe-Houghton Index from 1854 through 1949 indicated the presence of an 18-year cycle in stock prices in the United States.

Daniels stated that this periodicity may be a reflection of the building
cycle.

Daniels, 1955. (Figure)

436

From Standard and Poor's Corporation Common Stock Price Index, Szatrowski detected a cycle approximately 18 years in length that influenced stock
prices in the United States.

Szatrowski, 1948, as reported by King, 1958.

437

An 18—19-year rhythmic cycle in Stock Prices, U.S.A., no dates given, is
alleged.

Long stated that stock prices in the United States showed a direct correlation to building activity in the United States which, he says, fluctuates
in waves approximately 18 to 19 years long.

Long, 1940. pp. 113—115.

438

An 18 1/3-year rhythmic cycle in the Lows in Stock Prices, U.S.A., is alleged.

There has been a tendency for the lows in common stock prices (Axe-
Houghton Index, 1854—1945) to move in waves averaging 18 1/3 years.

Dewey and Dakin, 1947. p. 132. (Figure)

439

Common stock lows have tended to follow an 18 1/3-year rhythmic pattern.

Klemme, 1950.

440

An 18 1/3-year rhythmic cycle in Railroad Stock Prices, U.S.A., 1831—1936,
is alleged.

Dewey and Dakin, 1947. p. 131. (Figure)

441

An 18 1/3-year rhythmic cycle in Industrial Stock Prices, U.S.A., 1897—
1947, is alleged.

Bartlett stated that the major rhythm influencing industrial stock prices
(Dow-Jones Corporation Industrial Averages) measured 18 1/3 years.

Bartlett, 1947.

442

An 18 2/3-year rhythmic cycle in Highs in Stock Prices, U.S.A., 1853—

1953, is alleged.

The average cycle length that dominated highs in stock prices in the United States has been 18 2/3 years. Langham suggested a lunar correlation.

Langham, 1954

443

A 19.4-year rhythmic cycle in Railroad Stock Price, U.S.A., 1831–1950, is alleged

A 19.4-year cyclic pattern in railroad stock prices (Cleveland Trust Company Index, 1831–1870, and Standard and Poor's Corporation Railroad Stock Price Index, 1871–1950) was suggested by Dewey. Typical amplitude of this cycle is 31.8% above trend at time of ideal crest and 24.1% below trend at time of an ideal trough. Typical timing placed a crest ideally at 1966 and a trough ideally at 1956.

Dewey, 1951-M. (Figure)
Dewey, 1951-P.

444

A 20-year rhythmic cycle in Industrial Stock Prices, U.S.A., 1897–1946, is alleged.

A minor 20-year cycle was reported by Woods as one of the factors influencing trends in the industrial stock prices in the United States (Dow-Jones Corporation Industrial Averages).

Woods, 1946.

445

A 22-year rhythmic cycle in Combined Stock Prices, U.S.A., 1871–1956, is alleged.

An audit of a possible 21.0-year cycle in stock prices (Standard and Poor's Corporation Combined Stock Price Index), which was first noted by Dewey in 1944, revised the length to 22.0 years. Typical strength of this cycle averaged 21.6% above trend at time of ideal crest. Ideal timing placed a crest at 1952.6.

Dewey, 1957-L. (Figure)
Dewey, 1957-A.

446

A 22–24-year rhythmic cycle in Lows in Stock Prices, U.S.A., 1837–1949, is alleged.

A gradually decreasing cycle, 22–24 years in length, was evident in stock price lows (Leonard Ayres' Index of Stock Prices, 1831–1871, and Standard and Poor's Composite Index, 1871–1949). Lows occurred at June 1861, January 1885, November 1907, and November 1929.

Smith, 1949, as reported by King, 1958.

447

A 25.0-year rhythmic cycle in Cigarette Stock Prices, U.S.A., 1912—1961,
is alleged.

Wilson, 1962-A. p. 159.

448

A 27-year rhythmic cycle in Combined Stock Prices, U.S.A., 1871—1956, is
alleged.

One of the rhythmic patterns which influences combined stock prices (Standard and Poor's Combined Stock Price Index) appeared to measure approximately 27 years in length. The strength of this 27-year cycle averaged 14.3%
above trend at time of ideal crest.

Dewey, 1957-K. (Figure)
Dewey, 1957-A.

449

A 27-year rhythmic cycle in Industrial Stock Prices, U.S.A., 1921—1949, is
alleged.

An analysis of the Dow-Jones Industrial Averages indicated that a 27-year
cycle appears to influence industrial stock prices in the United States.
Crests in the ideal pattern occurred in 1929 and in 1956.

Harvey, 1958.

450

A 27-year rhythmic cycle in Ordinary Share Prices, England, 1870—1953, is
alleged.

For the purpose of this analysis, McDougall used the London and Cambridge
Economic Service Index of Industrial Shares for those periods during which
it was compiled and linked the Kitchin Index from 1915 to 1924 and Moody's
Share Index from 1950 to 1958. The analysis revealed that the price of industrial ordinary shares in England had been influenced by a 27-year cycle.
Peaks were reported at about 1873, 1900, 1927, and 1954; lows, at about
1887, 1914, and 1941.

McDougall, 1958-B. (Figure)

451

A 28-year rhythmic cycle in Industrial Stock Prices, U.S.A., 1864—1947, is
alleged.

Industrial stock prices (E. W. Axe Industrial Stock Averages) appear to
have been influenced by a 28-year cycle. Peaks occurred in 1864, 1892,
1919, and 1946. Lows were reported in 1877, 1903, and 1932.

Westendorf, 1948. (Figure)

452

A 28-year rhythmic cycle in Stock Prices, U.S.A., 1831–1948, is alleged.

Except for the war-year 1865, the 28-year cycle repeated itself at regular 28-year intervals beginning with a low in June of 1837. For this analysis, Smith used the Leonard Ayres Index from 1831 through 1871 and Standard and Poor's Composite Index from 1871 through 1948.

Smith, 1948, as reported by King, 1958. (Figure)

453

A 36-year rhythmic pattern in Percent of Change in Stock Prices, U.S.A., 1839–1947, is alleged.

Smith, 1959. p. 161. (Figure)

454

A 37-year rhythmic cycle in Railroad Stock Prices, U.S.A., 1831–1950, is alleged.

The 37-year cycle, discovered to exist in various phenomena, displayed itself in railroad stock prices in the United States from 1831 through 1950.

Dewey, 1951-S.

455

A 37-year rhythmic cycle in Industrial Stock Prices, U.S.A., 1871–1950, is alleged.

Dewey, 1951-S.

456

A 45-year rhythmic cycle in Stock Prices, U.S.A., 1851–1946, is alleged.

The major cycle dominating stock prices in the United States, according to Woods, measured approximately 45 years in length. Using the Dow-Jones Stock Price Index for the analysis, Woods noted that the major fluctuations of the 45-year cycle have closely followed the highs and lows of nearly all major price trends since 1851.

Woods, 1947.

457

A 50-year rhythmic cycle in Gold Stock Values, U.S.A., 1815–1932, is alleged.

Babson, 1932. pp. 143–144.

458

A 54-year rhythmic cycle in Industrial Stock Prices, U.S.A., 1897–1947, is alleged.

Bartlett stated that a 54-year wave influenced industrial stock prices (Dow-

Jones Corporation Industrial Averages) during the 50-year period under
observation.

Bartlett, 1947.

459

A 56-year rhythmic cycle in Industrial Stock Prices, U.S.A., 1875–1935, is
alleged.

Using the Annalist-Burgess Indices, McGrath found that the major price cycle in industrial stocks averaged 56 years in length.

McGrath, 1936.

460

An 89 1/2-year rhythmic pattern in Stock Prices, U.S.A., 1799–1958, is
alleged.

By examination of the annual lows in stock prices (data from the United
States Bank, 1799–1812, and the Union Bank of Boston, 1817–1830) and
by examination of the monthly averages of stock prices (Ayres Index, 1831–
1871, and Standard and Poor's All Stock Index, 1871–1958), Smith found
that stock prices tended to follow an 89 1/2-year rhythmic pattern.

Smith, 1954. pp. 72–75.
Smith, 1959. pp. 172–174, 177–181. (Figure)

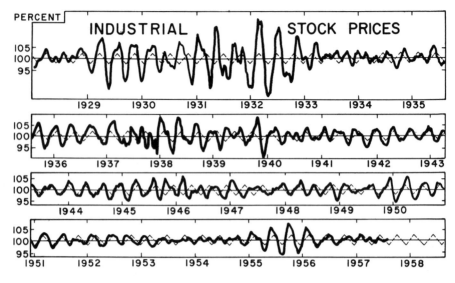

PRECIS 276

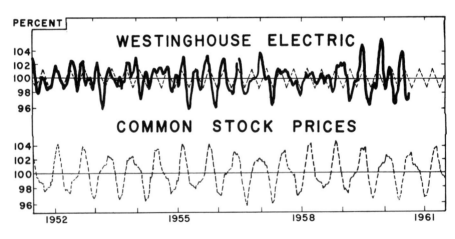

PRECIS 283

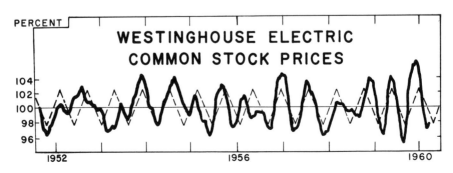

PRECIS 289

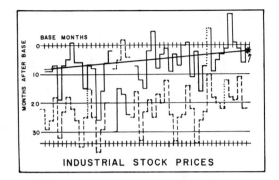

PRECIS 290

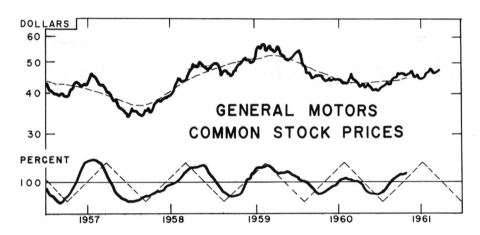

PRECIS 309

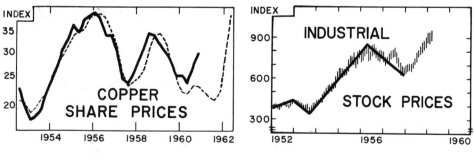

PRECIS 311   PRECIS 353

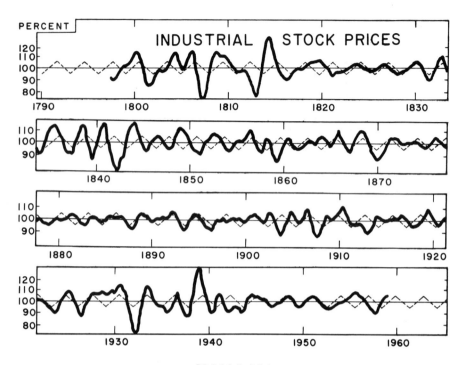

PRECIS 324

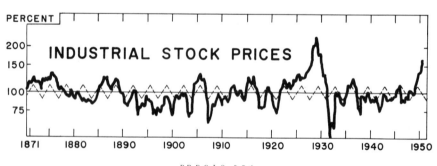

PRECIS 336

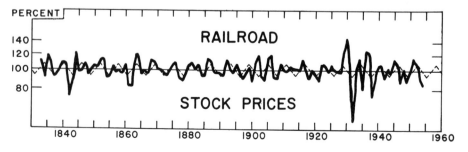

PRECIS 367

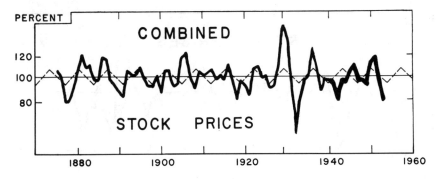

PRECIS 374

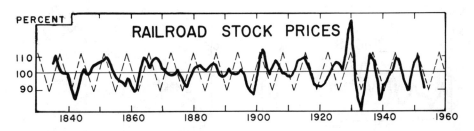

PRECIS 375

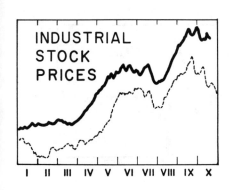

PRECIS 407

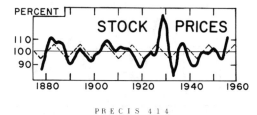

PRECIS 414

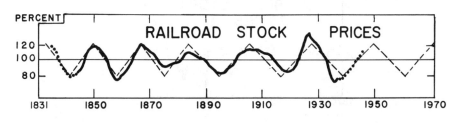

PRECIS 428

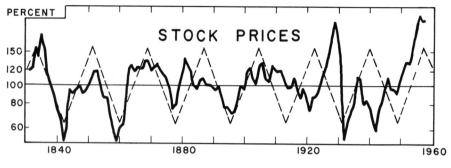

PRECIS 431

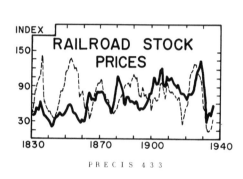

PRECIS 433

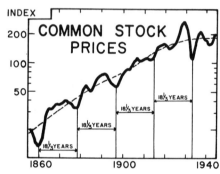

PRECIS 438

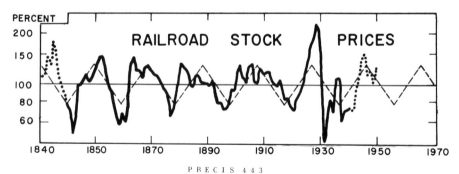

PRECIS 443

PRECIS 445

OTHER FINANCIAL DATA

BANK CLEARINGS AND CLEARINGS – DEBITS

461

A 3-month (13.04-week) rhythmic cycle in Clearings-Debits, U.S.A., 1867–1957, is alleged.

A systematic fluctuation in clearing-debits in the United States from 1867 through 1957 which measured approximately 3 months was discovered by means of spectral analysis. Friedman stated, however, that it had been produced because seasonal adjustment did not allow for variation in the number of Saturdays and Sundays in a month.

Friedman, 1959.

462

A 5-month (21.74-week) rhythmic cycle in Clearings-Debits, U.S.A., no dates given, is alleged.

In a series of some 40-odd years of data on clearings-debits in the United States, a spectral analysis by Friedman and Tukey revealed a fluctuation roughly 5 months in duration. Friedman felt this periodicity was produced by the effects of the bond campaigns, spaced at approximately that interval during the two World Wars.

Friedman, 1959.

463

A 31.08-month (2.59-year) rhythmic cycle in Reichsbank Clearings, Germany, 1884–1925, is alleged.

A minor cycle approximately 2.59 years in length was reported in Reichsbank clearings during the period under observation.

Wardwell, 1927. p. 76.

464

A 3-year rhythmic cycle in Bank Clearings, U.S.A., 1866–1914, is alleged.

A 3.00-year cycle in bank clearings outside New York City (data from the Philadelphia Clearing House Association, 1866–1878, and from the *Commercial and Financial Chronicle* for seven selected cities, 1879–1914) was reported by Frickey.

Frickey, 1935.

465

Various average cycles (shortest length: 37 months) in Deflated Clearings, U.S.A., March 1878–March 1933, are alleged.

The possibility of cycles with the lengths of 37, 41, 44, and 54 months having influenced deflated clearings in the United States was discussed.

Burns and Mitchell, 1946.

466

A 3.15-year (37.75-month) rhythmic cycle in Bank Clearings, U.S.A., 1875–1926, is alleged.

The average length of the minor cycle which influenced bank clearings in the United States was measured at 3.15 years.

Wardwell, 1927. p. 71.

467

A 3.33-year (40-month) rhythmic cycle in Bank Clearings, Great Britain and U.S.A., 1890–1922, is alleged.

There has been a tendency for bank clearings to follow a 40-month rhythmic pattern in both the United States and Great Britain. Kitchin also alleged a 40-month cycle in wholesale commodity prices and in interest rates.

Kitchin, 1923.

468

A 3.33-year (40-month) rhythmic pattern in Bank Clearings and Debits, New York, 1891–1940, is alleged.

Smith reported a 40-month rhythmic pattern in the 12-month percent of change in bank clearings and debits in New York City (daily average clearing for December, 1891–1919; daily average debits for December, 1919–1936; and total December debits, 1936–1940).

Smith, 1959. pp. 107, 114. (Figure)

469

A 6.5-year (78.0-month) average cycle in Discount Rates at the Central Bank, Great Britain, 1870–1914, is suggested.

Tinbergen, 1951. p. 133.

470

A 7.15-year (85.8-month) rhythmic cycle in Bank Clearings, New York, 1866–1914, is alleged.

New York City bank clearings (monthly data compiled by Matthews and Persons) appeared to follow a 7.15-year cycle from 1866 through 1914.

Frickey, 1935.

471

A 10-year rhythmic cycle in Bank Clearings and Debits, New York, 1891–1940, is alleged.

A recurrent 10-year cycle, which Smith called a Decennial Pattern, was evident in the 12-month percent of change in New York bank clearings and debits from 1891 through 1940.

Smith, 1959. pp. 107, 114. (Figure)

472

A 10.92-year rhythmic cycle in Reichsbank Clearings, Germany, 1884–1925, is alleged.

The major cycle influencing the Reichsbank clearings in Germany during the period under observation appeared to measure approximately 10.92 years in length.

Wardwell, 1927. p. 76.

473

A 14.50-year rhythmic cycle in Bank Clearings, U.S.A., 1875–1926, is alleged.

14.50 years appeared to be the length of the major cycle in bank clearings in the United States from 1875 through 1926.

Wardwell, 1927. p. 71.

474

A 50–60-year (average 54-year) rhythmic cycle in the Portfolio of the Bank of France, France, 1810–1925, is alleged.

Kondratieff, 1926.

BANK DEBITS AND CREDITS

475

A 3.33-year (40-month) rhythmic cycle in Bank Debits, New York, 1919–1940, is alleged.

Bank debits as well as bank clearings have appeared to follow a 40-month cycle.

Smith, 1959. pp. 107, 114.

476

A 3.33-year (40-month) rhythmic cycle in Rate of Change of Bank Debits, U.S.A., no dates given, is alleged.

Newbury, 1952. pp. 182–183.

477

A 3.42-year (41-month) rhythmic cycle in Bank Debits, U.S.A., no dates given, is alleged.

Dewey reported that bank debits in the United States have tended to fall in a 41-month pattern.

Dewey, 1951-H. p. 335.

478

A 4.01-year (48.1-month) rhythmic cycle in Bank Debits, Pittsburgh, 1919–1945, is alleged.

Neff and Weifenbach, 1949.

479

A 4.08-year (48.9-month) rhythmic cycle in Bank Debits, San Francisco, 1919–1945, is alleged.

Neff and Weifenbach, 1949.

480

A 4.12-year (49.4-month) rhythmic cycle in Bank Debits, Detroit, 1919–1945, is alleged.

Neff and Weifenbach, 1949.

481

A 5.38-year (64.5-month) rhythmic cycle in Bank Debits, Cleveland, 1919–1945, is alleged.

Neff and Weifenbach, 1949.

482

A 5.44-year (65.3-month) rhythmic cycle in Bank Debits, Chicago, 1919–1945, is alleged.

Neff and Weifenbach, 1949.

483

A 5.65-year (67.8-month) rhythmic cycle in Bank Debits, Los Angeles, 1919–1945, is alleged.

Neff and Weifenbach, 1949.

484

A 10-year rhythmic cycle in Bank Debits, New York, 1919–1940, is alleged.

Bank debits have appeared to move in a recurring 10-year cyclic pattern which Smith calls the Decennial Pattern.

Smith, 1959. pp. 107, 114.

485

An 18-year rhythmic cycle in Bank Credit, U.S.A., 1830–1936, is alleged.

Bank credit (total loans and discounts) in the United States showed a tendency to fluctuate with the building cycle.

Warren and Pearson, 1937. p. 142. (Figure)

BANK DEPOSITS
AND DEPOSIT VELOCITY

486

A 34.32-month (2.86-year) rhythmic cycle in Deposit Velocity, U.S.A., 1875–

1923, is alleged.

The minor cycle which appears to have governed deposit velocity measured approximately 2.86 years in length.

Wardwell, 1927. p. 72.

487

A 35.4-month (2.95-year) rhythmic cycle in Bank Deposits, U.S.A., 1869–1925, is alleged.

In the series of total deposits of all national banks in the United States, the minor influencing cycle was approximately 2.95 years long.

Wardwell, 1927. p. 71.

488

A 3.33-year (40-month) rhythmic cycle in Bank Deposits, U.S.A., 1885–1923, is alleged.

Deposits in national banks in the United States have shown a tendency to move in a 40-month cyclical pattern.

Ayres, 1939. p. 135. (Figure)

489

A 3.83-year (45.96-month) rhythmic cycle in the Ratio of Withdrawals to Deposits, Berlin, Germany, 1865–1920, is alleged.

The average length of the minor cycle in the ratio of withdrawals to deposits at the Berlin Municipal Savings Bank has been 3.83 years.

Wardwell, 1927. p. 75.

490

A 12-year rhythmic cycle in the Ratio of Withdrawals to Deposits, Berlin, Germany, 1865–1920, is alleged.

The major cycle influencing the ratio of withdrawals to deposits at the Berlin Municipal Savings Bank averaged 12 years in length.

Wardwell, 1927. p. 75.

491

A 12.08-year rhythmic cycle in Bank Deposits, U.S.A., 1869–1925, is alleged.

A 12.08-year major cyclic pattern has appeared to influence the total bank deposits of all national banks in the United States.

Wardwell, 1927. p. 71.

492

An 18.75-year rhythmic cycle in Deposit Velocity, U.S.A., 1875–1923, is

alleged.

The major cycle in deposit velocity in the United States measured approximately 18.75 years in length.

Wardwell, 1927. p. 72.

493

A 50–60-year (average 54-year) rhythmic cycle in Bank Deposits, France, 1844–1925, is alleged.

Kondratieff, 1926. p. 110.

BOND PRICES

494

A 10.8-month (.90-year) rhythmic cycle in Bond Prices, U.S.A., 1866–1914, is alleged.

From Moody's "typical corporation bond prices," monthly from 1866 through 1914, Frickey noted a tendency for bond prices to move in waves approximately .90 year long.

Frickey, 1935.

495

A 3.33-year (40-month) rhythmic cycle in Bond Prices, U.S.A., 1838–1939, is alleged.

A 40-month cycle in bond prices was observed by Ayres along with corresponding 40-month cycles in stock prices, interest rates, capital issues, loans and investments, and deposits. An interrelationship of these similar cycles was suggested.

Ayres, 1939. (Figure)

496

A 9 1/5-year rhythmic cycle in British Consol Prices, England, 1830–1958, is alleged.

McDougall, 1959-A. (Figure)

497

A 13-year rhythmic cycle in British Consol Prices, England, 1830–1958, is alleged.

An unusual complex 13-year cycle has appeared to influence the price of British consols.

McDougall, 1959-A. (Figure)

498

A 36-year rhythmic cycle in British Consol Prices, England, 1890–1958, is alleged.

A cyclical pattern very close to 36 years in length has been evident in the price of British consols for the period under observation.

McDougall, 1959-A. (Figure)

499

A 54-year rhythmic cycle in British Consol Prices, England, is alleged.

Kondratieff reported a 54-year cycle in the price of British consols from 1790 through 1918.

Kondratieff, 1926. pp. 253—256.

500

A 54-year cycle in the price of British consols from 1830—1958 revealed a peak in 1952 and a possible trough in 1979.

McDougall, 1959-A.

501

English consols appeared to be following a rigid 54-year wave through 1961.

Shirk, 1962-D. (Figure)

502

A 54.9-year rhythmic cycle in British Consol Prices, England, 1735—1955, is alleged.

Danson claimed to have isolated a 54.9-year cycle in the British Consols Price Series. This cycle appeared to be a major component in a compound cycle which dominates consol prices.

Danson, 1959. (Figure)

503

A 61.4-year rhythmic cycle in British Consol Prices, England, 1735—1955, is alleged.

A 61.4-year cycle in the British Consols Price Series was isolated by Danson who reported that this cycle appeared to be often compounded with the 54.9-year cycle.

Danson, 1959. (Figure)

BOND YIELDS AND
INTEREST RATES

504

Various average cycles (shortest length: 32 months) in Railroad Bond Yields, U.S.A., August 1860—May 1931, are suggested.

Cycles having the average length of 32 months, 42 months, 45 months, and 49 months were suggested as forces which exert influence on railroad bond yields.

Burns and Mitchell, 1946.

505

A 33.2-month (2.77-year) rhythmic cycle in Short-Term Interest Rates, France, January 1925—December 1938, is alleged.

Morgenstern, 1959. p. 92.

506

A 35.4-month (2.95-year) rhythmic cycle in Interest Rates, U.S.A., 1866—1926, is alleged.

The length of the minor cycle in 60—90-day interest rates in the United States appeared to be approximately 2.95 years.

Wardwell, 1927. p. 73.

507

Various average cycles (shortest length: 36 months) in Call Money Rates, U.S.A., October 1858—May 1931, are suggested.

Burns and Mitchell suggested that there may be three cycles of various average lengths (a 36-month, a 38-month, and a 40-month) present in call money rates in the United States.

Burns and Mitchell, 1946.

508

A 3—4-year rhythmic cycle in Short-Term Interest Rates, United Kingdom, 1870—1910, is alleged.

Tinbergen and Polak, 1950. p. 62.

509

A 3.02-year (36.2-month) rhythmic cycle in Call Money Rates, U.S.A., February 1878—August 1913, is alleged.

Morgenstern, 1959. p. 92.

510

A 3.02-year (36.26-month) rhythmic cycle in Bond Yields, U.S.A., 1890—1926, is alleged.

The minor cycle influencing bond yields in the United States showed an average length of 3.02 years.

Wardwell, 1927. p. 72.

511

A 3.05-year (36.6-month) rhythmic cycle in Commercial Paper Rates, U.S.A., February 1878—August 1913, is alleged.

Morgenstern, 1959. p. 92.

512

A 3.18-year (38.16-month) rhythmic cycle in Discount Rates in Private Banks, Berlin, Germany, 1876—1923, is alleged.

The average length of the minor cycle in discount rates in private banks in

Germany from 1876 through 1923 was 3.18 years.

Wardwell, 1927. p. 76.

513

A 3.22-year (38.6-month) rhythmic cycle in Short-Term Interest Rates, Germany, February 1878—August 1913, is alleged.

Morgenstern, 1959. p. 92.

514

A 3.31-year (39.7-month) rhythmic cycle in Short-Term Interest Rates, Great Britain, January 1925—December 1938, is alleged.

Morgenstern, 1959. p. 92.

515

A 3.33-year (40-month) rhythmic cycle in Bond Yields, U.S.A., 1836—1939, is alleged.

Ayres reported that bond yields in the United States have shown a tendency to follow a 40-month cyclic pattern. He also noted that the troughs of bond yields correspond with the crests of bond prices.

Ayres, 1939. (Figure)

516

A 3.33-year (40-month) rhythmic cycle in Commercial Paper Rates, U.S.A., 1831—1939, is alleged.

Discount rates on 4—6-month commercial paper in the United States from 1831 through 1939 showed a tendency to move in cycles approximately 40 months in duration.

Ayres, 1939. (Figure)

517

A 3.33-year (40-month) average cycle in Commercial Paper Rates, New York, is suggested.

By means of a periodogram analysis, Crum found evidence that an average 40-month cycle influenced commercial paper rates in New York from 1866 through 1922.

Crum, 1923. (Figure; data)

518

Using power spectrum analysis of New York commercial paper rates for the period from 1876 through 1914, Granger and Morgenstern found a suggestion of the conventional 40-month period in short-term interest rates.

Granger and Morgenstern, 1963. p. 6.

519

A 3.33-year (40-month) rhythmic cycle in Interest Rates, U.S.A., Great

Britain, is alleged.

In the 40-month cycle which Ayres found in interest rates in the United
States during the period from 1885 through 1923, the downswing averaged 23 months in length while the upswing averaged only 17 months.

Ayres, 1939. (Figure)

520

A 40-month rhythmic pattern was reported to be present in pre-World War I
interest rates in the United States.

Granger, 1960.

521

A 40-month cycle influenced interest rates in both Great Britain and the
United States during the period from 1890 through 1922. Kitchin also alleged a 40-month cycle in wholesale commodity prices and in bank clearings.

Kitchin, 1923. (Figure)

522

A 3.95-year (47.4-month) rhythmic cycle in Long-Term Interest Rates,
U.S.A., February 1878—August 1913, is alleged.

Long-term interest rates in the United States for the period from February
1878 through August 1913 (as measured by Macaulay's railroad bond yield
index) moved in cycles which averaged approximately 47.4 months in duration.

Morgenstern., 1959. pp. 451—453.

523

A 3.96-year (47.5-month) rhythmic cycle in Short-Term Interest Rates,
France, February 1878—August 1913, is alleged.

Morgenstern, 1959. p. 92.

524

A 4.10-year (49.2-month) rhythmic cycle in Long-Term Interest Rates,
France, February 1878—August 1913, is alleged.

The waves which were present in 3% rentes in France from February 1878
through August 1913 measured about 49.2 months in duration.

Morgenstern, 1959. pp. 451—453.

525

A 4.38-year (52.6-month) rhythmic cycle in Short-Term Interest Rates, Great
Britain, February 1878—August 1913, is alleged.

Morgenstern, 1959. p. 92.

526

A 4.58-year (55.0-month) rhythmic cycle in Short-Term Interest Rates, U.S.A., January 1925—December 1938, is alleged.

Morgenstern, 1959. p. 92.

527

A 5.95-year (71.4-month) rhythmic cycle in Long-Term Interest Rates, Great Britain, February 1878—August 1913, is alleged.

During the period from February 1878 through August 1913, 3% consols appeared to move in a cyclic pattern which averaged about 71.4 months in duration.

Morgenstern, 1959. pp. 451—453.

528

A 6.21-year (74.5-month) rhythmic cycle in Short-Term Interest Rates, Germany, January 1925—December 1938, is alleged.

Morgenstern, 1959. p. 92.

529

A 7.6-year (91.2-month) rhythmic cycle in Long-Term Interest Rates, Germany, February 1878—August 1913, is alleged.

Long-term interest rates in Germany as measured by the movements of 6% government bond yields and gold mortgage bond yields moved in waves approximately 91.2 months in duration during the period February 1878—August 1913.

Morgenstern, 1959. pp. 451—453.

530

An 8.02-year rhythmic cycle in Commercial Paper Rates, U.S.A., 1866—1914, is alleged.

Based on data supplied by W. L. Crum, Frickey determined a cycle approximately 8.02 years in length in commercial paper rates.

Frickey, 1935.

531

An 8.19-year rhythmic cycle in Discount Rates in Private Banks, Berlin, Germany, 1876—1923, is alleged.

The average length of the major cycle in discount rates in private banks in Germany was determined to be 8.19 years.

Wardwell, 1927. p. 76.

532

A 12.5-year rhythmic cycle in "Series B," U.S.A., 1911—1956, is alleged.

From "Series B" data supplied by a New York Financial House, Dewey found a 12.5-year cycle. Typical amplitude of this cycle was 1.9% above trend at time of an ideal crest and 1.8% below trend at time of an ideal trough.

Dewey, 1957-G. (Figure)

533

A 12.92-year rhythmic cycle in Bond Yields, U.S.A., 1890–1926, is alleged.

The average length of the major cycle in bond yields in the United States appeared to be 12.92 years.

Wardwell, 1927. p. 72.

534

A 17.05-year rhythmic cycle in Interest Rates, U.S.A., 1866–1926, is alleged.

A cycle approximately 17.05 years in length has appeared to influence 60–90-day interest rates in the United States.

Wardwell, 1927. p. 73.

535

A 50-year rhythmic cycle in Interest Rates, U.S.A., no dates given, is alleged.

Interest rates in the United States appeared to fluctuate in waves which measured from 40 to 70 years and which averaged 50 years.

Hamberg, 1951. p. 9.

536

A 50-year rhythmic cycle in the Yield of Consols, Great Britain, no dates given, is alleged.

According to the authors, the yields of consols in Great Britain appeared to display a 20–30-year upward movement.

Brown and Ozga, 1955.

537

An average 54-year rhythmic cycle in Interest Rates of British Consols, England, 1820–1918, is alleged.

Using data from statistical tables from *Commerce and Industry*, Kondratieff reported that an average 54-year cycle influenced interest rates of British consols during the period under observation, 1820–1918. It was also noted that the price of British consols shows an inverse relationship to interest rates of British consols.

Kondratieff, 1926. (Figure)

538

An average 54-year rhythmic cycle in Interest Rates of Rentes, France, 1816–1925, is alleged.

Data from the *Annuaire Statistique* revealed that the interest rates of

French rentes move in the same cyclical pattern as the interest rates of British consols.

Kondratieff, 1926. (Figure)

539

A 54-year rhythmic cycle in Interest Rates, U.S.A., 1857–1956, is alleged.

During the 100-year period under observation, Dewey found that interest rates in the United States (Macaulay Index of Yields, high grade railroad bonds, 1857–1926, and Moody's Aa Railroad Bond Yield Averages, 1919–1956) showed a tendency to move in a 54-year cyclic pattern. A crest in the ideal pattern of this cycle occurred at 1923.

Dewey, 1957-N. (Figure)

540

Klemme suggested that interest rates in the United States (no dates given) followed a 54-year rhythmic pattern.

Klemme, 1950.

541

A figure prepared by Moody's and based on Moody's Aa Railroad Bond Yield Averages illustrated the continuance of the 54-year cycle in interest rates in the United States.

Shirk, 1960-S. (Figure)

542

Domestic corporate, all grades, bond yields in the United States through August of 1962 appeared to be following the ideal pattern of the 54-year cycle. A crest in the ideal pattern was dated at 1978.

Shirk, 1962-V. (Figure)

BUSINESS FAILURES

543

A 3.22-year (39.84-month) rhythmic cycle in Liabilities of Failed Concerns U.S.A., 1875–1926, is alleged.

Wardwell reported that a 3.32-year minor cycle appeared to influence the liabilities of failed concerns in the United States.

Wardwell, 1927. p. 71.

544

A 3.42-year (41.04-month) rhythmic cycle in Business Failures, U.S.A., is alleged.

A 3.42-year minor cyclical pattern was evident in the liabilities of commercial and industrial failures in the United States during the period under observation even though it was overwhelmed by the upsurge of failures during the Civil War and the lack of failures during World War II. Typical amplitude of this cycle was measured at 15.8% above trend at time of an ideal crest and 13.7% below trend at time of an ideal trough. The 3.42-year cycle crested ideally at the end of 1893 and every 3.42 years forward and backward from that time.

Dewey, 1953-B. (Figure)

545

A later article extended data on the 3.42-year cycle through 1956. Dewey noted that a crest in the ideal pattern occurred at 1952.14.

Dewey, 1957-H. (Figure)

546

Various average cycles (shortest length: 3.42 years) in Business Failures, U.S.A., 1908–1959, were suggested.

The cycles which are listed below had been originally determined by Dewey in 1953, using data from the year 1857, on the liabilities of commercial and industrial failures.

Length in Years	% Above Trend at Crest	Ideal Crest
3.42	15.9	1958.98
5.9	12.5	1955.70
6.5	14.3	1961.50
9.2	38.0	1959.50
17.67	51.0	1946.50

Shirk, 1960-U. (Figure)

547

A 4 1/2-year rhythmic cycle in Business Failures, U.S.A., 1857–1950, is alleged.

A hint of a 4 1/2-year rhythm was found in an analysis of the 17 2/3-year cycle which appeared to influence the liabilities of commercial and industrial failures from 1857 through 1950.

Dewey, 1951-G.

548

A 5 1/2-year rhythmic cycle in Business Recessions, France, 1838–1920, is alleged.

Mitchell, 1927.

549

A 5.9-year (70.8-month) rhythmic cycle in Business Failures, U.S.A., 1857–1953, is alleged.

The 5.9-year cycle in the liabilities of commercial and industrial failures appeared to have some correlation with the 5.91-year cycle in cotton prices and sunspot numbers. Typical amplitude of this cycle was recorded as 12.5%

above trend at time of an ideal crest and 11.1% below trend at time of ideal trough.

Dewey, 1953-B. (Figure)

550

A later article carried data through 1956. A trough in the ideal pattern was dated at 1958.65.

Dewey, 1957-H. (Figure)
Dewey, 1957-I. (Figure)

551

A 6-year rhythmic cycle in Business Failures, U.S.A., 1857–1950, is alleged.

An average wave of 6 years duration was reported to be present in the liabilities of commercial and industrial failures in the United States during the period under observation.

Dewey, 1951-G.

552

A 6.5-year (78.0-month) rhythmic cycle in Business Failures, 1857–1953, is alleged.

One of the cycles which was clearly evident in Dewey's study of the liabilities of commercial and industrial failures in the United States measured 6.5 years in length. Typical amplitude of this cycle averaged 14.3% above trend at time of an ideal crest and 12.5% below trend at time of an ideal trough.

Dewey, 1953-B.

553

Dewey extended data through 1956 and reported that a crest in the ideal pattern occurred at 1948.5.

Dewey, 1957-H. (Figure)

554

A 7-year rhythmic cycle in Business Recessions, England, 1837–1920, is alleged.

Mitchell, 1927.

555

A 9-year rhythmic cycle in Business Failures, U.S.A., 1857–1950, is alleged.

A minor influence in the liabilities of commercial and industrial failures in the United States during the period under observation measured approximately 9 years in length.

Dewey, 1951-G.

556

A 9.2-year rhythmic cycle in Business Failures, U.S.A., 1857–1953, is

alleged.

There has been a tendency for the liabilities of commercial and industrial failures to move in a 9.2-year cyclical pattern. Typical amplitude of this 9.2-year cycle has been 38% above trend at time of ideal crest and 31% below trend at time of ideal trough. A crest of this cycle came ideally at mid-1913 and every 9.2 years forward and backward from that time.

Dewey, 1953-B. (Figure)

557

A later article carried the study of the 9.2-year cycle through 1954. A crest in the ideal pattern was reported at 1950.

Dewey, 1954-N. (Figure)

558

Dewey brought the figures up-to-date for the 9.2-year cycle in the liabilities of commercial and industrial failures.

Dewey, 1957-H. (Figure)

559

A 9.4-year rhythmic cycle in Business Failures, U.S.A., 1867—1932, is alleged.

In his Periodogram Analysis with Special Application to Business Failures in the United States, 1867—1932, Greenstein found a cycle of a typical duration of 9.4 years. Data used for the analysis was from Dun's Review—*Econometrica* for April 1935.

Greenstein, 1935, as reported by Schumpeter, 1939. p. 171.

560

An 11-year rhythmic cycle in Business Failures, U.S.A., no dates given, is alleged.

Stetson contended that there is a correlation between sunspot activity and the number of business failures in the United States.

Stetson, 1946.

561

A 17 2/3-year rhythmic cycle in Business Failures, U.S.A., 1857—1950, is alleged.

Analysis of annual data evidenced a major 17 2/3-year cycle in the liabilities of commercial and industrial failures in the United States as well as minor rhythms approximately 4 1/2, 6, and 9 years in length. A major 54-year rhythm was also suggested. This cycle displayed a typical amplitude of 51% above trend at time of ideal crest and 34% below trend at time of ideal trough. Mid-1893 dated a crest in the ideal pattern. This cycle was later refined to the length of 17 3/4 years.

Dewey, 1951-G. (Figure)

562

A 17 3/4-year rhythmic cycle in Business Failures, 1857–1950, is alleged.

This 17 3/4-year cycle is the refined length of the 17 2/3-year cycle. Dewey reported that the average amplitude of this cycle remained at 51% above trend at time of ideal crest and 34% below trend at time of ideal trough.

Dewey, 1953-B. (Figure)

563

An additional article carries data on the 17 3/4-year cycle in the liabilities of commercial and industrial failures through 1956. Minor influencing cycles are reported as measuring 9.2, 6.5, 5.9, and 3.42 years.

Dewey, 1957-H.

564

A 19.33-year rhythmic cycle in Liabilities of Failed Concerns, U.S.A., 1875–1926, is alleged.

The average length of the major cycle in the liabilities of failed concerns in the United States from 1875 through 1926 was approximately 19.33 years.

Wardwell, 1927. p. 71.

565

A 54-year rhythmic cycle in Business Failures, U.S.A., 1857–1950, is alleged.

Although the period under observation does not allow for a repeat cycle, a wave of approximately 54 years is seemingly present in the liabilities of commercial and industrial failures in the United States from 1857 through 1950.

Dewey, 1951-G.

INCOME AND WAGES

566

A 3.33-year (40-month) rhythmic cycle in Income, U.S.A., no dates given, is alleged.

Hubbard, 1942. p. 199.

567

A 3.35-year (40.16-month) rhythmic cycle in National Income, U.S.A., 1853–1958, is alleged.

Using data from the National Bureau of Economic Research, Coppock noted a possible 3.35-year rhythmic pattern in national income for the period from 1853 through 1958. This compares favorably, said Coppock, with the Klein-

Goldberger model findings.

Coppock, 1962. p. 464.

568

A 4–5-year rhythmic cycle in Personal Income, U.S.A., 1944–1959, is alleged.

According to the Woytinskys, personal income in the United States from 1944 through 1959 experienced a setback every fourth or fifth year. 1949–1950, 1953–1954, and 1958–1959 were listed as setback years.

Woytinsky and Woytinsky, 1959. pp. 4–5. (Figure)

569

A 7–10-year rhythmic cycle in National Income and Capital Formation, United Kingdom, 1870–1914, is alleged.

Movements of national income and capital formation in the United Kingdom for the period under observation followed a 7–10-year pattern. Matthews noted the following durations: for troughs – 6, 8, 10, and 5 years; for peaks – 9, 7, 10, and 7 years.

Matthews, 1959. p. 216. (Figure)

570

A 20-year rhythmic cycle in Income Growth, Japan, 1878–1942, is alleged.

Shinohara, 1962. pp. ii, 79.

571

A 50–60-year rhythmic cycle in the Weekly Wages of Textile Workers, England, 1790–1925, is alleged.

Kondratieff, 1926. (Figure)

572

A 50–60-year rhythmic cycle in the Weekly Wages of Textile Workers, France, 1810–1925, is alleged.

Kondratieff, 1926. (Figure)

573

A 50–60-year rhythmic cycle in the Weekly Wages of Coal Miners, France, 1849–1925, is alleged.

Kondratieff, 1926. (Figure)

INTEREST BEARING DEBT

574

A 59-year rhythmic cycle in Interest Bearing Debt, U.S.A., 1833–1936, is alleged.

Interest bearing debt of the United States appears to move in a cyclical pattern approximately 59 years long.

Dewey, 1958-B. (Figure)

INVESTMENT

575

A 3.33-year (40-month) rhythmic cycle in Dynamic Investment, U.S.A., no dates given, is alleged.

Hubbard, 1942. p. 199.

576

A 3.33-year (40-month) rhythmic cycle in Induced Investment, U.S.A., no dates given, is alleged.

Hubbard, 1942. p. 199.

577

A 5-year average cycle in Investments, Great Britain, 1870—1914, is suggested.

Tinbergen, 1951. p. 131.

578

A 7—10-year rhythmic cycle in Foreign Investments, United Kingdom, no dates given, is alleged.

Matthews, 1959. p. 216.

579

A 7—10-year rhythmic cycle in Fixed Investments, U.S.A., no dates given, is alleged.

There exists, says Matthews, a 7- to 10-year cycle in fixed investments which appears to be largely regulated in intensity by the phases of the building cycle.

Matthews, 1959. p. 211.

580

A 10-year average cycle in Demand for Investment Goods, United Kingdom, 1870—1914, is suggested.

Tinbergen, 1951. p. 127.

581

A 20-year rhythmic cycle in Foreign Investments, United Kingdom, no dates given, is alleged.

In addition to a 7—10-year cycle in foreign investments, a longer and more prominent 20-year cycle was evident.

Matthews, 1959. p. 216.

582

A 20-year rhythmic cycle in Investment and Migration, England, no dates given, is alleged.

According to Saul, Cairncross discovered a cycle of about 20 years duration in investment and migration in England.

Cairncross, 1953, as reported by Saul, 1962. p. 119.

LAPSE RATES

583

A 50-year rhythmic cycle in Lapse Rates, U.S.A., 1916—1942, is alleged.

Bowerman alleged a correlation between lapse rates in the United States and wholesale commodity prices.

Bowerman, 1945.

LOANS

584

A 27-month (2.25-year) rhythmic cycle in Loans, New York City, January 1866—June 1914, is alleged.

Using monthly data, Frickey found a 2.25-year cycle influencing loans of New York City clearing house banks.

Frickey, 1935.

585

A 35.76-month (2.98-year) rhythmic cycle in Ratio of Loans and Investments to Deposits, New York City, 1867—1925, is alleged.

The average length of the minor cycle in the ratio of loans and investments to deposits in New York City clearing house banks was calculated to be 2.98 years.

Wardwell, 1927. p. 72.

586

A 3—4-year rhythmic cycle in Public Borrowings, New Zealand, 1867—1911, is alleged.

Simkin, 1951. pp. 45, 51.

587

A 3.33-year (40-month) rhythmic cycle in Loans and Investments, U.S.A., 1885—1923, is alleged.

Ayres stated that loans and investments in the United States, as well as bond activity, interest rates, stock prices, and general bank activity, tended to follow a 40-month rhythmic pattern.

Ayres, 1939. (Figure)

588

A 15.35-year rhythmic cycle in Ratio of Loans and Investments to Deposits, New York City, 1867—1925, is alleged.

The major influence on the ratio of loans and investments to deposits in clearing house banks in New York City from 1867 through 1925 appeared to be a cycle measuring approximately 15.35 years.

Wardwell, 1927. p. 72.

589

An 18 1/3-year rhythmic cycle in Loans and Discounts, U.S.A., 1833–1936, is alleged.

Variations in the volume of loans and discounts, expressed as a percentage of the normal, seemed to move in the same cyclical pattern as building activity in the United States (18 1/3-year pattern).

Dewey, 1955-G. pp. 35, 59. (Figure)

590

Klemme also noted that loans and discounts in the United States tended to move in an 18 1/3-year cycle.

Klemme, 1950.

MISCELLANEOUS FINANCIAL

591

A 12 1/2-week (2.87-month) rhythmic cycle in Total Odd Lot Short Sales, New York, 1960–1961, is alleged.

Viele, 1962. (Figure)

592

A 12 1/2-week (2.87-month) rhythmic cycle in Odd Lot Sales Divided by Odd Lot Purchases, New York, 1960–1961, is alleged.

Viele, 1962. (Figure)

593

A 2–3-year rhythmic cycle in the Ratio of Net Changes in Installment Credit to Disposable Income, U.S.A., no dates given, is alleged.

Abramson and Mack, 1956. pp. 64–66.

594

A 3.4-year (40.8-month) rhythmic cycle in General Financial Activity, New Zealand, 1860–1911, is alleged.

General financial activity in New Zealand during the period from 1860 through 1911, as measured by ascertained receipts of New Zealand, appeared to move in waves which measured approximately 3.4 years although the duration of the waves ranged between two and seven years.

Simkin, 1951. pp. 93–94.

595

A 4.8-year (57.6-month) rhythmic cycle in Credit Money, New Zealand,

1860—1908, is alleged.

Although the waves found in credit money in New Zealand from 1860 through 1908 ranged in measurement from 3 to 9 years, the average duration of a wave averaged 4.8 years.

Simkin, 1951. p. 74.

596

A 4.8-year (57.6-month) rhythmic cycle of Circulating Money, New Zealand, 1870—1908, is alleged.

The range of wave lengths in circulating money in New Zealand from 1870 through 1908 was from 3 to 7 years. The average duration appeared to be 4.8 years.

Simkin, 1951. p. 75.

597

A 20-year rhythmic cycle in Economic Interaction, England and U.S.A., no dates given, is alleged.

Thomas was quoted by Saul as having found a cycle which measured approximately 20 years in duration in the interaction of the British and the American economies.

Thomas, 1954, as reported by Saul, 1962.

MORTGAGES

598

An 11-year rhythmic cycle in Residential Mortgage Loans, U.S.A., 1923—1942, is alleged.

Bowerman contended that the total mortgage loans by Savings and Loan Associations of the United States on residential building during the years under observation moved in an average 11-year cycle. A correlation of this movement with the cyclical pattern recorded in sunspot activity was suggested.

Bowerman, 1944.

599

An 18—20-year rhythmic cycle in New Mortgages, Berlin, Germany, 1844—1909, is alleged.

The increase in new mortgages in the vicinity of Berlin, Germany, showed a close relationship to the 18 1/3-year building cycle. Reich reported that a crest in the ideal pattern occurred at about 1890.

Reich, 1912, as reported by Warren and Pearson, 1937. (Figure)

600

An 18—25-year rhythmic cycle in Mortgage Financing, U.S.A., no dates

given, is alleged.

Downs, 1959. Chapter IV.

POSTAL RECEIPTS

601

A 22-year rhythmic cycle in Postal Receipts, Milwaukee, Wisconsin, no dates given, is alleged.

Dewey, 1950-D. p. 10.

SECURITY ISSUES

602

A 3.33-year (40-month) rhythmic cycle in Security Issues, U.S.A., 1863–1939, is alleged.

Ayres reported that he had found a 40-month cycle in security issues, as well as in bond prices, stock prices, bond yields, interest rates, loans and investments, general banking, and business activity.

Ayres, 1939.

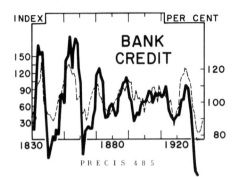

PRECIS 485

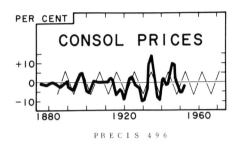

PRECIS 496

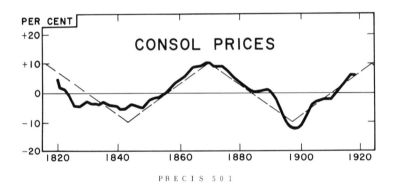

PRECIS 501

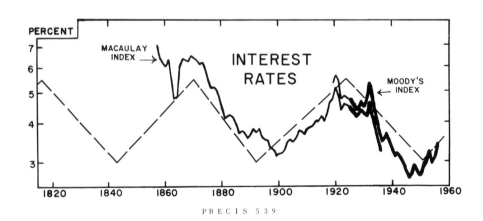

PRECIS 539

PRECIS 550

PRECIS 553

PRECIS 556

PRECIS 558

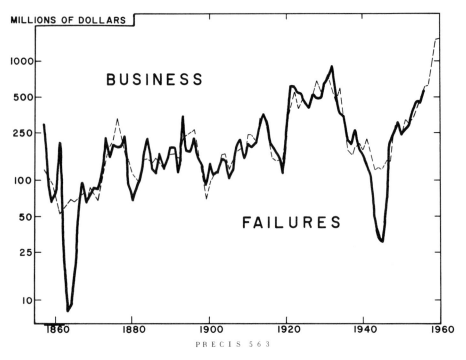

PRECIS 563

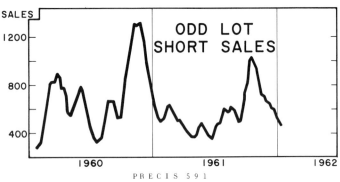

PRECIS 591

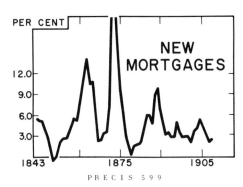

PRECIS 599

GENERAL BUSINESS

603

Various average cycles (shortest length: 8.6 months) in General Business Activity, U.S.A., no dates given, are suggested.

Flood found, by various methods, possible cycles in general business activity of the following durations: 8.6 months, 8.7 months, 9 months, 9.2 months, 28.9 months, 38 months, 41.6 months, and 46.5 months.

Flood, 1940.

604

A 15–18-month rhythmic cycle in General Business Activity, U.S.A., no dates given, is alleged.

Mack, 1958.

605

A 15.4- or 19-month average cycle in General Business Activity, U.S.A., 1875–1940, is suggested.

According to the author, "subcycles" or wavelets in general business activity in the United States averaged (but not periodically) 15.4 or 19.0 months in duration.

Mack, 1957.

606

A 17.94-month (1.49-year) rhythmic cycle in General Business Activity, U.S.A., no dates given, is alleged.

Clement, 1962. p. 247.

607

A 2–7-year rhythmic cycle in General Business Activity, U.S.A., 1911–1960, is alleged.

Alternating waves of expansion and contraction in general business activity in the United States during the period from 1911 through 1960 require from 2 to 7 years for completion, according to Gitlow. His analysis included data from retail sales, stock prices, freight car loadings, inventory accumulations, industrial production, gross national product, national income, and other economic criteria.

Gitlow, 1962.

608

A 34.7-month (2.89-year) rhythmic cycle in General Business Activity, U.S.A., January 1919–December 1932, is alleged.

The four upswings and three downswings which were present in general business activity in the United States from January 1919 through December 1932 displayed a cyclic pattern which averaged 34.7 months in duration.

Morgenstern, 1959. pp. 61–62.

609

A 35–46-month rhythmic cycle in General Business Activity, U.S.A., is alleged.

Bratt stated that Persons (using data for the period from 1878 through 1932) had found an average periodicity for the business cycle in the United States of 46 months when the cycle included only major depressions and one of 35 months when minor depressions were used in the calculations.

Bratt, 1937. pp. 169–172.

610

General business activity in the United States during the period from 1895 through 1925 appeared to move in waves which measured between 35 and 45 months. Peak years were listed as 1899, 1901, 1903, 1907, 1909, 1913, 1918, 1919, and 1923. Trough years, according to the authors, occurred in 1896, 1900, 1902, 1904, 1908, 1911, 1914, 1919, 1921, and 1924 with minor peaks coming in 1906 and 1917.

Hardy and Cox, 1928. p. 13.

611

A 36–40-month rhythmic cycle in General Business Activity, U.S.A., 1834–1958, is alleged.

Davis, Hughes and McDougall, 1961. p. 80.

612

A 36–42-month rhythmic cycle in General Business Activity, U.S.A., is alleged.

The authors noted that the minor cycle in general business activity in the United States runs its course, on the average, in 3 to 3 1/2 years.

Burns, Neal, and Watson, 1953.

613

The ups and downs of general business activity in the United States from 1790 through 1946, as measured by the Cleveland Trust Company Index, appeared to have been characterized by minor waves which averaged from about 3 to about 3 1/2 years in length. The waves lengthened during the years but the increase in length was not completely regular although it appeared to occur at intervals of about 34 years.

Yeatman, as reported by Dewey, 1950-C. (Figure)

614

An audit of the changing length 3–3 1/2-year cycle in general business activity in the United States revealed the following progression in the behavior pattern:

Period Under Observation	Number of Months	Number of Cycles	Average Cycle Length
July 1800–July 1832	384	11	34.09
July 1832–February 1869	439	12	36.58
February 1869–October 1905	440	11	40.00
October 1905–February 1947	469	12	41.33

Dewey, 1955-T. (Figure)

615

"The conclusion is clear that within the period and country represented by our indexes, business cycles, while varying in length from a year and a half to nearly seven years, have a model length in the neighborhood of three to three and one half years."

Mitchell, 1927. p. 343.

616

A 3–4-year rhythmic cycle in General Business Activity, U.S.A., is alleged.

General business activity in the United States appeared to move in waves which measure between 3 and 4 years in duration.

Dodd, Kennedy, and Olsen, 1962. p. 418.

617

According to Matthews, the existence of a 3–4-year (or roughly 40-month) periodicity in general business activity is well attested in American data from 1867 through 1954.

Matthews, 1959. p. 206. (Figure)

618

Newbury stated that a regular procession of short 3–4-year cycles during the period from 1898 through 1929 displayed a pattern of two years of good business followed by one year of poor business.

Newbury, 1952. p. 134.

619

General business activity in the United States appeared to be characterized by a 3–4-year rhythmic cycle.

Tinbergen and Polak, 1950. p. 60.

620

A 3–8-year rhythmic cycle in General Business Activity, U.S.A., no dates

given, is alleged.

Kuznets, 1930. p. 411.

621

A 3.3-year (39.56-month) rhythmic cycle in General Business Activity, U.S.A., 1879–1930, is alleged.

Using the Axe-Houghton-Annalist Index of Business Activity, King found a 39.56-month rhythmic wave present in American business activity for the period under observation.

King, 1931. pp. 812–813. (Figure)

622

A 3.32-year (39.8-month) rhythmic cycle in General Business Activity, France, January 1919–December 1932, is alleged.

General business activity in France displayed four full cycles which averaged 39.8 months in duration for the period from January 1919 through December 1932.

Morgenstern, 1959. pp. 61–62.

623

A 3.33-year (40.0-month) rhythmic cycle in General Business Activity, Great Britain, January 1919–December 1932, is alleged.

Four full cycles which averaged 40.0 months in length were present in general business activity in Great Britain from January 1919 through December 1932.

Morgenstern, 1959. pp. 61–62.

624

A 3.33-year (40-month) rhythmic cycle in General Business Activity, U.S.A., is alleged.

Percents by which general business activity in the United States rose or fell below the computed normal level each month from 1838 through 1939, according to the index of American Business Activity of the Cleveland Trust Company, appeared to move in 40-month rhythmic waves. The upswing of business activity measured about 27 months while the downswing measured only 13 months.

Ayres, 1939. (Figure)

625

"...the evidence is very strong that business activity has a cyclical component of about 3 1/3 years, which at times contributed a large part of the energy in the series, and probably at all times contributes as much as 12 percent."

Davis, 1941. p. 550.

626

The 40-month cyclic allegation is the adjusted length of the 4-year cycle in general business activity that Estey found in the data for the period 1790 through 1925.

Estey, 1941. p. 16.

627

General business activity in the United States appeared to be characterized by a 40-month rhythm.

Hubbard, 1942.

628

From 1877 through 1922, general business activity in the United States ran in a pattern which measured approximately 40 months from trough to trough. The periods, however, ranged from 2 to 7 years in duration.

Jordan, 1927. p. 42.

629

In addition to an 8—9-year cycle in general business activity in the United States from 1870 through 1960, "the picture is complicated by so-called minor cycles, which last an average of forty months."

McConnell, 1960. p. 203.

630

King reported that Mills had found a cycle which measured approximately 40 months in length in American business activity for the period from 1796 through 1923. Mills contended that there was "a distinct shortening of the average duration during the period of sharp industrial and economic transition." Mills reported that for the period from 1796 through 1845, the cycle averaged 4.45 years; for the period from 1845 through 1890, the cycle averaged 4.12 years; and for the period from 1890 through 1923, the cycle averaged 3.27 years.

Mills, as reported by King, 1931. p. 812.

631

Using five indexes of business activity, Mitchell found an average 40-month periodicity in general business activity in the United States from 1878 through 1923.

Mitchell, 1927. p. 343.

632

American business activity has followed a 40-month rhythmic pattern.

Newbury, 1938. Section II; p. 2.

633

A 3.33-year (40-month) rhythmic cycle in General Business Activity, North America, no dates given, is alleged.

Chambers, 1961. pp. 47, 50.

634

A 3.33-year (40-month) rhythmic cycle in General Business Activity, no
locale cited, no dates given, is alleged.

According to Fels, a 40-month cycle in general business activity is "fairly
representative."

Fels, 1952. p. 29.

635

A 3.35-year (40.16-month) rhythmic cycle in Business Activity, U.S.A.,
1855—1940, is alleged.

Using the Model Index of Business Activity, Hutner found that business
activity in the United States for the 86-year period under observation
showed a tendency to move in a cycle which measured 40.16 months long.

Hutner, 1940. pp. 832—833. (Figure)

636

A 3.42-year (41-month) rhythmic cycle in Business Activity, England, no
dates given, is alleged.

A tendency for English business activity to oscillate in waves averaging
41 months in length was noted by H. S. Jevons as early as 1909.

Jevons, H. S., 1909.

637

A 3.42-year (41-month) rhythmic cycle in General Business Activity, U.S.A.,
is alleged.

Business activity in the United States from 1891 through 1935 exhibited an
average period of approximately 41 months. Typical over-all amplitude of
this 41-month cycle averaged 6.79% of trend.

Armstrong, 1936. (Figure)

638

Although its movements were at times quite irregular, business activity in
the United States appeared to follow a 41-month repetitive pattern.

Kitchin, 1923.

639

Klemme said that a rhythmic pattern which measured approximately 41
months and kept within a 39—42-month limit has been evident in the activity
of many businesses in the United States.

Klemme, 1950. (Figure)

640

A 3.5-year (42-month) rhythmic cycle in General Business Activity, U.S.A.,

is alleged.

The timing of the swings in general business activity in the United States since World War II "coincides with the so-called 'minor' or 'inventory' cycle which has occurred in the U. S. on the average of every three and one half years since the Civil War."

Ernst, 1957. p. 1.

641

A 42-month rhythmic cycle was evident in the movement of American business activity during the period under observation.

Hald, 1954. p. 46.

642

From 1883 through 1930, a 3 1/2-year cyclical pattern appeared to characterize general business activity in the United States.

Haney, 1931. pp. 27, 160.

643

The minor fluctuation which appeared to be present in general business activity in the United States from 1857 through 1937 measured approximately 3 1/2 years in length.

Hansen, 1941, as reported by Achinstein, 1950. p. 19.

644

Hartkemeier stated that there was "strong evidence of a cyclical component" in general business activity in the United States which appeared to measure approximately 3 1/2 years in duration.

Hartkemeier, 1943.

645

A 3 1/2–4-year rhythmic cycle in General Business Activity, U.S.A., 1857–1957, is alleged.

During the period from 1857 through 1957, general business activity displayed 25 cyclical peaks which average between 3 1/2 and 4 years in duration. The authors stated that this basic pattern remains in American business activity during the period from 1929 through 1959.

Fishman and Fishman, 1962. pp. 229, 231, 1226.

646

A 3 1/2–4-year rhythmic cycle in General Business Activity, U.S.A., 1929–1957, is alleged.

Fishman and Fishman, 1962. p. 231.

647

A 3.58-year (42.9-month) rhythmic cycle in General Business Activity,

U.S.A., January 1879–December 1914, is alleged.

Ten cyclic patterns which measured approximately 42.9 months in length
were found in general business activity in the United States for the period
from January 1879 through December 1914.

Morgenstern, 1959. pp. 61–62.

648

A 43.5–48-month rhythmic cycle in General Business Activity, U.S.A.,
1854–1954, is alleged.

Fluctuations in general business activity in the United States from 1854
through 1954 showed an arithmetic average duration of about 4 years and a
median duration of 43.5 months. The extreme limits, however, ranged from
27 months to 99 months, according to Harris who said that the average expansion measured 29.8 months and the average contraction measured 20
months.

Harris, 1961.

649

A 44–48-month rhythmic cycle in General Business Activity, U.S.A., 1854–
1959, is alleged.

Haines noted that business in the United States from 1854 through 1959
moved in 25 cycles which varied in length from 2 to 8 years and averaged
44–48 months in duration.

Haines, 1961. pp. 395–396.

650

A 3.75-year (45-month) rhythmic cycle in General Business Activity, U.S.A.,
is alleged.

For the period from 1854 through 1933, general business activity in the
United States moved in cycles which measured approximately 45 months.
Crane noted that automobiles, chemicals, coppers, and lead and zinc pro-
ducing companies appeared to be closely tied to this rhythm.

Crane, 1959.

651

A 3 3/4-year repetitive pattern was reported by Mitchell in the movement of
general business activity in the United States during the period from 1837
through 1920.

Mitchell, 1927.

652

A 45–50-month rhythmic cycle in General Business Activity, U.S.A., 1854–
1958, is alleged.

In agreement with the business cycle alleged by the National Bureau of
Economic Research, Fellner stated that the business cycle in the U. S.
from 1854 through 1958 averaged between 45 and 50 months.

Fellner, 1960. pp. 336–337.

653

A 3.98-year (47.7-month) rhythmic cycle in General Business Activity,
U.S.A., 1854–1938, is alleged.

According to Dauten who used National Bureau of Economic Research figures in his calculations, the American business cycle from 1854 through
1938 varied in length from 27 to 99 months. Its average duration appeared
to measure 47.7 months.

Dauten, 1954. p. 17.

654

A 4-year rhythmic cycle in General Business Activity, U.S.A., is alleged.

An "ordinary business cycle" in the United States runs an average of four
years in duration.

Business Week, 1963.

655

Employing data from the National Bureau of Economic Research, Dauten
noted that American business cycles from 1790 through 1953 have varied in
length from one to eleven years. The average length of these cycles was 4
years; the most common length, 3 years.

Dauten, 1954. p. 17.

656

The "business cycle proper" had period fluctuations which ranged from 1
to 9 years (average, 4 years) in duration during the period from 1854 through
1951.

Encyclopedic Dictionary of Business, 1952. p. 114.

657

Estey asserted that, in addition to a longer cycle which measured about
8 6/7 years, a short 4-year cycle was present in general business activity
in the United States for the period from 1790 through 1925. Estey goes on
to say that later evidence, however, seems to support a 40-month cycle.

Estey, 1941. p. 16.

658

Gitlow stated that W. L. Thorp had found that, during the period from 1796
through 1923, American business activity displayed 32 waves which averaged about 4 years in duration.

Gitlow, 1962.

659

During the period from 1870 through 1938, general business activity in the
United States appeared to be characterized by a wave which measured approximately 4 years.

Long, 1940. pp. 102–107.

660

General business activity from 1796 through 1923 appeared to move in a 4-year pattern.

Thorp, 1926.

661

A 4.11-year (49.3-month) rhythmic cycle in General Business Activity, Germany, 1902–1914, is alleged.

The three cyclic fluctuations which transpired between 1902 and 1914 in German business activity appeared to measure approximately 49.3 months.

Schmidt, 1934. p. 131.

662

A 4.17-year (50-month) rhythmic cycle in General Business Activity, U.S.A., is alleged.

Using over 100 years of data, Bratt asserted that the expansions in general business activity in the United States averaged slightly less than 30 months while the contractions averaged not more than 20 months.

Bratt, 1958. p. 176.

663

General business activity in the United States from 1855 through 1957 moved in a cycle which 'measured approximately 50 months.

Business Week, 1958. (Figure)

664

According to Shiskin, during the period for which the National Bureau of Economic Research has compiled a chronology of business (1854–1961), cyclic expansions have averaged 30 months and cyclic contractions have averaged about 20 months.

Shiskin, 1961.

665

A 4.2-year (50.4-month) rhythmic cycle in General Business Activity, South Africa, 1806–1936, is alleged.

In addition to a major rhythm which measured approximately 7.6 years in length, general business activity in South Africa from 1806 through 1936 appeared to show a minor cycle approximately 4.2 years long.

Schumann, 1938. p. 252.

666

A 4.3-year (51.6-month) rhythmic cycle in General Business Activity, Japan, 1890–1920, is alleged.

Thorp, 1926.

667

A 4.38-year (52.6-month) rhythmic cycle in General Business Activity, Germany, January 1919—December 1932, is alleged.

Three full cycles which averaged approximately 52.6 months in duration were present in the data on general business activity in Germany for the period from January 1919 through December 1932.

Morgenstern, 1959. pp. 61—62.

668

A 4.5-year (54-month) rhythmic cycle in General Business Activity, U.S.A., 1854—1949, is alleged.

General business activity in the United States from 1854 through 1949 appeared to move in cycles approximately 4.5 years in duration. According to Adelman, the expansions averaged 2.8 years while the contractions averaged 1.7 years.

Adelman, 1960. (Figure; data)

669

A 4.75-year (57-month) rhythmic cycle in General Business Activity, U.S.A., 1933—1957, is alleged.

Since the Big Depression, according to Crane, general business had fluctuated in periods which measured approximately 57 months. Crane noted that automobiles, chemicals, coppers, and lead-producing and zinc-producing companies appeared to follow this pattern.

Crane, 1959.

670

A 4.86-year (58.3-month) rhythmic cycle in General Business Activity, Germany, 1879—1932, is alleged.

General business activity in Germany from 1879 through 1932 appeared to move in a cycle approximately 58.3 months in duration although the cycles ranged from 3 to 6 or 7 years. Schmidt noted peaks at the following dates: December 1879, January 1882, March 1890, March 1900, July 1903, July 1907, April 1913, June 1918, May 1922, March 1925, and March 1928. He placed troughs at February 1881, August 1886, February 1895, March 1902, February 1905, October 1908, July 1914, June 1919, November 1923, March 1926, and August 1932.

Schmidt, 1934. pp. 117, 131.

671

A 4.9-year (58.8-month) rhythmic cycle in General Business Activity, Russia, 1891—1925, is alleged.

Thorp, 1926.

672

A 5-year rhythmic cycle in General Business Activity, Argentina, 1890—

1920, is alleged.

Thorpe, 1926.

673

A 5-year rhythmic cycle in General Business Activity, Brazil, 1889–1924, is alleged.

Thorp, 1926.

674

A 5-year rhythmic cycle in Business Activity, Europe, no dates given, is alleged.

European business activity has shown a tendency to follow a 5-year cyclic pattern.

Tintner, 1935, as reported by Davis, 1941. p. 27.

675

A 5-year rhythmic cycle in General Business Activity, Germany, 1848–1925, is alleged.

Mitchell, 1927.

676

A 5-year rhythmic cycle in General Business Activity, Russia, 1891–1925, is alleged.

Mitchell, 1927.

677

A 5-year rhythmic cycle in General Business Activity, South Africa, 1890–1920, is alleged.

Thorp, 1926.

678

A 5-year rhythmic cycle in General Business Activity, U.S.A., no dates given, is alleged.

According to Douai, crises appear every five years or less and their magnitude of intensity varies greatly.

Douai, 1878. pp. 30, 35, 36, 39.

679

A 5.1-year (61.2-month) rhythmic cycle in General Business Activity, Canada, 1888–1924, is alleged.

Thorp, 1926.

680

A 5.1-year (61.2-month) rhythmic cycle in General Business Activity, Germany, 1848–1925, is alleged.

Thorp, 1926.

681

A 5.2-year (62.4-month) rhythmic cycle in General Business Activity, India,

1889—1920, is alleged.

Thorp, 1926.

682

A 5.2-year (62.4-month) rhythmic cycle in General Business Activity, 17 countries, 1888-1892—1920-1925, is alleged.

During the period under observation, Mills noted 105 waves in the data concerning general business activity in 17 different countries which averaged 5.2 years in duration.

Mills, 1926.

683

A 5.2-year (62.4-month) average cycle in Business Activity, 17 countries, varying dates, is suggested.

A study of business activity in 17 countries indicated the presence of an average 5.2-year cycle. The following countries and periods were used in this composite analysis:

Country	Period Under Observation	Country	Period Under Observation
United States	1796—1923	England	1793—1920
France	1838—1920	Sweden	1892—1920
Italy	1888—1920	Argentina	1890—1920
Germany	1848—1925	Austria	1866—1922
Russia	1891—1925	Australia	1890—1924
Brazil	1889—1924	Canada	1888—1924
Netherlands	1891—1920	China	1888—1920
South Africa	1890—1920	India	1889—1920
Japan	1890—1920		

Thorp and Mitchell, 1926, as reported by Davis, 1941. p. 548. (Figure)

684

A 5.5-year (66-month) rhythmic cycle in General Business Activity, France, 1838—1920, is alleged.

Thorp, 1926.

685

A 5.6-year (67.2-month) rhythmic cycle in General Business Activity, Austria, 1866—1922, is alleged.

Mitchell, 1927.
Thorp, 1926.

686

A 5.6-year (67.2-month) rhythmic cycle in General Business Activity, Sweden, 1892—1920, is alleged.

Thorp, 1926.

687

A 5.7-year (68.4-month) rhythmic cycle in General Business Activity,

Australia, 1890–1924, is alleged.

Thorp, 1926.

688

A 5 3/4-year (69.0-month) rhythmic cycle in General Business Activity, U.S.A., 1796–1923, is alleged.

Gitlow quotes W. L. Thorp as stating that a cycle which averaged 5 3/4 years in duration was present in general business activity in Great Britain from 1796 through 1923.

Gitlow, 1962.

689

A 5.8-year (69.6-month) rhythmic cycle in General Business Activity, England, 1793–1920, is alleged.

Thorp, 1926.

690

A 5.8-year (69.6-month) rhythmic cycle in General Business Activity, Netherlands, 1891–1920, is alleged.

Thorp, 1926.

691

A 5.82-year (69.9-month) rhythmic cycle in General Business Activity, France, January 1879–December 1914, is alleged.

Six repetitions of fluctuations which averaged about 69.9 months in duration were present in the data relating to general business activity in France from January 1879 through December 1914.

Morgenstern, 1959. pp. 61–62.

692

A 5.88-year (70.5-month) rhythmic cycle in General Business Activity, Great Britain, January 1879–December 1914, is alleged.

General business activity in Great Britain for the period from January 1879 through December 1914 displayed six waves which averaged approximately 70.5 years in length.

Morgenstern, 1959. pp. 61–62.

693

A 5.92-year (71-month) rhythmic cycle in General Business Activity, Germany, January 1879–December 1914, is alleged.

General business activity in Germany, January 1879–December 1914, showed six cyclic repetitions which averaged approximately 71.0 months in duration.

Morgenstern, 1959. pp. 61–62.

694

A 6-year rhythmic cycle in General Business Activity, Argentina, 1890–

1920, is alleged.

Mitchell, 1927.

695

A 6-year rhythmic cycle in General Business Activity, Netherlands, 1891–1920, is alleged.

Mitchell, 1927.

696

A 6-year rhythmic cycle in General Business Activity, Sweden, 1892–1920, is alleged.

Mitchell, 1927.

697

A 6–9-year rhythmic cycle in General Business Activity, U.S.A., no dates given, is alleged.

Newbury quotes Brandow as having found a 6–9-year rhythmic pattern in many economic series and in general business activity in the United States.

Brandow, 1939, as quoted by Newbury, 1952. p. 141.

698

Newbury reported that "a long component cycle" which measured 6–9 years in length was present in American business.

Newbury, 1947. p. 283.

699

A 6–12-year rhythmic cycle in General Business Activity, U.S.A., no dates given, is alleged.

Horton, 1948. p. 40.

700

A 6.3-year (75.6-month) rhythmic cycle in General Business Activity, Italy, 1888–1920, is alleged.

Mitchell, 1927.

701

A 6.4-year (76.8-month) rhythmic cycle in General Business Activity, China, 1888–1920, is alleged.

Thorp, 1926.

702

A 6.4-year (76.8-month) rhythmic cycle in General Business Activity, Italy, 1888–1920, is alleged.

Thorp, 1926.

703

A 7-year (84.0-month) rhythmic cycle in General Business Activity, Brazil, 1889–1924, is alleged.

Mitchell, 1927.

704

A 7-year (84.0-month) rhythmic cycle in General Business Activity, Great Britain, no dates given, is alleged.

According to Fritz, Sir William Petty, noted English political economist of the 17th century, studied business cycles in great detail and at that time estimated their length to be approximately 7 years.

Petty, 1662, as cited by Fritz, 1934.

705

A 7—10-year rhythmic cycle in General Business Activity, Great Britain, is alleged.

General business activity in Great Britain has shown a tendency to fluctuate in waves which average from 7 to 10 years in duration "though it may be interrupted by wars and other accidents by which credit movements are affected."

Hawtrey, 1913. pp. 125—126.
Hawtrey, 1927. pp. 471—482.

706

For the period between 1850 and 1940, general business activity in Great Britain appeared to be characterized by cyclic movements which measured between 7 and 10 years.

Matthews, 1959. p. 223.

707

A 7—10-year rhythmic cycle in General Business Activity, U.S.A., is alleged.

American business activity appears to follow a 7—10-year cyclic pattern.

Hald, 1954. p. 46.

708

"Historically speaking, the length of the business cycle has varied between 7 and 10 years..."

Halm, 1961. p. 343.

709

In addition to a minor 3 1/2-year cycle in general business activity in the United States, Haney noted that waves which measured between 7 and 10 years were also present. He called this the major business cycle.

Haney, 1931. p. 160.

710

A 7—11-year rhythmic cycle in General Business Activity, no locale cited, no dates given, is alleged.

Tinbergen and Polak, 1950. p. 60.

711

A 7—11-year rhythmic cycle in General Business Activity, Germany, 1800—1900, is alleged.

Wagemann, 1930. p. 78.

712

A 7.6-year (91.2-month) rhythmic cycle in General Business Activity, South Africa, 1806—1936, is alleged.

The major rhythm present in general business activity in South Africa from 1806 through 1936 appeared to measure approximately 7.6 years.

Schumann, 1938. p. 252.

713

An 8-year rhythmic cycle in General Business Activity, Great Britain, 1924—1935, is alleged.

Using various models to test the validity of the 8-year cycle in general business activity in Great Britain, Radice found that the waves generally fell in the range of 7 1/2 to 8 1/4 years — an average 8-year cycle.

Radice, 1939.

714

An 8-year rhythmic cycle in General Business Activity, U.S.A., is alleged.

A major cycle which measured about 8 years in length was present (along with a minor cycle of about 3 1/2 years) in general business activity in the United States during the period from 1858 through 1937.

Hansen, 1941, as reported by Achinstein, 1950.

715

According to Harris, Alvin H. Hansen dated seven "major cycles" in the general business activity of the United States from the time of the Civil War to the time of World War I. These major cycles averaged approximately 8 years in duration.

Harris, 1961.

716

An 8—9-year rhythmic cycle in General Business Activity, U.S.A., 1870—1960, is alleged.

"Major cyclical fluctuations (in general business activity) average eight or nine years over-all, though some are as short as six years and others as long as twelve."

McConnell, 1960. p. 203.

717

An 8 1/2-year rhythmic cycle in General Business Activity, Germany, 1848–1914, is alleged.

Business cycles in Germany from 1848 through 1914 appeared to range from 7 to 10 years in duration and to average approximately 8 1/2 years.

Wagemann, 1930. p. 93.

718

An 8 6/7-year rhythmic cycle in General Business Activity, U.S.A., 1790–1925, is alleged.

Estey, 1941. p. 16.

719

A 9-year rhythmic cycle in Business Activity, U.S.A., 1830–1930, is alleged.

Davis, 1941. p. 27.

720

A 9–10-year rhythmic cycle in General Business Activity, U.S.A., no dates given, is alleged.

The major cycle in general business activity in the United States, according to the authors, ranges in duration from 8 to 11 years and averages between 9 and 10 years.

Burns, Neal, and Watson, 1953.

721

A 9.93-year rhythmic cycle in Business Activity, U.S.A., 1855–1940, is alleged.

Hutner, using the Model Index of Business Activity, determined that there was distinct evidence that a wave having the length of just a little under 10 years, or 9.93 years, was present in American business activity from 1855 through 1940.

Hutner, 1940. (Figure)

722

A 10-year rhythmic cycle in General Business Activity, Great Britain, is alleged.

"I have long felt convinced that a well marked decennial periodicity can be traced in the activity of trade and the recurrence of commercial crises." Peaks in trade were noted at 1701, 1711, 1721, 1732, 1742, 1753, 1763, 1772, 1783, 1793, 1805, 1815, 1825, 1837, 1847, 1857, and 1866. Jevons also asserted that, "It is almost certain that two sets of phenomena, credit cycles and solar cycles, are connected as to cause and effect."

Jevons, 1878.

723

According to Mills, a "credit" or general business activity cycle was present in Great Britain during the period from 1815 through 1866. Crisis years occurred in 1815, 1825, 1836, 1847, 1857, and 1866.

Mills, 1867.

724

Tugan-Baranovski reported 7 and 11 years as the limits of the business activity cycle in England and stated that it averaged approximately 10 years.

Tugan-Baranovski, 1913. pp. 247—248.

725

A 10-year rhythmic cycle in General Business Activity, U.S.A., is alleged.

General business activity in the United States, according to Babson, displayed a tendency to move in cycles averaging 10 years in duration.

Babson, 1948. p. 45.

726

A study based upon Wilson's periodogram of business activity in the United States from 1790 through 1929 revealed "that there exists a permanent cyclical pattern in business indexes of around 10 years."

Davis, 1941. p. 551.

727

General business activity in the United States appeared to move in 10-year cycles.

Hubbard, 1942.

728

A 10-year rhythmic cycle in General Business Activity, no locale cited, no dates given, is alleged.

Cardozo, South Carolina economist and journalist, spoke of "those cycles (commercial) of speculation destined to visit about every decade."

Cardozo, 1857. p. 342.

729

In addition to a long cycle of approximately 60 years and a short cycle of about 40 months, Fels thought a 10-year rhythmic wave was also present in general business activity.

Fels, 1952. p. 29f.

730

An 11-year rhythmic cycle in General Business Activity, U.S.A., is alleged.

Silberling reported a relationship between the sunspot cycle and a general business activity index for the period from 1750 through 1940.

Silberling, 1943, as reported by Williams, 1961. p. 83. (Figure)

731

A correlation between sunspot activity and general business activity in the United States was suggested.

Stetson, 1946.

732

Silberling's chart, 1750—1940, was brought up through 1960 by Williams by adding the Cleveland Trust Company index from 1940 through 1960. Zurich sunspot numbers and general business activity continued to show a close relationship.

Williams, 1962. pp. 96—97. (Figure)

733

An 11-year-plus rhythmic cycle in Non-Agricultural Business Activity, U.S.A., no dates given, is alleged.

Garcia-Mata and Shaffner alleged a correlation between the major cycles of non-agricultural business activity in the United States and sunspot activity.

Garcia-Mata and Shaffner, 1934. p. 26.

734

An 11.14-year rhythmic cycle in Business Activity, U.S.A., 1855—1940, is alleged.

Business activity in the United States, as gauged by the Model Index of Business Activity, appeared to be characterized by a cycle which averaged 11.14 years in length. A correlation of this 11.14-year cycle and sunspot activity was suggested.

Hutner, 1940. (Figure)

735

A 13.81-year rhythmic cycle in Business Activity, U.S.A., no dates given, is alleged.

During a 79-year period, six extremely regular, repetitive waves of 13.81 years duration were evident in business activity in the United States.

Williams, 1947. p. 3.

736

A 15-year rhythmic cycle in Business Activity, U.S.A., 1890—1949, is alleged.

Klemme stated that a 15-year cycle was not uncommon in various types of business activity for the period from 1890 through 1949.

Klemme, 1950. (Figure)

737

A 15–20-year rhythmic cycle in General Business Activity, U.S.A., no dates given, is alleged.

Gordon, 1961. p. 246.

738

An 18 1/2-year rhythmic pattern in General Business Activity, U.S.A., 1784–1936, is alleged.

An 18 1/2-year rhythmic pattern in "business generations" was discovered by Hays for the period in the United States which began in 1784 and ended in 1936. This 18 1/2-year periodicity was comprised of three minor cycles which measured 7 years, 5 1/2 years, and 6 years, respectively.

Hays, 1937. (Figure)

739

A 20-year rhythmic cycle in General Business Activity, Germany, 1870–1933, is alleged.

Noting peak years as 1873, 1890, 1906, and 1927, Matthews traced a 20-year rhythm in general business activity in Germany for the period under consideration.

Matthews, 1959.

740

A 20-year rhythmic cycle in General Business Activity, Japan, 1878–1942, is alleged.

Shinohara, 1962. pp. ii, 79.

741

A 20-year rhythmic cycle in General Business Activity, U.S.A., is alleged.

In addition to the "ordinary business cycle" of about 4 years, a long cycle which averages about 20 years in duration is present in general business activity in the United States.

Business Week, 1963.

742

A long cycle which characterizes general business activity in the United States and which is often called the "Kuznets cycle" measures approximately 20 years.

Kuznets, as cited by *Business Week*, 1963.

743

Horace White testified in 1878 at a House of Representative's Hearing on "Depressions in Labor and Business" that commercial crises "held to a twenty-year period.''

White, 1878. pp. 29—30.

744

A 20—30-year rhythmic cycle in General Business Activity, Western Europe, 1822—1913, is alleged.

Haberler quotes Spiethoff as alleging that business cycles in Western Europe from 1822 through 1913 measured approximately 20—30 years. The four waves during the period under observation were: 1822—1842, 1843—1873, 1874—1894, and 1895—1913.

Haberler, 1958. p. 273.

745

A 40-year rhythmic cycle in General Business Activity, no locale cited, no dates given, is alleged.

Tinbergen and Polak, 1950. p. 60.

746

A 50-year rhythmic cycle in General Business Activity, England and France, no dates given, is alleged.

General business activity in England and in France moved in long waves which appeared to have a duration of a little over 50 years.

Clough and Cole, 1952.

747

A 50-year rhythmic cycle in General Business Activity, U.S.A., no dates given, is alleged.

General business activity in the United States appeared to move in long waves that ''run for about 50 years.''

Encyclopedic Dictionary of Business, 1952. p. 114.

748

A 50-year-plus rhythmic cycle in General Business Activity, U.S.A., no dates given, is alleged.

The authors noted that general business activity in the United States appeared to fluctuate in cycles which measured over 50 years in duration.

Dodd, Kennedy, and Olsen, 1962. p. 419.

749

A 53-year rhythmic cycle in Business Activity, U.S.A., 1709—1940, is alleged.

Business cycles in the United States have shown a tendency to move in repetitive patterns which average 53 years in length.

Hoskens, 1953.

750

A 54-year rhythmic cycle in General Business Activity, U.S.A., no dates given, is alleged.

Business activity in the United States, as well as wholesale commodity prices and wheat prices, appears to be characterized by a 54-year cyclic pattern.

Klemme, 1951. p. 1263.

751

A 56-year rhythmic cycle in General Business Activity, U.S.A., 1761–1946, is alleged.

In connection with work performed by J. M. Funk in 1933, Williams found that business activity in the United States from 1761 through 1946 was "dominated by a 56-year rhythm."

Williams, 1947.

752

A 60-year rhythmic cycle in General Business Activity, no locale cited, no dates given, is alleged.

Fels redated the timing of the Kondratieff cycle and called it a 60-year cycle in general business activity.

Fels, 1952. p. 29.

AGRICULTURE

AGRICULTURE

APPLE PRODUCTION

753

A 24-month (2-year) rhythmic cycle in Apple Production, U.S.A., no dates given, is alleged.

Huntington, 1945. p. 457.

754

A 20–25-year rhythmic cycle in Apple Production, U.S.A., no dates given, is alleged.

Warren, 1913, as reported by Pearson and Myers, 1957. p. 5496.

BARLEY PRODUCTION
(see CROP PRODUCTION AND YIELDS)

CATTLE PRODUCTION

755

A 14-year rhythmic cycle in Cattle Production, U.S.A., 1880–1951, is alleged.

Crests in a 14-year rhythmic pattern which was evident in cattle production in the United States through 1951 occurred in 1890, 1904, 1918, 1934, and 1946.

Zimmerman, 1951. p. 308. (Figure)

756

A 14-year rhythmic cycle in Cattle Numbers, U.S.A., is alleged.

The number of cattle on farms in the United States from 1885 through 1955 appeared to fluctuate in a 14-year rhythmic pattern.

Bassie, 1958. pp. 61–62. (Figure)

757

The total number of cattle on farms in the United States, 1880–1947, showed a tendency to move with the cycle characteristic of the purchasing power of cattle, namely an average 14-year cycle. Peaks were reached in 1890, 1904, 1918, 1934, and 1946; lows, in 1896, 1912, 1928, and 1938.

Hadorn, 1947. pp. 1–2. (Figure)

758

A 14–16-year rhythmic cycle in Changes in the Number of All Cattle on Farms, U.S.A., 1880–1944, is alleged.

Pearson, Myers, and Lorie, 1945. p. 3698. (Figure)

759

A 14–16-year rhythmic cycle in Number of Beef Cattle on Farms, U.S.A., is alleged.

The number of beef cattle on farms on January 1 in the United States from 1870 through 1950 appeared to move in a cycle which averaged from 14 to 16 years in length.

Ross, 1951. (Figure)

760

Total beef cattle population in the United States from 1865 through 1958 has fluctuated in cycles which have measured approximately from 14 to 16 years. According to the authors, these cycles appear to be shortening.

Snapp and Naumann, 1960. p. 25. (Figure)

761

A 15-year rhythmic cycle in Cattle Numbers, U.S.A., 1890–1944, is alleged.

The number of cattle on farms on January 1 as well as the value per head of cattle appeared to move in 15-year cycles for the period from 1890 through 1944.

Shepherd, 1947. pp. 42–43. (Figure)

762

A 15-year rhythmic cycle in Beef Cattle Production, U.S.A., is alleged.

Beef cattle produced in the United States appeared to move in a cyclic pattern which measured approximately 15 years in duration.

Ross, 1951.

763

"In the case of cattle, it takes about 15 years to go from a period of low production to a period of high production and finally back to low production."

Spaid, 1949. p. 4414.

764

A 16–18-year rhythmic cycle in the Number of Cattle on Farms, U.S.A., 1890–1940, is alleged.

Annual changes in the number of cattle on farms in the United States from

1890 through 1940 appeared to move in a 16—18-year rhythmic cycle which followed the pattern found in the purchasing power of cattle. In 1899, 1914, 1930, and 1939, when the purchasing power of the price of cattle was high, cattle on farms were retained in order to replenish herds; in 1893, 1908, 1924, and 1935, when the purchasing power was low, cattle were sold in excess of normal.

Pearson, Myers, and Curtiss, 1940. (Figure)

765

A 17-year average cycle in Cattle Supply and Demand, U.S.A., 1893—1953, is alleged.

During the period from 1893 through 1953, demand and supply of live cattle on the hoof showed a tendency to move in an average 17-year cycle.

Pearson, Myers, and Vial, 1945. p. 5081. (Figure)

CHEESE CONSUMPTION

766

A 4-year rhythmic cycle in Cheese Consumption, U.S.A., 1867—1953, is alleged.

Data available on civilian per capita consumption of cheese in the United States from 1867 through 1953 indicated that there was a tendency for such cheese consumption to follow a 4-year rhythmic pattern. Typical timing placed a crest in the ideal pattern at 1870.0. Strength of this 4-year cycle averaged 2.6% above trend at time of ideal crest and 2.6% below trend at time of ideal trough.

Dewey, 1955-D. (Figure)

CHICKEN PRODUCTION

767

A 3—4-year rhythmic cycle in Changes in the Number of Chickens on Farms, U.S.A., 1909—1944, is alleged.

Pearson, Myers, and Lorie, 1945. p. 3699. (Figure)

COFFEE PRODUCTION

768

A 15-year rhythmic cycle in Coffee Production, Brazil, no dates given, is alleged.

Dauten, 1954. pp. 101—102.

CORN PRODUCTION
(also see CROP PRODUCTION AND YIELDS)

769

A 5 1/2-year rhythmic cycle in Corn Production, U.S.A., 1862—1875, is alleged.

A 5 1/2-year cycle (an 11-year pattern comprised of alternating 5-year and 6-year waves) appeared to be present in corn production during the period under observation.

Benner, 1875. pp. 76—90. (Figure)

770

An 11-year rhythmic cycle in Corn Production, U.S.A., no dates given, is alleged.

Morris reported that Wylie had found an inverse relationship between corn production in Iowa and the sunspot frequency cycle.

Wylie, 1948, as reported by Morris, 1948. p. 2.

COTTON PRODUCTION

771

A 24-month (2-year) rhythmic cycle in Cotton Production, U.S.A., is alleged.

Cotton production, measured in bales, has displayed a regular 2-year cyclic pattern from 1900 through 1952. Production appeared to be greater in even years and lower in odd years.

Dewey, 1953-O. (Figure)

772

Cotton production in the United States during the period beginning with the crop year 1903—1904 and ending with the crop year 1911—1912 appeared to fluctuate in a 2-year rhythmic cycle.

Tinbergen and Polak, 1950. pp. 93—94. (Figure)

773

A 6-year rhythmic cycle in Cotton Production, U.S.A., 1900-1901—1943-1944, is alleged.

There has been a definite tendency for cotton production to move in a regular recurring pattern that measured 6 years from crest to crest. Typical wave amplitude averaged approximately 10% above trend at time of an ideal crest.

Dewey, 1949-B. (Figure)

774

A later article brought the series on cotton production up through 1952. The 6-year cycle continued to assert itself.

Dewey, 1953-O. (Figure)

CROP PRODUCTION AND YIELDS

775

An 8-year rhythmic cycle in Crop Yields, U.S.A., 1882–1914, is alleged.

Moore, 1923. p. 33. (Figure)

776

An 8–9-year rhythmic cycle in Crop Production, no locale cited, 1830–1916, is alleged.

Teknisk Tidskrift (Veckoupplagen, 1916) is quoted by Mitchell as finding a cycle which measured between 8 and 9 years in crop production.

Mitchell, 1927.

777

An 11-year rhythmic cycle in Crop Yields, U.S.A., is alleged.

Crop yields in the Great Lakes region from 1792 through 1953 have shown a direct correlation with high water levels in the Great Lakes which in turn have shown a correlation with the sunspot cycle.

Musham, 1943.

778

Crop yields in Wisconsin, according to Morris, have shown a correlation with the sunspot cycle. Corn, tobacco, and rye show an inverse relationship to sunspot activity while barley, oats, potatoes, tame hay, tobacco, and wheat coincide with sunspot behavior.

Morris, 1948. (Figure)

779

An 11-year rhythmic cycle in Crop Yields, Canada, 1898–1938, is alleged.

Johnson maintained that crop yields of wheat, oats, and barley in semi-arid regions of Alberta and Saskatchewan were influenced by the sunspot cycle.

Johnson, 1940. (Figure; data)

780

A 33-year rhythmic cycle in Crop Production, Germany, 1862–1832, is alleged.

Lösch, 1937.

GENERAL AGRICULTURE ACTIVITY

781

A 24-month rhythmic cycle in the Production of Agricultural Produce, no locale cited, no dates given, is alleged.

Tinbergen and Polak, 1950. p. 239.

782

A 3 1/2-year (42-month) rhythmic cycle in General Agricultural Activity, Great Britain, no dates given, is alleged.

According to Von Haberler, Jevons alleged a 3 1/2-year cycle in harvest activity in Great Britain.

Jevons, H. S., 1910, as quoted by Von.Haberler, 1958.

783

A 3 1/2-year (42-month) rhythmic cycle in Hog-Corn Price Ratios, U.S.A., no dates given, is alleged.

Bassie, 1958. p. 61.

784

An 8-year rhythmic cycle in General Agricultural Activity, U.S.A., no dates given, is alleged.

Moore alleged that "an agricultural cycle...generates other economic cycles." This agricultural cycle, according to Moore, had a duration of about 8 years and was cosmic in origin.

Moore, 1923, as quoted by Garcia-Mata and Shaffner, 1934. p. 4.

785

A 15–25-year rhythmic cycle in Agricultural Production, U.S.A., no dates given, is alleged.

Babson, 1932. pp. 142–144.

786

A 29.7-year rhythmic cycle in Famines, Japan, no dates given, is alleged.

Nakame, as reported by Nishioka, 1957. p. 6.

787

A 242-year rhythmic cycle in Famines, no locale cited, no dates given, is alleged.

Grassmann, as reported by Nishioka, 1957. p. 5.

788

A 700-year rhythmic cycle in Famines, no locale cited, 700–1947, is alleged.

Yamamoto, as reported by Nishioka, 1957. p. 5.

GRASS SEED PRODUCTION

789

A 3.9-year (46.8-month) rhythmic cycle in Kentucky Bluegrass Seed Production, U.S.A., 1919-1920—1959-1960, is alleged.

Production of Kentucky Bluegrass seed in the United States for the crop years 1919—1920 through 1959—1960 has moved in a repetitive pattern with waves approximately 46.8 months long. A crest in the ideal pattern was dated at 1959.

Shirk, 1959-F. (Figure)

HAY (TAME) PRODUCTION
(see CROP PRODUCTION AND YIELDS)

HOG PRODUCTION

790

A 30—36-month rhythmic cycle in Hog Numbers, Chicago, 1897—1914, is alleged.

Elliott reported that there has been a "definite shifting up and down in the supply of hogs about every 15 to 18 months..."

Elliott, 1927. p. 533.

791

A 3-year rhythmic cycle in Hog Production, U.S.A., no dates given, is alleged.

Pearson and Myers reported that Warren had found a 3-year cycle in the production (over and under) of hogs.

Warren, 1913, as reported by Pearson and Myers, 1957. p. 5496.

792

A 3—4-year rhythmic cycle in Hog Production, Germany, 1900—1913, is alleged.

Hanau, 1927, as quoted by Tinbergen and Polak, 1950. p. 92. (Figure)

793

A 3—4-year rhythmic cycle in Hog Production, no locale cited, no dates

given, is alleged.

Hog production in many countries over long periods of time have shown evidence of a 3—4-year cycle.

Tinbergen and Polak, 1950. p. 92.

794

A 3—5-year rhythmic cycle in Hog Production, U.S.A., no dates given, is alleged.

Dauten, 1954. p. 101.

795

A 4-year rhythmic cycle in Hog Production, U.S.A., is alleged.

Hog production in the United States (U. S. Department of Agriculture data on number of pigs saved per month) appeared to be influenced by a 48-month rhythm during the period from 1948 through 1957.

Abel, 1962.

796

Harlow asserted that hog production in the United States appeared to be characterized by a 48-month cycle.

Harlow, 1960.

797

Although Maki believed that the beef and pork cycles are largely disappearing in the United States and elsewhere, he cited a 4-year cycle in hog production in the United States and said it appeared to be reliable.

Maki, 1962. pp. 741—742.

798

A well-defined cycle of 4 years duration has characterized the hog production in the United States during the period from 1861 through 1919.

Ross, 1951. (Figure)

799

Shepherd noted that the timing of the 4-year cycle in heavy hog production in the United States appeared as an inverted 4-year cycle in heavy hog prices at Chicago during the period from 1861 through 1945.

Shepherd, 1947. pp. 29—30.

800

A wave which measured approximately 4 years long was reported to be present in hog production in the United States during the period from 1860 through 1931.

Zimmerman, 1951. p. 308.

801

A 4–5-year rhythmic cycle in Hog Production, U.S.A., 1930–1948, is alleged.

The hog cycle in the United States, according to Spaid, averaged between 4 and 5 years in duration during the period under observation.

Spaid, 1949. pp. 4414–4415. (Figure)

802

A 4–6-year rhythmic cycle in Hog Numbers, U.S.A., 1880–1940, is alleged.

The annual changes in the number of hogs on farms in the United States from 1880 through 1940 appeared to move in waves approximately 4–6 years in length. A correlation between hog numbers and purchasing power in terms of 30 basic commodities was noted.

Pearson, Myers, and Curtiss, 1940. pp. 2918–2919. (Figure)

803

A 4–6-year rhythmic cycle in Changes in the Number of Hogs on Farms, U.S.A., 1880–1944, is alleged.

Pearson, Myers, and Lorie, 1945. p. 3704. (Figure)

804

A 4.08-year (49-month) average cycle in the Number of Hogs Slaughtered, U.S.A., 1879–1935, is suggested.

Using the Schuster method of periodogram analysis, Bradley and Crum found evidence of a fairly strong cycle in the range of 48–52 months. This average 49-month period was the most conspicuous period in the analysis.

Bradley and Crum, 1937.

HORSE PRODUCTION

805

A 10-year rhythmic cycle in Horse Production, U.S.A., no dates given, is alleged.

Warren, 1913, as reported by Pearson and Myers, 1957. p. 5496.

806

A 25-year rhythmic cycle in Number of Horses, U.S.A., 1880–1931, is alleged.

Zimmerman, 1951. p. 308. (Figure)

LEMON PRODUCTION

807

A 25–30-year rhythmic cycle in Lemon Production, California, 1924-25–1961-62, is alleged.

French and Bressler, 1962. p. 1035.

OAT PRODUCTION
(see CROP PRODUCTION AND YIELDS)

PECAN PRODUCTION

808

A 24-month (2-year) rhythmic cycle in Pecan Production, U.S.A., no dates given, is alleged.

Huntington, 1945. p. 457.

POTATO PRODUCTION
(see CROP PRODUCTION AND YIELDS)

POULTRY PRODUCTION

809

A 3–4-year rhythmic cycle in Changes in the Number of Chickens on Farms, U.S.A., 1909–1944, is alleged.

Pearson, Myers, and Lorie, 1945. p. 3699. (Figure)

810

A 3–5-year rhythmic cycle in Poultry Production, U.S.A., 1930–1948, is alleged.

Production of chickens and turkeys in the United States from 1930 through 1948 appeared to move in a cycle which averaged 3–5 years in length.

Spaid, 1949. pp. 4414–4415. (Figure)

RYE PRODUCTION
(see CROP PRODUCTION AND YIELDS)

SHEEP PRODUCTION

811

Various average cycles (shortest length: 6.8 years) in Sheep Population,

England and Wales, 1867—1939, are suggested.

Several possible cyclic patterns in sheep population in England and Wales
for the period from 1867 through 1939 were found by Kendall who used
several methods of analysis. The mean period appeared to be about 7.25
years long; that given by regression constants appeared to be about 6.8
years long; and that given by correlogram appeared to measure about 8.5
years.

Kendall, 1960. pp. 366, 385—418. (Figure; data)

812

A 7—12-year rhythmic cycle in Sheep Production, U.S.A., no dates given, is
alleged.

Ross, 1951.

813

An 8-year rhythmic cycle in Changes in the Number of Sheep on Farms,
U.S.A., 1880—1944, is alleged.

Pearson, Myers, and Lorie, 1945. p. 3699. (Figure)

SOY BEAN PRODUCTION

814

A 24-month (2-year) rhythmic cycle in Soy Bean Production, U.S.A., no
dates given, is alleged.

Dauten, 1954. p. 100.

TOBACCO PRODUCTION
(see CROP PRODUCTION AND YIELDS)

WHEAT PRODUCTION
(also see CROP PRODUCTION AND YIELDS)

815

A 3 1/2-year rhythmic cycle in Australian Wheat Production, U.S.A., 1860—
1939, is alleged.

Timoshenko, 1942.

816

A 3 1/2-year rhythmic cycle in Australian Wheat Yields, U.S.A., 1860—1939,
is alleged.

Timoshenko, 1942.

817

A 9.6-year rhythmic cycle in Acreage of Wheat Harvested for Grain, U.S.A.,

1866—1949, is alleged.

Acreage of wheat harvested for grain in the United States from the earliest available figures (1866) through 1949 displayed a 9.6-year cyclic pattern. Over-all amplitude of this cycle measured 11.4% of trend.

Dewey, 1951-X. (Figure; data)

818

A later article brought the series on acreage of wheat harvested for grain up through 1952. The 9.6-year cycle continued to assert itself.

Dewey, 1954-U. (Figure)

819

A 9.6-year rhythmic cycle in Acreage of Wheat Planted, Western United States, no dates given, is alleged.

Dewey, 1957-Q.

820

An 11-year rhythmic cycle in Wheat Production, Eastern England, 1885—1906, is alleged.

Shaw, as reported by Nishioka, 1957. p. 6.

821

An 18.3-year rhythmic cycle in Wheat Acreage, New York, 1880—1929, is alleged.

Using data published by Warren and Pearson, King ascribed a length of 18.3 years to wheat acreage in New York for the period from 1880 through 1929.

King, 1938. p. 231.

822

An 18 1/3-year rhythmic cycle in Wheat Acreage, New York, 1880—1930, is alleged.

Dewey and Dakin, 1947. p. 120. (Figure)

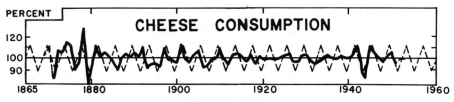

PRECIS 766

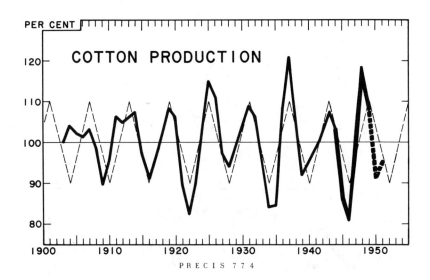

PRECIS 774

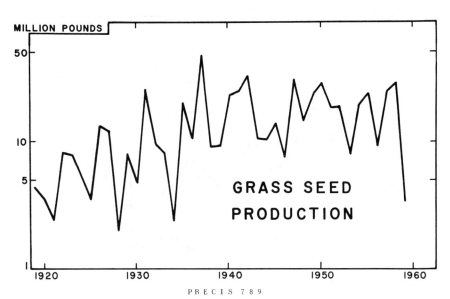

PRECIS 789

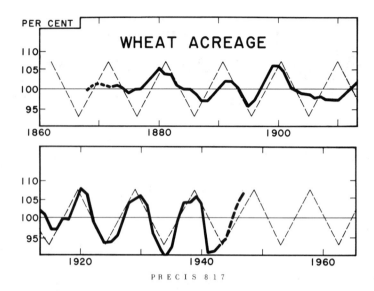

PRECIS 817

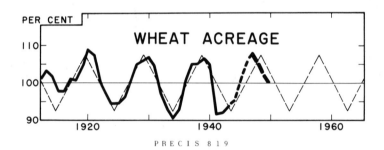

PRECIS 819

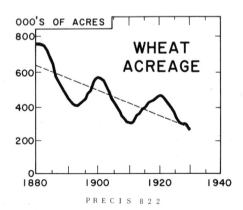

PRECIS 822

BUILDING CONSTRUCTION AND REAL ESTATE

BUILDING CONSTRUCTION AND REAL ESTATE

COMMERCIAL (NON-RESIDENTIAL) CONSTRUCTION

823

A 21-month (1.75-year) rhythmic cycle in Non-Residential Construction Contracts, U.S.A., January 1952—July 1960, is alleged.

A 21-month cycle (along with a seasonal cycle) appeared to be present in the dollar amount of non-residential construction contracts, let, by months from January 1952 through July 1960 (F. W. Dodge Corporation figures).

Shirk, 1960-H. (Figure)

824

An 18-year rhythmic cycle in Large Building Construction, U.S.A., 1830—1936, is alleged.

Peaks in the cycle present in large building construction appeared to occur in 1836, 1853, 1871, 1890, 1909, and 1925. This 18-year cycle appeared to lag behind the cycle dominating general building activity.

Warren and Pearson, 1937. pp. 110—113. (Figure)

825

An 18—20-year rhythmic cycle in Non-Residential Building, U.S.A., no dates given, is alleged.

Non-residential building in the United States, according to Hamberg, followed the same pattern as residential building in the United States which was an 18—20-year fluctuation.

Hamberg, 1951. p. 13.

RESIDENTIAL CONSTRUCTION

826

A 32.3-month (2.69-year) rhythmic cycle in Residential Building Contracts, U.S.A., 1923—1957, is alleged.

Residential building contracts, as measured in dollars by the F. W. Dodge Corporation, appeared to follow a 32.3-month cyclic pattern. 1956.87 dated a trough in the ideal pattern. Typical strength of this cycle averaged 15% above trend at time of an ideal crest and 15% below trend at time of an ideal trough.

Dewey, 1957-O. (Figure)

827

A later article compared actual behavior of this 32.3-month cycle in residential building contracts with ideal behavior through 1960.

Shirk, 1961-Q. (Figure)

828

Residential construction contracts as compiled by the F. W. Dodge Corporation appeared to be following the 32.3-month cyclic pattern although the trend continued to rise.

Shirk, 1962-F. (Figure)

829

A 33-month (2.75-year) rhythmic cycle in Residential Building Construction, U.S.A., is alleged.*

From 1919 through 1937, the minor cycle in residential building activity averaged 33 months in length. A crest in the ideal pattern occurred at January 1920 and every 33 months thereafter.

Pearson, Myers, and Brandow, 1939. p. 2695.

830

A continuation of the 33-month cyclic pattern alleged by Pearson, Myers, and Brandow illustrated that the crest due in April 1950 fell at that exact time.

Dewey, 1951-T. pp. 138—139. (Figure)

831

A later article lengthened the period under observation back through January 1923 and up through August 1957. Dewey refined the length of the study, based on the additional data, to 32.3 months.

Dewey, 1957-O. pp. 283—294. (Figure)

832

Four distinct periods in residential construction in the United States were noted by the author in the period from 1946 through 1959. The duration of these periods appeared to average 33 months.

Guttentag, 1961. p. 278.

---

* Although each separate precis under each individual allegation usually has been placed in alphabetical order throughout this catalogue, an exception has been made in this instance wherein, for the sake of clarity, chronological order has been employed.

833

According to Dewey, the 33-month rhythmic cycle in residential building construction was badly distorted during World War II but reverted to its old timing after the end of hostilities. Highs and lows conformed to a pattern which had been established and projected before the war had started.

Dewey, 1962-C.

834

A 10—20-year rhythmic cycle in Residential Building Construction, U.S.A., no dates given, is alleged.

Residential building construction in the United States has been characterized by "typical major swings" which measure 10 to 20 years in length.

Roos, as reported by Long, 1940. p. 158.

835

A 12—18-year rhythmic cycle in Number of Houses Constructed, Netherlands, 1900—1936, is alleged.

Warren and Pearson, 1937, as cited by Long, 1940. p. 158.

836

A 14—18-year rhythmic cycle in New Family Accomodations, St. Louis, Missouri, 1886—1936, is alleged.

Peaks in the 14—18-year cycle in new family accomodations in St. Louis, from 1886 through 1936 occurred in 1893, 1907, and 1925; lows, in 1900, 1918, and 1933.

Wenzlick, 1932—1934-C, as reported by Warren and Pearson, 1937. (Figure)

837

A 15—20-year rhythmic cycle in Residential Building Activity, U.S.A., no dates given, is alleged.

Gordon, 1961. pp. 243—246.

838

A 15—22-year rhythmic cycle in Residential Building, U.S.A., 1900—1940, is alleged.

Derkson, 1940. p. 97. (Figure)

839

A 16-year rhythmic cycle in Residential Construction, U.S.A., no dates given, is alleged.

Tinbergen and Polak, 1950. p. 94.

840

An 18-year rhythmic cycle in Residential Building Construction, U.S.A., is alleged.

Residential construction in the United States during the period from 1830 through 1937 appeared to be characterized by an 18-year rhythmic cycle.

Bassie, 1958. p. 311.

841

A cyclical movement which measured between 15 and 20 years and averaged 18 years was evident in building construction in the United States from 1853 through 1933.

Grebler, Blank, and Winnick, 1956. pp. 37—43. (Figure)

842

From 1830 through 1937, residential building construction in the United States appeared to move in waves which measured approximately 18 years.

Newbury, 1952. p. 136.

843

The major cycle characterizing residential building construction in the United States during the period from 1830 through 1937 displayed a duration of 18 years.

Pearson, Myers, and Brandow, 1939. p. 2687. (Figure)

844

An 18—20-year rhythmic cycle in Residential Building Construction, U.S.A., is alleged.

Housebuilding in the United States appears to move in cycles which average between 18 and 20 years in length.

Davis, Hughes, and McDougall, 1961. p. 80.

845

American construction of residential buildings follow an 18—20-year cyclic pattern.

Gertler, 1946. p. 8.

846

According to Hamberg, residential building in the United States tended to move in a cyclic pattern which displayed waves which varied in length from 14 (or 16) years to 23 years. The average duration of this movement in residential building was between 18 and 20 years.

Hamberg, 1951. p. 13.

847

Residential building construction in the United States displays a rhythmic pattern which averages 18—20 years in length.

Pearson, Myers, Paarlberg, and DeGraff, 1952. p. 168.

848

An 18-30-year rhythmic cycle in the Number of New Houses Built, London, 1871—1935, is alleged.

Warren and Pearson, 1937, as cited by Long, 1940. p. 158.

849

An 18 1/3-year rhythmic cycle in Residential Building Construction, U.S.A., is alleged.

During the period from 1856 through 1950, a regular 18 1/3-year cyclic pattern appeared to characterize residential building construction. Dewey reported that crests in this cycle occur at the same time as crests in general building construction but that the troughs have a tendency to lag about 1.2 years behind the troughs in general building construction.

Dewey, 1951-C. (Figure)

850

The range of the durations of fluctuations in residential construction in the United States appeared to be from 15 to 22 years and appeared to average 18 1/3 years.

Maisel, 1957. pp. 230—232. (Figure)

851

A 20-year rhythmic cycle in House Building, varying locales, varying dates, is alleged.

Citing Warren and Pearson's figures, Matthews noted that a 20-year cycle appeared to be present in the number of houses built in Germany, in Sweden, and in Canada during the period from 1830 through 1937.

Matthews, 1959. p. 98.

852

Saul stated that a long cycle was evident in house building in England during the period from 1890 through 1914 which had a duration of approximately 20 years.

Saul, 1962.

853

A 20-year rhythmic cycle in the Number of Houses Built, U.S.A., 1856—1957,

is alleged.

Matthews talked of a "seemingly regular" 20-year cycle in the number of houses built in the United States from 1856 through 1957.

Matthews, 1959. p. 98.

854

A 20-year rhythmic cycle in Residential Building Construction, Great Britain and United States, 1890–1950, is alleged.

Using the indexes of rents and of building costs, Thomas found cyclical fluctuations of about 20 years duration in building construction in Great Britain and the United States during the period from 1890 through 1950.

Thomas, 1954.

855

A 20–30-year rhythmic cycle in the Number of Houses Built, Great Britain, 1856–1957, is alleged.

Matthews, 1959. p. 98. (Figure)

856

A 20–35-year rhythmic cycle in the Number of Houses Built, Glasgow, Scotland, 1863–1936, is alleged.

Warren and Pearson, 1937, as cited by Long, 1940. p. 158.

857

A 25-year rhythmic cycle in Residential Building, all Swedish urban communities, 1860–1910, is alleged.

Silk wrote that residential building in all Swedish urban communities from 1860 through 1910 moved in rhythmic fluctuations which measured approximately 25 years. Peaks were noted in 1876–80 and in 1901–05; troughs, in 1866–70 and in 1891–95.

Silk, 1948.

858

A 30-year rhythmic cycle in Residential Building Construction, Glasgow, Scotland, 1863–1936, is alleged.

Caincross, 1934, as reported by Warren and Pearson, 1937. (Figure)

TOTAL OR UNSPECIFIED CONSTRUCTION

859

A 30–40-month rhythmic cycle in Construction, U.S.A., no dates given, is alleged.

Newbury, 1952. p. 174.

860

A 4-year rhythmic cycle in Building Activity, U.S.A., 1870–1938, is alleged.

Building activity in the United States from 1870 through 1938 was characterized by cycles which averaged approximately 4 years in duration. Long compared this cycle in building activity with several business indexes and found that the timing of the cycle as well as the length conformed to the cyclic pattern found in general business.

Long, 1940. pp. 102–107. (Figure; data)

861

A 5-year rhythmic cycle in Building Activity, U.S.A., 1875–1932, is alleged.

In addition to a major cycle of approximately 15–21 years in building activity in the United States from 1875 through 1932, a minor cycle which averaged almost 5 years in duration was revealed.

Newman, 1935. p. 11.

862

An 11 1/2-year rhythmic cycle in Building Activity, U.S.A., 1925–1937, is alleged.

Cooley, 1944-A. p. 46.

863

A 12.5–22.5-year rhythmic cycle in Vacancies, Hamburg, Germany, 1866–1928, is alleged.

A chart illustrated the duration between troughs and crests in the number of vacancies in Hamburg, Germany, from 1866 through 1928. The vacancy cycle had an average length of 17.5 years and appeared to lag several years behind the building cycle.

Feig and Meves, 1911. (Figure)

864

A 15–20-year rhythmic cycle in Building Activity, U.S.A., is alleged.

Fellner stated that a 15–20-year rhythmic pattern appeared to be present in building activity in the United States for the period from 1850 through 1950. He cited Burns and Mitchell's turning points as backup material.

Fellner, 1956. p. 57.

865

The six long building cycles which emerged in the United States from the 1830's to the 1930's appeared to fluctuate in waves which measured approximately 15–20 years in length.

Isard, 1942-A. pp. 90–112.

866

A 15–21-year rhythmic cycle in Building Construction, U.S.A., is alleged.

Bassie reported that a 15–21-year rhythmic cycle was present in building construction in the United States.

Bassie, 1958. p. 61.

867

For the period from 1875 through 1932, building construction in the United States appeared to be characterized by a cycle which measured between 15 and 21 years in length.

Newman, 1935. p. 8.

868

A 16-year rhythmic cycle in Building Construction, U.S.A., 1870–1940, is alleged.

Barger noted that 16 years was the average length of the cycle in building construction in the United States. Peaks occurred in 1871, 1890, 1909, and 1925; troughs, in 1878, 1900, 1918, and 1933.

Barger, 1962. pp. 556–557.

869

A 16–19-year rhythmic cycle in Building Activity, U.S.A., is alleged.

"Hoyt developed data on construction activity (1880–1933) in Chicago, which indicate that the peaks of construction are 16 to 19 years apart."

Hoyt, 1933, as quoted by Warren and Pearson, 1937. (Figure)

870

Newbury asserted that the major cycle present in the construction industry measured approximately 16 to 19 years.

Newbury, 1947. p. 283.

871

Wenzlick published a preliminary index of the volume of new building in the United States from 1875 through 1936 which showed peaks of construction occurring in 1890, 1909, and 1925.

Wenzlick, 1936-A. (Figure)

872

A 16–20-year rhythmic cycle in Building Construction, U.S.A., 1864–1945, is alleged.

According to Hamilton, there were about 4 full building cycles in the United States from 1864 through 1945. Measured from trough to trough, these have

been 1864–1880, 1880–1900, 1900–1918, and 1918–1934. Hamilton also
notes the possibility of a short cycle from 1934–1945.

Hamilton, 1962.

873

A 16–21-year rhythmic cycle in Total Number of New Buildings Constructed,
Hamburg, Germany, 1885–1935, is alleged.

Warren and Pearson, 1937, as cited by Long, 1940. p. 158.

874

Various rhythmic cycles (shortest length: 16 1/2 years) in Building Construction, U.S.A., varying dates, are alleged.

Burns and Mitchell reported on the following long cycles of "remarkably
regular duration" in the building industry in the United States.

Series	Period Covered	No. of Cycles	Average Duration Months	Average Duration Years
Per Capita Permits				
Unadjusted	1830–1933	6	206	17 1/6
Unadjusted	1878–1933	3	220	18 1/3
Adjusted	1830–1933	6	206	17 1/6
Adjusted	1878–1933	3	220	18 1/3
Adjusted Per Capita Permits by Region				
New England	1879–1933	3	216	18
Middle Atlantic	1878–1933	3	220	18 1/3
South Atlantic	1879–1933	3	216	18
East N. Central	1878–1933	3	220	18 1/3
West N. Central	1877–1932	3	220	18 1/3
South Central	1878–1933	3	220	18 1/3
Western	1878–1932	3	216	18
New Building Permits				
Manhattan	1877–1933	3	224	18 2/3
Brooklyn	1879–1933	3	216	18
Chicago	1862–1933	4	213	17 3/4
Philadelphia	1900–1933	2	198	16 1/2
Detroit	1878–1933	2	330	27 1/2
St. Louis	1878–1932	3	216	18
Minneapolis	1897–1933	2	216	18
Pittsburgh	1918–1934	1	192	16
Residential Permits				
Manhattan	1877–1932	3	220	18 1/3
Philadelphia	1900–1933	2	198	16 1/2
St. Louis	1900–1933	2	198	16 1/2

Series	Period Covered	No. of Cycles	Average Duration Months	Average Duration Years
Commercial and Industrial Permits				
Manhattan	1877–1933	2	336	28
Philadelphia	1908–1935	1	324	27
Subdivision Activity				
Chicago	1843–1932	5	214	17 5/6
Detroit area	1841–1918	4	231	19 1/4
Pittsburgh area	1831–1932	6	202	16 5/6

Burns and Mitchell, 1946. pp. 418–421.

875

A 17-year rhythmic cycle in Total Building Construction, U.S.A., 1830–1932, is alleged.

Riggleman, in a comprehensive study of data covering over 100 years, found six long cycles in total building in the United States which varied from 13 to 23 years and averaged 17 years in duration.

Riggleman, 1934, as reported by Long, 1940. pp. 158–159.

876

A 17-year rhythmic cycle in the Value of Building Permits, Canada, 1912–1929, is alleged.

Allen and Hope, in comparing the behavior of the number of buildings erected in Montreal and the value of permits for 35 cities, noted that the value of building permits appeared to follow a 17-year cyclic pattern.

Allen and Hope, 1937, as reported by Warren and Pearson, 1937; p. 127.

877

A 17.9-year rhythmic cycle in Building Activity Per Capita, U.S.A., 1830–1935, is alleged.

To the Riggleman index of building activity per capita in the United States for the period from 1830 through 1935, King attributed a length of 17.9 years. A crest in the ideal pattern was noted at 1928.

King, 1938. p. 232.

878

An 18-year rhythmic cycle in Building Activity and Construction, U.S.A., is alleged.

General construction activity in the United States appeared to be characterized by an 18-year rhythmic cycle.

Controllership Foundation, 1950. p. 70.

879

An 18-year rhythmic pattern appeared to be present in building construction in the United States.

Daniels, 1955.

880

One of the influencing cycles present in building activity in the United States was one measuring approximately 18 years.

Dauten, 1954. p. 95.

881

The major cycle found in building construction in the United States from 1830 through 1937 averaged 18 years in length.

Pearson, Myers, and Brandow, 1939. (Figure)

882

A composite study, in which the Riggleman index, the Wenzlick index, and the Warren and Pearson index for 120 cities were used, indicated an 18-year cycle in building activity in the United States from 1830 through 1936. Peaks of construction came 17, 18, 19, 19, and 16 years apart.

Warren and Pearson, 1937. pp. 132—133. (Figure)

883

An 18-year rhythmic cycle in Building Material Consumption, Great Britain, 1785—1849, is alleged.

Cairncross and Weber, 1956. (Figure; data)

884

An 18-year rhythmic cycle in Building Permits Per Capita, U.S.A., 1830—1935, is alleged.

Riggleman prepared an index of the purchasing power of building permits per capita for a number of cities in the United States which indicated that peaks in construction occurred in 1836, 1853, 1871, 1890, 1909, and 1925. Troughs were dated at 1843, 1864, 1878, 1900, 1918, and 1934. The duration of the dominating cycle averaged 18 years in length.

Riggleman, 1935, as reported by Warren and Pearson, 1937. (Figure)

885

An 18-year rhythmic cycle in Construction Material Consumption, U.S.A., no dates given, is alleged.

Construction material consumption in the United States appears to follow

the same 18-year cyclic pattern that has been found in general construction
activity.

Controllership Foundation, 1950. p. 70.

886

An 18-year rhythmic cycle in the Number of Rooms in New Buildings, Stockholm, Sweden, 1890—1936, is alleged.

Warren and Pearson, 1937. pp. 132—133.

887

An 18-year rhythmic cycle in Total Building Permits Issued, U.S.A., 1853—
1933, is alleged.

According to Hald, a "remarkably uniform cyclical pattern" has been evident
in the total building permits issued for residential and business construction
in the United States from 1853 through 1933.

Hald, 1954. p. 31.

888

An 18—19-year rhythmic cycle in Building Activity, U.S.A., 1865—1940, is
alleged.

The average length of fluctuations in all types of building in the United
States since the Civil War has been 18 to 19 years. Close agreement between the different types of building activity was noted.

Long, 1940. p. 160.

889

An 18—20-year rhythmic cycle in New Building Construction, Hamburg, Ger--
many, 1885—1935, is alleged.

From data taken from the *Statistische Landesamt*, Warren and Pearson found
that peaks in the construction of new buildings in Hamburg, Germany, occurred in 1890, 1910, and 1928. The peaks, 20 and 18 years apart, approximately coincided with the peaks of activity in the United States.

Warren and Pearson, 1937. p. 123. (Figure)

890

An 18—20-year rhythmic cycle in the Number of Buildings Demolished, Hamburg, Germany, 1885—1935, is alleged.

The number of buildings demolished in Hamburg, Germany, from 1885 through
1935 followed the pattern of the new building construction cycle in Hamburg.
Major peaks were reported in 1908 and in 1929, years which also marked
peaks in building activity.

Warren and Pearson, 1937. pp. 123—124. (Figure)

891

An 18—25-year rhythmic cycle in New Building Construction, U.S.A., no
dates given, is alleged.

Downs, 1959. Chapter IV.

892

An 18.2-year rhythmic cycle in Building Construction, Hamburg, Germany,
1885—1935, is alleged.

A cycle which measured approximately 18.2 years in duration was present in
building construction in Hamburg, Germany, during the period from 1885
through 1935. A crest in the ideal pattern was dated at 1963.8.

Dewey, 1955-G. pp. 35—36.

893

An 18.3-year rhythmic cycle in Building Activity, U.S.A., 1795—1937, is
alleged.

Cooley, 1944-B. p. 45.

894

An 18 1/3-year rhythmic cycle in Building Activity, U.S.A., 1830—1936, is
alleged.

Ideal highs in an 18 1/3-year cycle in American building activity were reported at 1834.3, 1852.6, 1871.0, 1889.3, 1907.6, 1926.0, and 1944.3.

Dewey and Dakin, 1947. pp. 118—119. (Figure)

895

An 18 1/3-year rhythmic cycle in Building Construction, U.S.A., 1830—1945,
is alleged.

From Warren and Pearson's 120 City Index and from the value of all construction contracts awarded in 37 states, Dewey found a cycle of about
18 1/3 years present in American building construction from 1830 through
1945.

Dewey, 1955-G. pp. 35, 36, 59. (Figure)

896

A 19-year rhythmic cycle in Building Activity, Montreal, Canada, 1865—
1936, is alleged.

Building activity in Montreal, Canada, appeared to follow a 19-year cyclic
pattern from 1865 through 1936. Peaks occurred at about 1871, 1888, 1911,
and 1928; lows, at about 1880, 1900, 1918, and 1936.

Allen and Hope, 1937. (Figure)

897

A 19-year rhythmic cycle in Building Activity, Montreal, Canada, 1865—1936, is alleged.

According to Warren and Pearson, "The peaks of building activity in the city of Montreal averaged 19 years apart; the low points, 19 years."

Warren and Pearson, 1937. p. 127.

898

A 20-year rhythmic cycle in Building Activity and Construction, U.S.A., is alleged.

General building activity in the United States appeared to fluctuate in 20-year periods. This 20-year cyclic pattern measured twice the length which Babson attributed to the general business cycle in the United States.

Babson, 1948. p. 45.

899

Fellner stated that an analysis of the historical records of building construction in the United States revealed a cycle of from 15 to 20 years in duration, most of the waves measuring 20 years in length.

Fellner, 1960. p. 343.

900

A 20-year rhythmic pattern in general building construction in the United States was reported by Newbury.

Newbury, 1952. p. 136.

901

"The building industry has a comparatively regular cycle of about 20 years, which can be depended upon to have alternate peaks and troughs every 9 to 10 years."

Pearson, Myers, and Lorie, 1945-A. p. 3747.

902

A 22-year rhythmic cycle in Building Activity, Great Britain, no dates given, is alleged.

Beveridge, 1944. p. 307.

903

A 27-year rhythmic cycle in the Number of Rooms in New Buildings Completed, Stockholm, Sweden, 1880—1936, is alleged.

According to Long, Warren and Pearson alleged the existence of a 27-year cycle in the number of rooms in new buildings completed in Stockholm, Sweden, during the period from 1880 through 1936. Warren and Pearson noted in their book that peaks of this cycle occurred in 1885, 1904, and 1932; troughs, in 1893, and 1920.

Warren and Pearson, 1937, as cited by Long, 1940. p. 159.

904

A 33-year rhythmic cycle in Building Construction, Germany, 1862–1932, is alleged.

Lösch, 1937.

REAL ESTATE

905

A 15–17-year rhythmic cycle in Real Estate Activity, Greater St. Louis, 1868–1932, is alleged.

Wenzlick, 1933. pp. 201–202. (Figure)

906

A 17–18-year rhythmic cycle in Deeds Recorded, San Francisco, 1866–1936, is alleged.

A study of the real estate situation in San Francisco from 1866 through 1936 revealed that the deeds recorded per capita followed a 17–18-year repetitive pattern.

Maverick, 1932. p. 199. (Figure)

907

A 17–18-year rhythmic cycle in Real Estate Activity, U.S.A., 1875–1936, is alleged.

Wenzlick assembled a composite of real estate transfers in relation to the number of families for cities throughout the United States which he called the Wenzlick Index of National Cycles in Real Estate Activity. From this index, he found a 17–18-year rhythmic cycle in national real estate activity for the period beginning in 1875 and ending in 1936.

Wenzlick, 1936-B. (Figure)

908

An 18-year rhythmic cycle in New Family Accomodations, St. Louis, 1900–1936, is alleged.

New family accomodations provided for by all new buildings in St. Louis from 1900 through 1936 appeared to move in an 18-year cyclic pattern.

Wenzlick, 1934. pp. 224, 264. (Figure)

909

An 18-year rhythmic cycle in Property Vacancies, St. Louis, 1900–1936, is

alleged.

A study of the percentage of vacancies in St. Louis from 1900 through 1936 indicated a correlation between such vacancies and the building cycle.

Wenzlick, 1932–1934-A. (Figure)

910

An 18-year rhythmic cycle in Real Estate Activity, Chicago, 1832–1932, is alleged.

Real estate activity in the Chicago metropolitan area moved in cycles approximately 18 years in length. Peaks occurred in 1836, 1856, 1872, 1890–1892, and 1925–1926; lows, in 1842, 1861, 1877, 1897, and 1933.

Hoyt, 1933. (Figure)

911

An 18-year rhythmic cycle in Urban Real Estate, U.S.A., 1915–1960, is alleged.

Based on data from the Urban Land Institute, the authors found that urban real estate in the United States showed a tendency to move in 18-year cycles. Peaks occurred in 1818, 1836, 1854, 1872, 1890, 1907, and 1925.

Colean, Fisher, and Gaffney, 1960. (Figure)

912

An 18–20-year rhythmic cycle in Foreclosures, St. Louis and St. Louis County, 1868–1936, is alleged.

The foreclosures per 100,000 families in St. Louis and St. Louis County appeared to follow an 18–20-year cyclic pattern for the period from 1868 through 1936. Peaks were reported in 1878, 1898, 1915, and 1932.

Wenzlick, 1932–1934-D. (Figure)

913

An 18–25-year rhythmic cycle in Foreclosures, U.S.A., no dates given, is alleged.

Downs, 1959.

914

An 18–25-year rhythmic cycle in Real Estate Activity, U.S.A., no dates given, is alleged.

Downs, 1959.

915

An 18–25-year rhythmic cycle in Real Estate Sales, U.S.A., no dates given, is alleged.

Downs, 1959.

916

An 18—25-year rhythmic cycle in Real Estate Security Prices, U.S.A., no
dates given, is alleged.

Downs, 1959.

917

An 18—25-year rhythmic cycle in Rent Prices, U.S.A., no dates given, is alleged.

Downs, 1959.

918

An 18—25-year rhythmic cycle in Residential Occupancy, U.S.A., no dates
given, is alleged.

Downs, 1959.

919

An 18—35-year rhythmic cycle in Land Values, Chicago, no dates given, is
alleged.

Kuznets, 1930. p. 411.

920

An 18.2-year rhythmic cycle in Real Estate Activity, U.S.A., 1851—1954, is
alleged.

For the period from 1851 through 1954, real estate activity in the United
States adhered to a cyclic pattern which measured slightly longer than 18
years. Typical amplitude of this 18.2-year cycle averaged approximately
37% above trend at time of an ideal crest and 41% below trend at time of
an ideal trough. A crest in the ideal pattern occurred at 1852.0 and every
18.2 years thereafter.

Dewey, 1955-G. (Figure)

921

An 18.3-year rhythmic cycle in Real Estate Activity, U.S.A., 1875—1937, is
alleged.

King refined the 17—18-year cycle attributed by Wenzlick to the movement
of real estate activity in the United States to 18.3 years in duration. A crest
in the ideal pattern was dated at 1890.

King, 1938. p. 232.

922

An 18 1/3-year rhythmic cycle in Real Estate Activity, U.S.A., is alleged.

Real estate activity in the United States from 1796 through 1946 moved in
cycles which measured approximately 18 1/3 years in length. A crest in the
ideal pattern occurred at 1943.6; a trough in the ideal pattern, at 1934.5. In
1955, Dewey refined this length to 18.2 years.

Dewey and Dakin, 1947. pp. 116—117. (Figure)

923

Downs cited Wenzlick's figures in real estate activity in the United States as showing a distinct 18 1/3-year rhythmic pattern for the period beginning 1870 and ending 1959.

Downs, 1959.

924

According to Seager, real estate activity in the United States displayed a tendency to move in 18 1/3-year cycles.

Seager, 1962.

925

The number of voluntary transfers of real estate in relation to the number of families in urban areas in the United States from 1795 through 1958 appeared to move in a cyclical pattern which measured 18 1/3 years. During the period under observation, eight repetitions of the 18 1/3-year cycle were observed.

Shirk, 1959-B. (Figure)

926

A 19–20-year rhythmic cycle in Real Estate Activity, Manhattan, 1875–1936, is alleged.

A correlation between building activity and a 19–20-year rhythmic cycle in the number of voluntary transfers of real estate per 100,000 families in Manhattan Island, New York, from 1875 through 1936, was suggested. Peaks were reported to average 19–20 years apart while lows were reported to average 19 years apart.

Wenzlick, 1936. p. 544. (Figure)

927

A 54-year rhythmic cycle in Real Estate Activity, U.S.A., 1795–1950, is alleged.

A 54-year cycle was reported to be present in real estate activity in the United States for the period from 1795 through 1950. This 54-year cycle was composed of minor cycles averaging 18 years in duration. These minor cycles all measured between 16 to 20 years.

Bodfish, 1951.

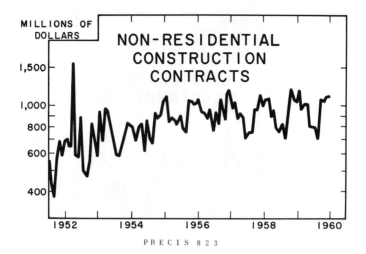

MILLIONS OF DOLLARS

NON-RESIDENTIAL CONSTRUCTION CONTRACTS

PRECIS 8 2 3

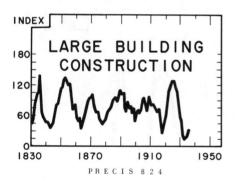

INDEX

LARGE BUILDING CONSTRUCTION

PRECIS 8 2 4

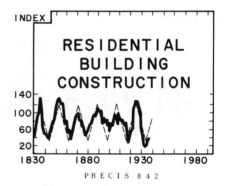

INDEX

RESIDENTIAL BUILDING CONSTRUCTION

PRECIS 8 4 2

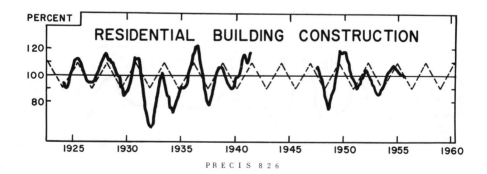

PERCENT

RESIDENTIAL BUILDING CONSTRUCTION

PRECIS 8 2 6

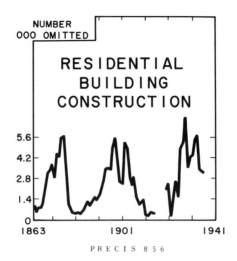

PRECIS 856

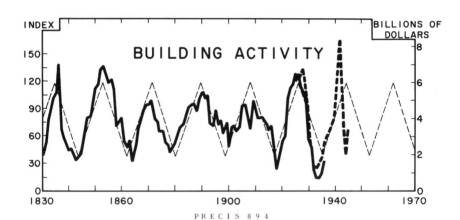

PRECIS 894

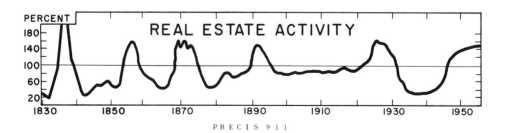

PRECIS 911

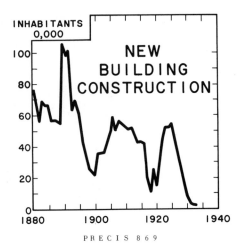

PRECIS 869

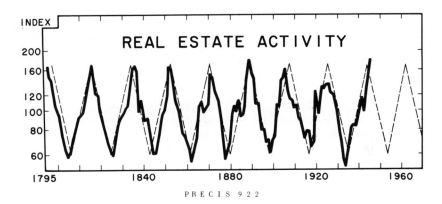

PRECIS 922

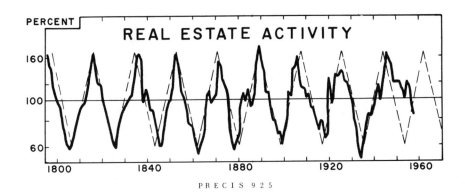

PRECIS 925

MANUFACTURING

MANUFACTURING

AGRICULTURAL EQUIPMENT

928

A 6-year rhythmic cycle in Allis-Chalmers Manufacturing Company Sales, U.S.A., 1916–1945, is alleged.

Dollar sales billed at the Allis-Chalmers Manufacturing Company have appeared to move in cycles approximately 6 years in length. Typical amplitude of the 6-year cycle influencing Allis-Chalmers sales averaged about 15% above trend at time of an ideal crest and about 20% below trend at time of an ideal trough. 1948 dated a crest in the ideal pattern.

Dewey, 1950-G. pp. 4, 11. (Figure)

929

A later article showed that the 6-year cycle in dollar sales billed at Allis-Chalmers Manufacturing Company had continued to assert itself through 1954.

Dewey, 1955-J. (Figure)

930

Pinkham analyzed and correlated the 6-year cycle in 32 various time series discovered by Dewey, one of which was the dollar sales billed at Allis-Chalmers Manufacturing Company. It was reported that a crest in the ideal pattern occurred at 1948.5; a trough in the ideal pattern, at 1945.5. Pinkham suggested that there may be a correlation between these 6-year cycles and the 6-year cycle found in barometric pressure in the United States.

Pinkham, 1956.

ALUMINUM

931

A 6.4-year (76.8-month) rhythmic cycle in Primary Aluminum Production, U.S.A., 1886–1957, is alleged.

A 6.4-year cycle has appeared to be present in primary aluminum production in the United States since the beginning of the industry in 1885. This cycle crested ideally at 1956.3 and displayed typical amplitude of 26% above trend at time of an ideal crest and 21% below trend at time of an ideal trough.

Dewey, 1958-D. (Figure)

932

Shirk reported that the refined strength of this cycle averaged 25.9% above trend at time of an ideal crest and 20.6% below trend at time of an ideal trough.

Shirk, 1958-E. (Figure; data)

933

A chart was published which displayed the performance of the 6.4-year cycle in primary aluminum production from January 1952 through January 1959.

Shirk, 1959-J. (Figure)

934

An additional article reported that the actual behavior of primary aluminum production showed a departure from the ideal behavior.

Shirk, 1961-A. (Figure)

935

Dewey brought the data on the 6.4-year rhythmic cycle in aluminum production in the United States through 1962.

Dewey, 1963-A. (Figure; data)

936

A 13—14-year rhythmic cycle in Primary Aluminum Production, U.S.A., 1886—1957, is alleged.

From data compiled for the 6.4-year rhythmic cycle in primary aluminum production, a longer cycle of considerable strength measuring approximately 13—14 years in length became evident.

Shirk, 1958-E. pp. 51—54. (Data)

AUTOMOBILES

937

A 23 2/3-month (1.97-year) rhythmic cycle in Passenger Car Sales, U.S.A., 1913—1953, is alleged.

The factory sales of passenger cars in the United States have shown a tendency to move in a cyclical pattern approximately 23 2/3 months long. Typical amplitude of this cycle averaged 14.5% above trend at time of an ideal crest and 12.7% below trend at time of an ideal trough. March 1955 dated a crest in the ideal pattern. Dewey reported that this cycle measures exactly one-third of the well-known 5.91-year cycle, which, in turn, measures exactly one-third the length of the 17 2/3-year cycle. The relationship of this three-fold progression, he asserted, could not easily be the result of chance.

Dewey, 1954-C and 1954-D. (Figure)

938

A composite line made up of the 23 2/3-month cycle, the 6 1/3-year cycle, the seasonal cycle, and trend in automobile factory sales in the United States through December 1961 was charted. Actual behavior continued to follow in the ideal pattern.

Shirk, 1962-K. (Figure)

939

A 32.64-month (2.72-year) rhythmic cycle in Passenger Car Sales, U.S.A., 1893—1957, is alleged.

One of the cycles characterizing the factory sales of passenger cars measured approximately 2.72 years in length. This cycle displayed an average strength of 6.2% above trend at time of an ideal crest. A crest in the ideal pattern occurred at 1956.08.

Dewey, 1958-F. (Data)

940

An article, combining the 2.72-year cycle in factory sales of passenger cars in the United States with three other cycles (3.00-year, 3.41-year, and 6.33-year), was published.

Shirk, 1958-A. (Figure)

941

A 33-month (2.75-year) rhythmic cycle in Passenger Car Sales, U.S.A., 1913—1953, is alleged.

From monthly figures on factory sales of passenger cars from 1913 through 1953, Dewey found a cycle approximately 33 months long. This cycle was later refined to a length of 36 months.

Dewey, 1954-B. (Figure)

942

A 33-month (2.75-year) average cycle in Unit Sales of General Motors Corporation, U.S.A., 1910—1955, is alleged.

A periodogram analysis of unit sales of passenger cars and trucks at General Motors from 1910 through 1955 revealed an average wave which measured approximately 2.75 years. Typical over-all amplitude of this cycle averaged 14% of trend. A crest in the ideal pattern occurred at 1953.50.

Hughey, 1956. (Figure; data)

943

A 3.0-year rhythmic cycle in Passenger Car Sales, U.S.A., 1895—1954, is alleged.

Detailed analysis revealed that the 33-month cycle found by Dewey actually measured 36 months. Ideal timing placed a crest at January 1914 and every 36 months thereafter. Typical amplitude of the 36-month cycle in factory sales of passenger cars averaged 14% above trend at time of an ideal crest and 12% below trend at time of an ideal trough.

Dewey, 1954-C. (Figure)

944

Further study determined that the 36-month cycle evident in the factory
sales of passenger cars in the United States crested ideally at 1955.875
and at 36-month intervals forward and backward from that time. Typical
amplitude was reported to be 7.6% above trend at time of an ideal crest.

Dewey, 1958-F. (Data)

945

A 3.0-year rhythmic cycle in Automobile Production, U.S.A., no dates given,
is alleged.

"The so-called automobile cycle is about three years long."

Pearson, Myers, and Lorie, 1945. p. 3747.

946

A 3—4-year rhythmic cycle in Automobile Production, U.S.A., 1919—1936, is
alleged.

Although often irregular and violent in movement, automobile production in
the United States (Federal Reserve Index of Production of Automobile Passenger Cars and Trucks) appeared to move in a cycle 3 to 4 years in length.

Warren and Pearson, 1937. pp. 158—159. (Figure)

947

A 3.33-year (40-month) rhythmic cycle in Automobile Production, U.S.A.,
1919—1938, is alleged.

From 1919 through 1938, automobile production in the United States, following a pattern found in general business, appeared to move in waves approximately 40 months long.

Pearson, Myers, and Brandow, 1939. pp. 2696—2697. (Figure)

948

A 3.42-year (41-month) rhythmic cycle in Passenger Car Sales, U.S.A.,
1895—1953, is alleged.

Factory sales of passenger cars have been characterized by a 41-month cyclical movement which displayed typical amplitude of about 9.7% above
trend at time of an ideal crest. Although the cyclical pattern was disturbed
by World War II activity, it reasserted itself after the war in accordance with
the timing established before the war.

Dewey, 1954-B and 1954-S. (Figure; data)

949

A later article carried data pertaining to the 41-month cycle in factory sales
of passenger cars in the United States through 1957. The cycle crested ideally at 1954.2 and every 3.41 years forward and backward from that time.
Typical amplitude averaged 7.2% above trend at time of an ideal crest.

Dewey, 1958-F. (Figure)

950

A 3.5-year (42-month) average cycle in Unit Sales of General Motors Corporation, U.S.A., 1910—1955, is alleged.

A 3.5-year cycle in the unit sales of passenger cars and trucks at General
Motors Corporation from 1910 through 1955 was revealed by means of a periodogram analysis. Typical amplitude of this cycle was indicated as 11.5%
of trend at time of an ideal crest. 1954.75 dated a crest in the ideal pattern.

Hughey, 1956. (Figure; data)

951

A 6-year rhythmic cycle in Unit Sales of General Motors Corporation, U.S.A.,
1919—1954, is alleged.

Dewey reported that the annual unit sales of General Motors passenger cars
and trucks moved in a definite 6-year cycle prior to World War II. After World
War II, the cycle was also evident but with timing opposite to that of the
pre-war period. The 6-year cycle is the revised length of the 6 1/8-year cycle alleged by Dewey in 1950. The length was later revised to a length of
6 1/3 years.

Dewey, 1955-K. (Figure; data)

952

A 6 1/8-year (73.4-month) rhythmic cycle in Passenger Car Sales, U.S.A.,
1893—1949, is alleged.

A 6 1/8-year cycle (length later revised to 6 1/3 years) appeared to influence the factory sales of passenger cars in the United States from 1893
through 1949. Typical timing placed a crest in the ideal pattern at 1899.
Typical amplitude averaged 16% above trend at time of an ideal crest.

Dewey, 1950-A. (Figure)

953

A 6.33-year (76.0-month) rhythmic cycle in Passenger Car Sales, U.S.A.,
1893—1957, is alleged.

One of the cycles isolated by Dewey from the factory sales of passenger
cars in the United States measured 6 1/3 years long. It displayed an average strength of 23% above trend at time of an ideal crest. 1955.28 dated a
crest in the ideal pattern.

Dewey, 1958-F. (Figure; data)

954

A combined 6 1/3-year, 23 2/3-month, and seasonal cycle along with a trend line were charted through December 1961 for automobile factory sales in the United States. Actual behavior continued to follow ideal behavior.

Shirk, 1962-K. (Figure)

955

A 6.5-year average cycle in Unit Sales of General Motors Corporation, U.S.A., 1910–1955, is alleged.

Through a periodogram analysis, Hughey isolated a 6.50-year cycle in the unit sales of passenger cars and trucks at General Motors Corporation. Typical over-all amplitude was 24% of annual trend. A crest in the ideal pattern occurred at 1955.625.

Hughey, 1956. (Figure; data)

956

A 9.25-year average cycle in Unit Sales of General Motors Corporation, U.S.A., 1910–1955, is alleged.

A periodogram analysis of unit sales of passenger cars and trucks at General Motors Corporation from 1910 through 1955 revealed the presence of a 9.25-year cycle. Typical over-all amplitude of this cycle averaged 31.5% of annual trend. A crest in the ideal pattern occurred at 1954.50.

Hughey, 1956. (Figure; data)

957

An 11-year rhythmic cycle in Automobile Production, U.S.A., 1925–1936, is alleged.

Stetson alleged that automobile production in the United States moves in a pattern similar to the activity pattern found in sunspot numbers.

Stetson, 1937. p. 71. (Figure)

958

A 12.0-year average cycle in Unit Sales of General Motors Corporation, U.S.A., 1910–1955, is alleged.

Hughey, by means of a periodogram analysis of the unit sales of passenger cars and trucks at General Motors Corporation, isolated a 12.0-year cycle. This cycle displayed typical over-all amplitude of 43% of annual trend. January 1952 dated a crest in the ideal pattern.

Hughey, 1956. (Figure; data)

959

A 13.0-year rhythmic cycle in Passenger Car Sales, U.S.A., 1893–1952, is alleged.

A cycle which measured approximately 13.0 years in length was evident in

the factory sales of passenger automobiles since the beginning of the industry. Typical amplitude ranged from 39% above trend at the time of an ideal
crest to 28% below trend at time of an ideal trough. Typical timing placed
1900 as an ideal crest.

Dewey, 1952-R. (Figure)

960

A diagram traced the ideal movement of this cycle as well as the 6-year and
the 3.4-year cycles and illustrated the movement of a combination of these
cycles and the residual.

Dewey, 1954-B. (Figure)

BRICKS AND TILES

961

A 16–18-year rhythmic cycle in Brick Production Per Capita, England and
Wales, 1785–1849, is alleged.

There was a definite tendency for per capita brick production (number of
bricks produced on which taxes were paid) in England and Wales from 1785
through 1849 to follow a cyclical pattern about 16 to 18 years in length.

Shannon, 1934, as reported by Warren and Pearson, 1937. (Figure)

962

An 18-year rhythmic cycle in Quantity of Bricks Charged to Duty, Great
Britain, 1785–1849, is alleged.

Cairncross and Weber, 1956.

963

An 18-year rhythmic cycle in Quantity of Tiles Charged to Duty, Great
Britain, 1785–1832, is alleged.

Cairncross and Weber, 1956.

CEMENT

964

An 18-year rhythmic cycle in Cement Production and Consumption, U.S.A.,
no dates given, is alleged.

Newbury, 1952. p. 139.

CHEMICALS

965

A 3 1/2-year (42-month) rhythmic cycle in E. I. du Pont de Nemours and
Company Sales, U.S.A., 1925–1953, is alleged.

Dollar sales to customers of E. I. du Pont de Nemours and Company have been characterized by a minor cycle approximately 3 1/2 years long. This cycle crested ideally in 1954 and every 3 1/2 years forward and backward from that time. Typical amplitude averaged 5.9% above trend at time of an ideal crest and 5.9% below trend at ideal trough.

Dewey, 1954-G. (Figure)

966

A 6-year rhythmic cycle in E. E. du Pont de Nemours and Company Sales, U.S.A., 1928–1945, is alleged.

A 6-year cycle in dollar sales to customers of E. I. du Pont de Nemours and Company was evident during the period from 1928 through 1945. Typical wave amplitude was approximately 19% above trend at time of an ideal crest and 16% below trend at time of an ideal trough. A crest in the ideal pattern occurred in 1947.

Dewey, 1950-G. pp. 4, 8. (Figure)

967

A subsequent article reported that the 6-year cycle in dollar sales of E. I. du Pont de Nemours and Company showed an indication of fading. Based on additional data, the typical amplitude of this cycle was changed to 15% above trend at time of an ideal crest and 15% below trend at time of an ideal trough.

Dewey, 1954-G. (Figure)

968

A 6-year rhythmic cycle in Monsanto Chemical Company Sales, U.S.A., 1930–1945, is alleged.

Dollar sales at Monsanto Chemical Company from 1930 through 1945 were reported to have moved in waves approximately 6 years in length. A crest in the ideal pattern came at 1947. Typical amplitude averaged approximately 7% above trend at time of an ideal crest.

Dewey, 1950-G. pp. 4, 10. (Figure)

969

An audit of the 6-year cycle in dollar sales at Monsanto Chemical Company with data extended through 1953 indicated that the ideal timing of the cycle should be placed one-half year later than previously stated. A crest in the ideal pattern, therefore, came at the end of 1953. Typical amplitude was reported to average 11 1/2% above trend at time of an ideal crest and 11 1/2% below trend at time of an ideal trough.

Dewey, 1954-T. (Figure)

970

A 7.3-year rhythmic cycle in E. I. du Pont de Nemours and Company Sales, U.S.A., 1925–1953, is alleged.

A 7.3-year rhythmic pattern was evident in the dollar sales to customers of

E. I. du Pont de Nemours and Company during the period under observation. This 7.3-year cycle crested ideally in mid-1951 and displayed a typical amplitude of 18% above trend at time of an ideal crest and 18% below trend at time of an ideal trough.

Dewey, 1954-G. (Figure)

CIGARETTES

971

An 8-year rhythmic cycle in Cigarette Production, U.S.A., 1880—1948, is alleged.

Cigarette production in the United States has shown a tendency to move in a repetitive pattern that measures approximately 8 years from crest to crest. Typical timing placed an ideal crest in 1888. This 8-year cycle in cigarette production displayed average ideal strength of 6.9% above and below trend.

Dewey, 1950-B. (Figure)

972

An audit of the 8-year cycle in cigarette production with data extended through 1952 illustrated that the cycle continued to follow ideal timing. 1944 dated the actual as well as the ideal crest.

Dewey, 1952-B. (Figure)

973

Although the 8-year cycle in cigarette production continued to follow the ideal pattern through 1955, Dewey stated that a refined measurement of 7.95 years appeared to be the true length of the cycle.

Dewey, 1956-B. (Figure; data)

974

This cycle, first discovered in 1949, continued to follow the ideal pattern for more than 1 1/2 waves after discovery.

Dewey, 1962-A. (Figure)

COPPER

975

A 4.7-year (56.4-month) rhythmic cycle in Copper Production, U.S.A., 1880—1924, is alleged.

Kuznets, 1930. p. 297. (Data)

976

A 54-year rhythmic cycle in Copper Production, U.S.A., 1845—1952, is alleged.

Dewey reported that copper, produced in tons, in the United States was one of the 12 series studied as part of the extensive manufacturing production analysis. From 1845 through 1952, copper appeared to fall into a 54-year pattern.

Dewey, 1953-J. p. 301.

CORK

977

A 3.42-year (41-month) rhythmic cycle in Armstrong Cork Company Production, U.S.A., 1860—1946, is alleged.

Wright, 1947. p. 85—86.

978

A 10-year rhythmic cycle in Armstrong Cork Company Production, U.S.A., 1860—1946, is alleged.

One of the component cycles found in production by the Armstrong Cork Company from its founding through 1946 was a 10-year cycle. Wright stated, however, that the cycle may be somewhere between 10 and 15 years.

Wright, 1947. p. 86.

DURABLE GOODS

979

A 9-month (39.13-week) rhythmic cycle in Heavy Durable Goods Production, U.S.A., no dates given, is alleged.

Brandow, 1939, as quoted by Newbury, 1952. p. 145.

980

A 15—18-month rhythmic cycle in Production of Durable Goods, U.S.A., no dates given, is alleged.

Mack, 1958.

981

A 25.5-month (2.12-year) rhythmic cycle in New Orders for Durable Goods, U.S.A., 1951—1959, is alleged.

A strong cycle which measured about 25.5 months from crest to crest appeared to be present in new orders for durable goods in the United States during the period from 1951 through 1959.

Shirk, 1960-D. (Figure)

982

New orders for durable goods, after adjustment for seasonal variation, appeared to be slightly out of phase in the 25.5-month cyclic pattern which had characterized its past movements.

Shirk, 1962-E. (Figure)

983

A 40—75-month rhythmic cycle in the Manufacture of Heavy Durable Goods,
U.S.A., no dates given, is alleged.

Abramson and Mack, 1956. pp. 64—66.

984

A 4.17—4.67-year (50—56-month) rhythmic cycle in New Orders for Durable
Goods, U.S.A., 1951—1959, is alleged.

Although only two repetitions of the 50—56-month rhythmic cycle in new
orders for durable goods were possible during the period of available data
(1951—1959), such a pattern appeared to be real and continuous.

Shirk, 1960-D. (Figure)

ELECTRICAL EQUIPMENT

985

A 3.33-year (40-month) rhythmic cycle in the Rate of Change of Westinghouse
Electric and Manufacturing Company Orders, U.S.A., 1921—1942, is alleged.

Newbury, 1952. p. 166.

986

A 6-year rhythmic cycle in General Electric Company Orders Received,
U.S.A., 1893—1946, is alleged.

Dollar orders received at General Electric Company from 1893 through 1946
have appeared to move in a 6-year cyclical pattern. 1948 dated a crest in
the ideal pattern of this 6-year cycle and typical amplitude measured approximately 12% above trend at time of an ideal crest.

Dewey, 1949-C. (Figure)

987

A 6-year rhythmic cycle in General Electric Company Sales, U.S.A., 1899—
1954, is alleged.

A study of General Electric Company sales, using data from 1899 through
1954, revealed that the 6-year cycle continued to perform in the ideal pattern. This cycle crested ideally at 1900.8 and every 6 years thereafter.
Typical amplitude measured 26.9% above trend at time of an ideal crest and
21.3% below trend at time of an ideal trough.

Dewey, 1955-O. (Figure)

988

An 8 1/2-year rhythmic cycle in General Electric Company Sales, U.S.A.,
1899—1954, is alleged.

The sales of General Electric Company showed a tendency to move in

waves measuring about 8 1/2 years in length during the period under observation. Typical strength of this cycle averaged 18.3% above trend at time of
an ideal crest and 15.3% below trend at time of an ideal trough. 1902.75
dated a crest in the ideal pattern; 1907.0, a trough in the ideal pattern.

Dewey, 1955-O. pp. 204—205.

FOODS (RAW AND PROCESSED)

989

A 6-year rhythmic cycle in Armour and Company Sales, U.S.A., 1904—1945,
is alleged.

A 6-year repetitive pattern in the dollar sales grossed at Armour and Company for the years 1904 through 1945 was evidenced. Typical timing placed
a crest in the ideal pattern at 1948 and every 6 years backward and forward
from that date. Typical amplitude averaged 10% above trend at time of an
ideal crest.

Dewey, 1950-G. pp. 4, 11. (Figure)

990

Additional study, using data through 1952, indicated that the 6-year rhythmic
cycle in dollar sales at Armour and Company had continued. Typical amplitude was re-evaluated and found to average 15% above trend at time of an
ideal crest and 22% below trend at time of an ideal trough.

Dewey, 1952-L and 1953-M. (Figure)

991

A 6-year rhythmic cycle in Swift and Company Sales, U.S.A., 1900—1945, is
alleged.

Dollar sales of Swift and Company from 1900 through 1945 were characterized by a 6-year cycle. 1949 dated a crest in the ideal pattern. Typical amplitude was measured to be about 8% above trend at time of an ideal crest.

Dewey, 1950-G. pp. 5, 14. (Figure)

992

Employing a longer series of figures, 1892—1954, Dewey reported an apparent continuance of a 6-year rhythm in Swift and Company sales. Typical average amplitude was measured as 12% above trend at time of an ideal crest
and 12% below trend at time of an ideal trough.

Dewey, 1955-M. (Figure)

993

A 6-year rhythmic cycle in Wilson and Company Sales, U.S.A., 1930—1945,

is alleged.

A 6-year cyclic pattern appeared to be present in the dollar sales of Wilson and Company for the period from 1930 through 1945. A crest in the ideal pattern of this 6-year cycle occurred in 1948. Typical timing averaged 12% above trend at time of an ideal crest.

Dewey, 1950-G. pp. 5, 14. (Figure)

994

Additional study which brought the series through 1949 appeared to verify the continuance of the 6-year cycle in Wilson and Company dollar sales. Typical amplitude continued to average 12% above trend at time of an ideal crest and 18% below trend at time of an ideal trough.

Dewey, 1953-Q. (Figure)

FREIGHT CARS
(also see TRANSPORTATION)

995

Various rhythmic cycles (shortest length: 32 months) in Freight Car Orders, U.S.A., 1870–1933, are suggested.

Four cycles, the waves of which measured approximately 32 months, 39 months, 40 months, and 49 months, were suggested as forces which may exert influence on freight car orders in the United States from the fourth quarter of 1870 through the first quarter of 1933.

Burns and Mitchell, 1946. p. 484.

FURNITURE

996

An 18 1/3-year rhythmic cycle in Furniture Production, U.S.A., no dates given, is alleged.

Dewey and Dakin, 1947. pp. 128–129.

GLASS

997

A 6-year rhythmic cycle in Pittsburgh Plate Glass Company Sales, U.S.A., 1908–1945, is alleged.

Pittsburgh Plate Glass Company's net dollar sales from 1908 through 1945 appeared to have been characterized by a cyclic pattern approximately 6 years long. Typical amplitude of this cycle was about 11% or 12% above trend at time of an ideal crest. A crest was dated ideally at 1947.

Dewey, 1950-G. pp. 4, 10. (Figure)

998

A later article illustrated that the 6-year cycle had continued to perform in the ideal pattern through 1951.

Dewey, 1952-N. (Figure)

999

An audit of the 6-year cycle in net dollar sales of Pittsburgh Plate Glass Company using data through 1952 revealed that the typical amplitude of this cycle measured 15.8% above trend at time of an ideal crest and 13.2% below trend at time of an ideal trough.

Dewey, 1954-P. (Figure)

1000

An 18-year rhythmic cycle in Quantity of Crown and German Sheet Glass Retained for Home Consumption, Great Britain, 1789—1844, is alleged.

Cairncross and Weber, 1956.

IRON

1001

A 3 1/3-year (40-month) rhythmic cycle in Pig Iron Production, U.S.A., 1891—1940, is alleged.

The twelve-month percent of change (December figures) in pig iron production in the United States for the period from 1891 through 1940 appeared to fluctuate in rhythmic waves approximately 3 1/3 years in duration when measured from crest to crest. Smith attempted to correlate the rhythmic behavior in pig iron production with a rhythmic pattern of similar length in weather — April and October rainfall at Bern, Switzerland.

Smith, 1959. pp. 114, 118—119. (Figure)

1002

Various average cycles (shortest length: 3.4 years) in Pig Iron Production, U.S.A., 1854—1933, are suggested.

Frickey found evidence of several possible cycles in the production of pig iron in the United States from 1854 through 1933. These suggested cycles are listed below.

10.1 or 8.9 years	4.6 or 4.1 years
7.9 or 6.5 years	3.9 or 3.7 years
5.7 or 4.9 years	3.5 or 3.4 years

Frickey, 1942.

1003

A 3.42-year (41-month) rhythmic cycle in Pig Iron Production, U.S.A., is alleged.*

During the period from 1901 through 1938, pig iron production in the United States appeared to fluctuate in waves which measured approximately 41 months in duration.

Hoskins, 1938. (Figure; data)

1004

Dewey and Dakin augmented the study of pig iron production which was originally performed by Hoskins. Because the 41-month cycle was somewhat obscured in the actual production figures, the authors, using data through 1946, plotted the cycle as a percent of the rate of change in actual production for each month to the corresponding month one year prior.

Dewey and Dakin, 1947. pp. 106–107. (Figure)

1005

Dewey reported in a later article that the 41-month cycle in pig iron production had been obscured but it appeared that it was still continuing but with reduced amplitude and late timing.

Dewey, 1954-M. (Figure)

1006

A 3.48-year (41.8-month) rhythmic cycle in Pig Iron Production, U.S.A., no dates given, is alleged.

One of the minor cyclic patterns which appeared to modify the behavior of the 41-month cycle in pig iron production in the United States measured approximately 41.8 months in duration.

Dewey, 1954-M.

1007

A 3.58-year (43-month) rhythmic cycle in Pig Iron Production, U.S.A., January 1879—March 1933, is alleged.

Burns and Mitchell, 1946. pp. 375, 484. (Data)

1008

A 3.67-year (44-month) rhythmic cycle in Pig Iron Production, U.S.A., January 1879—March 1933, is alleged.

Burns and Mitchell, 1946. p. 484. (Data)

1009

An 8-year rhythmic cycle in Pig Iron Production, U.S.A., no dates given, is

---

*Although each separate precis under each individual allegation has been placed in alphabetical order throughout this catalogue, an exception has been made in this instance wherein, for the sake of clarity, chronological order has been employed.

alleged.

Moore, 1923. p. 32.

1010

A 10-year rhythmic pattern in Pig Iron Production, U.S.A., 1891—1940, is alleged.

The twelve-month percent of change in pig iron production for successive Decembers from 1891 through 1940 appeared to follow the Decennial Pattern. A correlation between weather patterns (April and October rainfall reported at Bern, Switzerland) and pig iron production was suggested.

Smith, 1959. pp. 114, 118—119. (Figure)

1011

An 11.2-year rhythmic cycle in Pig Iron Production, U.S.A., 1844—1958, is alleged.

An 11.2-year cycle was evident in pig iron production in the United States during the period from 1844 through 1958. Typical over-all strength of this cycle measured about 10% of ideal trend per year.

Shirk, 1959-C. (Figure)

1012

An 18-year rhythmic cycle in Pig Iron Production and Consumption, U.S.A., no dates given, is alleged.

Newbury, 1952. p. 139.

1013

A 22-year rhythmic cycle in Pig Iron Production, U.S.A., 1854—1924, is alleged.

Kuznets, 1930. p. 94.

1014

A 50—60-year rhythmic cycle in Pig Iron Production, U.S.A. and England, varying dates, is alleged.

Kondratieff, 1935. (Figure)

1015

A 50—60-year rhythmic cycle in Pig Iron Production, worldwide, 1872—1914, is alleged.

Kondratieff, 1935. (Figure)

1016

A 54-year rhythmic cycle in Pig Iron Production, U.S.A., 1810—1952, is alleged.

While analyzing manufacturing production in the United States, Dewey used as one criteria, pig iron production in the United States for the period from 1810 through 1952. This pig iron series appeared to move in waves which measured approximately 54 years in duration — a finding which upheld Kondratieff's studies in this area.

Dewey, 1953-J.

LEAD

1017

A 6-year rhythmic cycle in National Lead Company Sales, U.S.A., 1933–1945, is alleged.

Net sales of National Lead Company from 1933 through 1945 appeared to move in a 6-year cyclical pattern. Typical amplitude of this cycle averaged 12% above trend at time of an ideal crest. A crest was ideally dated at 1949.

Dewey, 1950-G. pp. 5, 14. (Figure)

1018

A subsequent article reported on the conformance of the actual net sales of National Lead Company to the ideal pattern for the years 1930 through 1953.

Dewey, 1954-T. pp. 358–360. (Figure)

1019

A 50–60-year rhythmic cycle in Lead Production, England, 1870–1925, is alleged.

Kondratieff, 1935. (Figure)

1020

A 54-year rhythmic cycle in Lead Production, U.S.A., 1825–1952, is alleged.

Lead production was one of the series studied by Dewey in order to confirm the presence of a 54-year cycle in manufacturing production.

Dewey, 1953-J. p. 301.

LEATHER
(also see SHOES)

1021

A 15–18-month rhythmic cycle in Leather Output, U.S.A., no dates given, is alleged.

Mack, 1958.

1022

A 23-month (1.92-year) rhythmic cycle in Leather and Shoe Production, U.S.A., no dates given, is alleged.

Newbury quotes Roos as having found a 23-month cycle in the production of leather and shoes in the United States.

Roos, 1948, as quoted by Newbury, 1952.

LUMBER

1023

An 18 1/3-year rhythmic cycle in Lumber Production, U.S.A., no dates
given, is alleged.

Dewey and Dakin, 1947. pp. 128—129.

1024

A 54-year rhythmic cycle in Lumber Production, U.S.A., 1809—1952, is alleged.

Lumber production, in board feet, appeared to move in a 54-year cyclic pattern.

Dewey, 1953-J. p. 300.

MACHINERY

1025

A 23-month (1.92-year) rhythmic cycle in the Manufacture of Textile Machinery, U.S.A., no dates given, is alleged.

Newbury, 1952. p. 147.

MANUFACTURING PRODUCTION — GENERAL

1026

A 9-month rhythmic cycle in Industrial Production, Pittsburgh area, 1886—
1942, is alleged.

Newbury noted that a 9-month cyclic pattern that appeared and disappeared
was present in industrial production in the Pittsburgh area during the period
from 1886 through 1942.

Newbury, 1952. p. 139. (Figure)

1027

A 9-month rhythmic cycle in Industries Producing Capital Goods, Pittsburgh, 1880—1938, is alleged.

Newbury, 1938. Section I; p. 1. (Figure)

1028

A 15—18-month rhythmic cycle in Industrial Production, U.S.A., no dates
given, is alleged.

Mack, 1958.

1029

A 30-month (2.5-year) rhythmic cycle in Industrial Production, 1949–1956, is alleged.

A study of the Federal Reserve Board Index of Industrial Production revealed the presence of a 30-month cycle.

Chapman, 1957. (Figure)

1030

A 3-year rhythmic cycle in Industrial Production, U.S.A., 1919–1930, is alleged.

As in steel-ingot production, industrial production in the United States appeared to move in 3-year cycles for the period from 1919 through 1930 with peaks appearing in 1920, 1923, 1926, and 1929.

Haney, 1931. p. 59. (Figure)

1031

A 3.33-year (40-month) rhythmic cycle in Consumption, U.S.A., no dates given, is alleged.

Hubbard, 1942. p. 199.

1032

A 3.33-year (40-month) rhythmic cycle in Heavy Industry Production, U.S.A., 1855–1938, is alleged.

Newbury, 1952. p. 139.

1033

A 3.33-year (40-month) rhythmic cycle in Industrial Production, Japan, 1878–1942, is alleged.

Shinohara, 1962. pp. ii, 79.

1034

A 3.33-year (40-month) rhythmic cycle in Industrial Production, Pittsburgh area, 1886–1942, is alleged.

Newbury, 1952. p. 139. (Figure)

1035

A 3.33-year (40-month) rhythmic cycle in Industries Producing Capital Goods, Pittsburgh, 1880–1938, is alleged.

Newbury, 1938. Section I. (Figure)

1036

A 3.33-year (40-month) rhythmic cycle in the Rate of Change in Industrial Production, Pittsburgh district, 1885–1937, is alleged.

Newbury, 1952. pp. 168–169.

1037

A 3.33-year (40-month) rhythmic cycle in Rate of Change in Industrial Production, U.S.A., no dates given, is alleged.

The rate of change in industrial production in the United States as gauged by the Federal Reserve Board's Index of Industrial Production appeared to move in waves which measured approximately 40 months.

Newbury, 1952. pp. 182–183.

1038

A 3.42-year (41-month) rhythmic cycle in Industrial Production, U.S.A., no dates given, is alleged.

"Industrial production, for as far back as figures are available, shows a 41-month cycle."

Dewey, 1951-H. p. 331.

1039

A later article indicated that industrial production in general, as measured by the Federal Reserve Board Index, 1944–1953, continued to follow the 41-month cycle but with reduced amplitude and with delayed turning points.

Dewey, 1954-M. pp. 115–116. (Figure)

1040

A 41-month rhythmic cycle appeared to be present in industrial production in the United States.

Wright, 1947. p. 83.

1041

A 3 1/2-year (42-month) rhythmic cycle in Industrial Production, U.S.A., is alleged.

A 42-month cycle was found "to parallel the growth cycle" of industrial production in the United States from 1949 through 1956, as measured by the Federal Reserve Board Index.

Chapman, 1957. (Figure)

1042

Although somewhat obscured in the actual production figures as measured by the Federal Reserve Board Index, a 42-month cycle in industrial production for the period from 1919 through 1945 became apparent when graphed as rate of change in production.

Hoskins, 1938, as reported by Dewey and Dakin, 1947. (Figure)

1043

McGrath stated that the volume of manufactured goods produced in the United States (no dates given) moves in cycles which average 42 months in length when measured from peak to peak.

McGrath, 1936.

1044

A 3 1/2-year (42-month) rhythmic cycle in Heavy Industrial Production, U.S.A., 1867–1946, is alleged.

A "short component" cycle, the average length of which was 3 1/2 years, appeared to characterize heavy industrial production in the United States from 1867 through 1946.

Newbury, 1947. pp. 283–285. (Figure)

1045

A 42–43-month rhythmic cycle in Industrial Production and Trade, U.S.A., 1878–1932, is alleged.

Using Person's Index, Bratt noted the existence of a 42–43-month periodicity in industrial production and trade in the United States for the period under observation. He noted that the average length of the total period was 43 months while the average length of the period from 1900–1932 was 42 months and concluded that this may indicate a shortening of the waves.

Bratt, 1937. pp. 166–167.

1046

A 4-year rhythmic cycle in Industrial Output, U.S.A., 1944–1958, is alleged.

Industrial output as measured by the manufacture of durable and nondurable goods appeared to move in cycles which measured approximately 4 years in duration. Troughs were noted in 1949, 1954, and 1958.

Woytinsky and Woytinsky, 1959. pp. 66–68. (Figure)

1047

A 4.7-year (56.4-month) rhythmic cycle in Manufacturing Production, U.S.A., 1900–1950, is alleged.

In the fifty years under observation, manufacturing production in the United States appeared to follow a 4.7-year cyclic pattern in which the rise measured about twice as long as the fall.

Woytinsky and Associates, 1953. pp. 54–56.

1048

A 4.7-year (56.4-month) average cycle in British Consumption, Great Britain, 1870–1914, is suggested.

Tinbergen, 1951. p. 132.

1049

A 5.6-year (67.2-month) rhythmic cycle in Manufacturing Production, U.S.A.,

1860—1950, is alleged.

In the 5.6-year pattern which is found in manufacturing production in the
United States for the period from 1860 through 1950, the rise appears to last
twice as long as the fall.

Woytinsky and Associates, 1953. pp. 54—56.

1050

A 6-year rhythmic cycle in Heavy Industrial Production, U.S.A., 1900—1946,
is alleged.

Newbury stated that one of the significant cycles found in heavy industrial
production was a "long component cycle" which averaged 6 years in length.

Newbury, 1947. p. 283.

1051

A 6—9-year rhythmic cycle in Heavy Industrial Production, Great Britain, no
dates given, is alleged.

"The 6 to 9-year component cycle of American business is apparently the
complete cycle of British industry."

Newbury, 1947. p. 283.

1052

A 6.25-year (75-month) rhythmic cycle in Industrial Production, Pittsburgh
area, 1886—1942, is alleged.

Newbury, 1952. p. 139. (Figure)

1053

A 6.25-year (75-month) rhythmic cycle in Industries Producing Capital
Goods, Pittsburgh, 1880—1938, is alleged.

Newbury, 1938. Section I; p. 1. (Figure)

1054

An 8-year average cycle in Demand for Consumer Goods, United Kingdom,
1870—1914, is suggested.

Tinbergen, 1951. p. 126.

1055

An 8—9-year rhythmic cycle in Industrial Production, no locale cited, 1830—
1916, is alleged.

An 8—9-year rhythmic pattern in industrial production was found by *Tecknisk
Tidskrift* (Veckoupplagen, 1916), according to Mitchell.

Mitchell, 1927.

1056

An 8—11-year rhythmic cycle in Industrial Activity, no locale cited, no
dates given, is alleged.

"...a short industrial cycle covering usually from 8 to 11 years" was reported by Kondratieff.

Kondratieff, 1922, as reported by Kuznets, 1930.

1057

A 9-year rhythmic cycle in Industrial Production, U.S.A., no dates given, is
alleged.

Klemme, 1950.

1058

A 9-plus-fraction-year rhythmic cycle in Heavy Industry — Capital Goods,
U.S.A., no dates given, is alleged.

Seager, 1962.

1059

A 9.3-year rhythmic cycle in Manufacturing Production, U.S.A., 1864—1943,
is alleged.

A rhythmic 9.3-year cycle has been present in manufacturing production from
1864, when figures are first available, through 1943. A crest in the ideal
pattern falls at 1862.65 and every 9.3 years thereafter. Typical amplitude
was measured as 5.9% above trend at time of an ideal crest and 5.6% below
trend at time of an ideal trough.

Dewey, 1953-D. (Figure)

1060

A later article showed that the 9.3-year cycle in manufacturing production
in the United States had continued through February 1956.

Dewey, 1956-H. pp. 150—151. (Figure)

1061

A 10-year rhythmic cycle in Industrial Production, U.S.A., no dates given,
is alleged.

Wright, 1947. p. 83.

1062

A 10-year rhythmic cycle in Life of Machinery, no locale cited, no dates
given, is alleged.

"Ten years seems to be, not merely the average, but also the markedly pre-
dominant" length of life of machinery, a measure of industrial fluctuations.

Pigou, 1920.

1063

An 11.20-year rhythmic cycle in the Physical Production of Manufactures, U.S.A., is alleged.*

Using data supplied by Persons and following procedures discovered by Macaulay, Garcia-Mata and Shaffner found an average cycle of 11.20 years duration in the physical production of manufactures in the United States from 1875 through 1930. A correlation with sunspot differences was suggested.

Garcia-Mata and Shaffner, 1934. pp. 13—15, 20. (Figure)

1064

According to Dewey, the 11.2-year cycle discovered by Garcia-Mata and Shaffner continued to follow ideal behavior through 1953. Ideal crests occurred at 1871.4 and every 11.2 years thereafter. Typical strength of the 11.2-year cycle averaged 9.6% above trend at time of an ideal crest and 8.8% below trend at time of an ideal trough.

Dewey, 1953-J. pp. 302—306. (Figure)

1065

A 13.0-year rhythmic cycle in Manufacturing Production, U.S.A., 1864—1953, is alleged.

A strong rhythmic cycle which measured approximately 13 years in length was evident in manufacturing production in the United States from 1864 forward. This cycle displayed an over-all average amplitude of 12.9%.

Dewey, 1953-D. (Figure)

1066

A 15—20-year rhythmic cycle in Industrial Production, U.S.A., is alleged.

Industrial production in general appeared to follow closely the movements of the building cycle which fluctuates in repetitive waves which measure between 15 and 20 years in length.

Davis, 1941. p. 27.

1067

Harris reported that Arthur F. Burns found a 15—20-year rhythmic cycle in industrial production during the period from 1870 through 1930.

Harris, 1961.

1068

A 15—25-year rhythmic cycle in Industrial Production, U.S.A., no dates

---

* Although each separate precis under each individual allegation has been placed in alphabetical order throughout this catalogue, an exception has been made in this instance wherein, for the sake of clarity, chronological order has been employed.

given, is alleged.

Babson, 1932. pp. 142–144.

1069

An 18 1/3-year rhythmic cycle in Industrial Production, U.S.A., no dates given, is alleged.

Klemme, 1950.

1070

A 20-year rhythmic cycle in Output, U.S.A., 1870–1955, is alleged.

"The possibility, therefore, arises that there is a significant cycle in the secular trend of output — meaning by this, movements which persist over a period longer than a business cycle — with an approximate duration of twenty years."

Abramovich, 1956. p. 20. (Figure)

1071

A 20-year rhythmic cycle in Manufacturing Production, U.S.A., 1860–1957, is alleged.

Matthews stated that a 20-year periodicity existed in manufacturing production in the United States for the period from 1860 through 1957. He also contended that this periodicity is "well-supported by evidence of fluctuations before the Civil War."

Matthews, 1959. p. 209. (Figure)

1072

A 33-year rhythmic cycle in Industrial Production, Germany, 1862–1932, is alleged.

Lösch, 1937. pp. 649–662. (Figure)

1073

A 36-year rhythmic cycle in Manufacturing Production, U.S.A., 1809–1953, is alleged.

A repetitive cycle which measured approximately 36 years in length appeared to characterize manufacturing production in the United States from 1809 through 1953. This 36-year cycle displayed typical amplitude of about 21% above trend at time of an ideal crest and 18% below trend at time of an ideal trough. 1775 dated a crest in the ideal pattern.

Dewey, 1954-E. (Figure)
Dewey, 1954-F. (Figure)

1074

A re-evaluation of the 36-year cycle in manufacturing production using the Federal Reserve Board Index reaffirmed both the timing and the amplitude which was determined in 1954. A crest in the ideal pattern was timed at 1955.

Dewey, 1958-E. (Figure)

1075

A 50-year rhythmic cycle in Manufacturing Production, U.S.A., 1809–1953, is alleged.

A cycle approximately 50 years long appeared to be evident in manufacturing production in the United States during the period from 1809 through 1953. Typical wave amplitude averaged 19% above trend at time of an ideal crest and 16% below trend at time of an ideal trough.

Dewey, 1954-E. (Figure)
Dewey, 1954-F. (Figure)

1076

Using the Federal Reserve Board Index, Dewey recomputed the cyclic trend in manufacturing production in the United States from 1809 through 1953. This recomputation changed neither the length nor the timing. 1953 dated a crest in the ideal pattern of this cycle.

Dewey, 1958-E. (Figure)

1077

A 54-year rhythmic cycle in Manufacturing Production, U.S.A., 1815–1947, is alleged.

The so-called 54-year cycle "seems to be present in manufacturing production, but in physical production the timing is very different from the timing in prices, ideal lows coming about 20 years earlier...."

Dewey, 1951-F. p. 203.

1078

From 1810 through 1953, manufacturing production in the United States appeared to follow a 54-year cycle. 1852 dated a crest in the ideal pattern and typical strength was measured at 6.4% above trend at time of an ideal crest and 6.0% below trend at time of an ideal trough. The length of this cycle was later revised to 50 years.

Dewey, 1953-J. (Figure)

1079

A 60-year rhythmic cycle in Certain Industrial Production, no locale cited, no dates given, is alleged.

"A long wave spanning up to 60 years" is identifiable in certain significant industrial production data drawn from industrial nations, according to Chambers.

Chambers, 1961. p. 50.

MANUFACTURING – UNDISCLOSED COMPANIES

1080

A 3-month (13.04-week) rhythmic cycle in the Sales of a Single Industrial

Company, U.S.A., 1931–1940, is alleged.

A figure illustrated a 3-month cycle in the sales of a large industrial company in the United States (a textile company in Boston).

Dewey and Dakin, 1947. pp. 138–139. (Figure)

1081

Various rhythmic cycles (shortest length: 4.05 months) in the Sales of
Company G, U.S.A., January 1913–February 1951, are alleged.

In addition to a seasonal cycle in the sales of Company G for the period
under observation, 22 additional cycles appeared to be present.

Cycle Length	Cycle Length	Cycle Length	Cycle Length
4.05 months	12.57 months	27.7 months	44.0 months
7.4 months	14.04 months	30.62 months	52.5 months
7.92 months	15.0 months	32.85 months	61.2 months
9.36 months	18.67 months	37.75 months	72.0 months
9.87 months	20.0 months	40.8 months	96.0 months
11.52 months	22.7 months		

A diagram illustrating the timings, amplitudes, and shapes of these ideal-
ized cycles was given, as well as a synthesis of the aggregate waves and
the trend.

Dewey, 1951-D. (Figure)

1082.

A 12.595-month (1.05-year) rhythmic cycle in the Sales of Company G,
U.S.A., June 1903–July 1950, is alleged.

Although originally computed to have a length of 12.576 months, the sales
of Company G from June 1903 through July 1950 moved in waves which
measured 12.595 months long. Typical amplitude at the time of an ideal
crest was 7.9%. A crest in the ideal pattern occurred at February 1946.

Dewey, 1952-Q and 1952-T. (Figure)

1083

A 15-month (1.25-year) rhythmic cycle in the Sales of a Single Industrial
Company, U.S.A., 1927–1941, is alleged.

Evidence of a 15-month cycle was found in the series of data pertaining to
the sales of an industrial company in the United States (a textile company
in Philadelphia) from 1927 through 1941. Cyclic waves which measured 24
months, 33 months, 41 months, and 10 years were also reported to have been
present in sales of this company prior to this study.

Dewey and Dakin, 1947. pp. 184–187. (Figure)

1084

A 22.7-month (1.89-year) rhythmic cycle in the Sales of Company G,
U.S.A., January 1904—August 1950, is alleged.

A 22.7-month cycle, which evidenced remarkable behavior when the ideal
and actual movements were compared, was isolated in the sales of Company
G. Typical over-all strength of the wave was reported to be 21.0% of trend.
Ideal timing placed a crest in the ideal pattern at September 1942 and every
22.7 months before and after that date.

Malinowski, as reported by Dewey, 1951-W. pp. 10—11. (Figure)
Dewey, 1951-Q. p. 13.

1085

A 24-month rhythmic cycle in the Sales of a Single Industrial Company,
U.S.A., 1927—1941, is alleged.

A 24-month cyclic pattern was found to be one of the regular cycles present
in the sales of a single industrial company in the United States from 1927
through 1941.

Dewey and Dakin, 1947. pp. 182, 184—187. (Figure)

1086

A 32.86-month (2.74-year) rhythmic cycle in the Sales of Company G,
U.S.A., 1904—1950, is alleged.

Sales of Company G for the period from 1904 through 1950 appeared to have
been characterized by a 2.74-year cycle. This cycle crested ideally at July
1906. Typical amplitude was measured at 13.19% above trend at time of an
ideal crest and 11.65% below trend at time of an ideal trough.

Dewey, 1951-U. (Figure)

1087

In a later article, data were carried through 1952. Dewey reported that the
sales of Company G through 1952 continued to move in an ideal 32.86-month
pattern.

Dewey, 1952-S. (Figure)

1088

A 33-month (2.75-year) rhythmic cycle in the Sales of a Single Industrial
Company, U.S.A., 1927—1941, is alleged.

One of the regular cycles present in the sales of a single industrial company in the United States from 1927 through 1941 measured 33 months in
length.

Dewey and Dakin, 1947. pp. 182, 184—187. (Figure)

1089

A 3.42-year (41-month) rhythmic cycle in the Sales of a Single Industrial

Company, U.S.A., 1927–1941, is alleged.

A 41-month cycle appeared as one of the regular cycles in the sales of a single industrial company in the United States from 1927 through 1941.

Dewey and Dakin, 1947. pp. 182, 184–187. (Figure)

1090

An 8-year rhythmic cycle in the Sales of Company G, U.S.A., 1913–1955, is alleged.

Dewey reported that an 8-year rhythmic cycle was present in the sales of Company G during the period from 1913 through 1955. This cycle crested in the ideal pattern at 1953.25.

Dewey, 1956-I. pp. 272–273.

1091

A 9-year rhythmic cycle in the Sales of Company A, U.S.A., 1875–1936, is alleged.

The sales of Company A followed closely a 9-year cyclic pattern for the period 1875 through 1936.

Dewey and Dakin, 1947. pp. 94–95. (Figure)

1092

A 9-year rhythmic cycle in the Sales of Company B, U.S.A., 1845–1939, is alleged.

The sales of Company B, which represented a totally different industry from Company A, also appeared to follow a 9-year cyclic pattern for the period under observation.

Dewey and Dakin, 1947. p. 95. (Figure)

1093

A 9 1/3-year rhythmic cycle in the Sales of a Single Industrial Company, U.S.A., 1871–1940, is alleged.

A regular 9 1/3-year cycle appeared to be present in the sales of a single industrial company in the United States from 1871 through 1940.

Dewey and Dakin, 1947. pp. 182–183. (Figure)

1094

A 10-year rhythmic cycle in the Sales of a Single Industrial Company, U.S.A., 1927–1941, is alleged.

One of the regular cycles which characterized the sales of a single industrial company in the United States from 1927 through 1941 measured approximately 10 years in length.

Dewey and Dakin, 1947. pp. 182, 184—187. (Figure)

1095

A 12.5-year rhythmic cycle in the Sales of Company G, U.S.A., 1903—1956, is alleged.

Sales of Company G, a manufacturing company located in the United States, for the period from 1903 through 1956, appeared to have moved in a cyclic pattern approximately 12.5 years in length. Typical amplitude of this cycle averaged 35.2% above trend at time of an ideal crest and 26.0% below trend at time of an ideal trough. 1954.5 dated a crest in the ideal pattern.

Dewey, 1957-G. (Figure)

1096

An 18 1/3-year rhythmic cycle in the Sales of a Single Industrial Company, U.S.A., 1872—1939, is alleged.

An 18 1/3-year cyclic pattern was evident in the sales of a large industrial company in the United States from 1870 through 1938.

Dewey and Dakin, 1947. pp. 129, 133, 183. (Figure)
Dewey, 1955-G. p. 35.

METAL PRODUCTION
(also see individual metals by name)

1097

A 15—18-month rhythmic cycle in Ferrous and Nonferrous Metal Production, U.S.A., no dates given, is alleged.

Mack, 1958.

1098

A 15—18-month rhythmic cycle in Ferrous and Nonferrous Metal Shipments, U.S.A., no dates given, is alleged.

Mack, 1958.

1099

A 6-year rhythmic cycle in Iron and Steel Production, U.S.A., no dates given, is alleged.

West, 1941.

NONDURABLE GOODS

1100

A 15—18-month rhythmic cycle in Production of Nondurable Goods, U.S.A., no dates given, is alleged.

Production of nondurable goods (other than food) in the United States appeared to follow a "subcycle" pattern of 15 to 18 months duration.

Mack, 1958.

OIL

1101

A 3 1/2-year (42-month) rhythmic cycle in Continental Oil Company Income,
U.S.A., 1930—1952, is alleged.

Gross operating income (used as a measure of productivity) of Continental
Oil Company from 1930 through 1952 moved in a 3 1/2-year cycle. This cycle which dated an ideal crest during the second half of 1930, displayed an
average amplitude of 6% above trend at the time of an ideal crest.

Dewey, 1953-C. (Figure)

1102

A later article revealed that refined analysis measured typical amplitude
at ideal crest at 5.3%. The timing of turnings remained the same.

Dewey, 1954-A. (Figure)

1103

A 6-year rhythmic cycle in Continental Oil Company Income, U.S.A., 1933—
1945, is alleged.

A 6-year cycle characterized the gross operating income of Continental Oil
Company from 1933 through 1945. Typical amplitude at time of an ideal crest
measured 6% above trend. A crest in the ideal pattern occurred in 1943.

Dewey, 1950-G. pp. 5, 14. (Figure)

1104

Subsequent studies of data through 1953 revealed a revised amplitude at
ideal crest of 10.0% but no change in the timing of turning points.

Dewey, 1953-C. (Figure)
Dewey, 1954-A. (Figure)

1105

A 6-year rhythmic cycle in Income of Standard Oil Company of California,
U.S.A., 1929—1945, is alleged.

Gross operating income of Standard Oil Company of California from 1929
through 1945 moved in a cyclic pattern measuring 6 years. Typical amplitude
was reported to be about 5% above trend at time of an ideal crest. Such

an ideal crest was dated at 1949.

Dewey, 1950-G. pp. 5, 17. (Figure)

1106

An 8-year rhythmic cycle in Oil Company Sales, U.S.A., no dates given, is alleged.

"The sales of certain oil companies show evidence of an eight-year cycle."

Dewey, 1952-C. p. 8.

PUBLISHING

1107

A 2-year rhythmic cycle in the Number of Books Published, U.S.A., 1929—1959, is alleged.

The number of books published for each active adult in the United States from 1929 through 1959 has appeared to move in cyclic waves approximately 2 years long.

Shirk, 1960-Y. (Figure)

RUBBER

1108

A 6-year rhythmic cycle in B. F. Goodrich Company Sales, U.S.A., 1915—1945, is alleged.

Net dollar sales of B. F. Goodrich Company from 1915 through 1945 evidenced a 6-year cyclic movement. Typical amplitude of this 6-year cycle averaged 12% above trend at time of an ideal crest. A crest in the ideal pattern occurred at 1943.

Dewey, 1950-G. pp. 5, 15. (Figure)

1109

A 6-year rhythmic cycle in Goodyear Tire and Rubber Company Sales, U.S.A., 1929—1945, is alleged.

A 6-year rhythmic cycle was isolated in the net dollar sales of Goodyear Tire and Rubber Company for the period from 1929 through 1945. The year 1943 dated a crest in the ideal pattern of this 6-year cycle. Typical amplitude at time of an ideal crest measured about 13%.

Dewey, 1950-G. pp. 5, 16. (Figure)

1110

Using four additional years of data, Dewey refined the amplitude and timing of the 6-year cycle in Goodyear Tire and Rubber Company net dollar sales. Mid-1954 dated a crest in the ideal pattern. The 6-year cycle had typical strength of 7.7% above trend at time of an ideal crest and 7.7% below trend at time of an ideal trough.

Dewey, 1954-H. (Figure)

1111

A 6-year rhythmic cycle in United States Rubber Company Sales, U.S.A., 1904–1944, is alleged.

Net dollar sales of United States Rubber Company for the years from 1904 through 1944 appeared to move in a 6-year cyclic pattern. Typical amplitude at time of an ideal crest appeared to average 13% above trend. A crest in the ideal pattern occurred at 1943.

Dewey, 1950-G. pp. 5, 17. (Figure)

1112

An 8-year rhythmic cycle in Goodyear Tire and Rubber Company Sales, U.S.A., 1926–1952, is alleged.

An 8-year cycle of considerable importance appeared to be present in the net dollar sales of Goodyear Tire and Rubber Company from 1926 (the earliest figures available) through 1952. This 8-year cycle in net dollar sales showed an average strength of 28.6% above trend at time of an ideal crest and 28.6% below trend at time of an ideal trough. A crest in the ideal pattern was reported in the third quarter of 1952.

Dewey, 1954-H. (Figure)

SEMI-DURABLE GOODS

1113

A 23-month (1.92-year) rhythmic cycle in Semi-durable Goods Production, U.S.A., 1910–1938, is alleged.

In addition to the 7–10-year and the 40-month cycles which Newbury said were present in the semi-durable goods industry from 1910 through 1938, a short 23-month cycle was reported.

Newbury, 1952. p. 146.

1114

A 2-year rhythmic cycle in Semi-durable Goods Production, U.S.A., 1830–1937, is alleged.

Newbury, 1952. p. 136.

1115

A 3.33-year (40-month) rhythmic cycle in Semi-durable Goods Production, U.S.A., 1910–1938, is alleged.

The intermediate component of the semi-durable goods industry measured approximately 40 months.

Newbury, 1952. p. 146.

1116

A 7–10-year rhythmic cycle in Semi-durable Goods Production, U.S.A., 1910–1938, is alleged.

One of the long component cycles present in the semi-durable goods industry from 1910 through 1938 measured approximately 7–10 years, according to Newbury.

Newbury, 1952. p. 146.

SHIPBUILDING

1117

A 2-year rhythmic cycle in Shipbuilding, Norway, 1884–1932, is alleged.

In addition to the 5-year major shipbuilding cycle in Norway from 1884 through 1932, Einarsen found a secondary 2-year cycle.

Einarsen, 1938. p. 133.

1118

A 5-year rhythmic cycle in Shipbuilding, Great Britain and Ireland, 1894–1932, is alleged.

Einarsen, 1938. pp. 133–135. (Figure)

1119

A 5-year rhythmic cycle in Shipbuilding, Norway, 1884–1932, is alleged.

Peaks in a 5-year rhythmic pattern which was present in Norwegian ship-building for the period from 1884 through 1932 occurred in 1884, 1890, 1895, 1899, 1906, 1912, 1916, 1920, 1925, and 1929. Troughs occurred in 1887, 1893, 1897, 1902, 1909, 1914, 1918, 1923, 1927, and 1932.

Einarsen, 1938. pp. 99, 133–135, 144–146. (Figure)

1120

A 5-year rhythmic cycle in Shipbuilding, worldwide, 1894–1932, is alleged.

Einarsen, 1938. pp. 133–135. (Figure)

1121

A 54-year rhythmic cycle in Vessels Built, U.S.A., 1800–1952, is alleged.

Vessels built, measured in gross tons, was one of a series utilized in order to confirm a 54-year cycle in manufacturing production.

Dewey, 1953-J. p. 300.

SHOES
(also see LEATHER)

1122

A 27-month (2.25-year) rhythmic cycle in Shoe and Slipper Production, U.S.A., 1942–1959, is alleged.

A 27-month cyclic pattern, along with a 12-month seasonal cycle, appeared to be present in shoe and slipper production in the United States for the period from 1942 through 1959. October 1959 dated a crest in the ideal pattern. On the average, typical amplitude of this cycle was 5% above trend at time of an ideal crest and 5% below trend at time of an ideal trough.

Shirk, 1960-L. (Figure)

1123

The 27-month cycle in shoe and slipper production in the United States combined with a seasonal cycle and trend appeared to be reinforced by conformance of the actual with the ideal through July 1962.

Shirk, 1962-T. (Figure)

SOAP AND RELATED PRODUCTS

1124

A 6-year rhythmic cycle in Procter and Gamble Sales, U.S.A., 1915–1945, is alleged.

Gross dollar sales of Procter and Gamble Company showed a tendency to move in waves approximately 6 years in duration during the period under observation. Typical strength of the 6-year cycle averaged 15% above trend at time of ideal crest. A crest in the ideal pattern occurred at 1943.

Dewey, 1950-G. pp. 5, 16. (Figure)

1125

A later article verified the continuance of the 6-year cycle in gross dollar sales of Procter and Gamble Company after discovery. A refinement, using four additional years of data, placed a crest in the ideal pattern at 1919. Typical amplitude was refined to 13 1/2% above trend at time of an ideal crest and 16 1/2% below trend at time of an ideal trough.

Dewey, 1953-P. (Figure)

STEEL

1126

A 3-year rhythmic cycle in Steel-Ingot Production, U.S.A., 1919–1930, is

alleged.

From 1919 through 1930, steel-ingot production in the United States appeared to move in waves which measured approximately 3 years. Peaks were observed at 1920, 1923, 1926, and 1929.

Haney, 1931. p. 59. (Figure)

1127

A 3.33-year (40-month) rhythmic cycle in Rate of Change in Steel-Ingot Production, U.S.A., no dates given, is alleged.

Newbury, 1952. pp. 182—183.

1128

A 6-year rhythmic cycle in Armco Steel Corporation Sales, U.S.A., 1904—1944, is alleged.

Dollar sales of Armco Steel Corporation for the period from 1904 through 1944 followed a 6-year rhythmic pattern. The average wave amplitude was approximately 12% above trend at time of an ideal crest. A crest in the ideal pattern occurred at 1949.

Dewey, 1950-G. pp. 5, 15. (Figure)

1129

A subsequent article, using figures from 1901 through 1951, showed that the 6-year cycle in dollar sales of Armco Steel Corporation had continued since discovery. Typical amplitude remained at 12% above trend at time of an ideal crest and was reported to average 27% below trend at time of an ideal trough. The timing of turning points remained the same as in the original study.

Dewey, 1953-N. (Figure)

1130

A 6-year rhythmic cycle in Bethlehem Steel Corporation Production, U.S.A., 1908—1947, is alleged.

For the period from 1908 through 1947, net ton production of Bethlehem Steel Corporation appeared to move in waves approximately 6 years long. Typical amplitude of this 6-year cycle averaged 18% above trend at time of an ideal crest. The year 1947 dated a crest in the ideal pattern.

Dewey, 1950-G. pp. 4, 8. (Figure)

1131

A later article reported that typical amplitude of the 6-year cycle in net ton production of Bethlehem Steel Corporation for the period from 1905 through 1952 averaged 16.7% above trend at time of an ideal crest. Timing of ideal troughs were reported to fall four years after time of ideal crests.

Dewey, 1953-A. (Figure)

1132

A 6-year rhythmic cycle in Inland Steel Company Sales, U.S.A., 1924–1945, is alleged.

Net dollar sales of Inland Steel Company for the period from 1924 through 1945 were characterized by a 6-year cycle. Typical wave amplitude of the ideal cycle was reported to be about 17% above trend at time of an ideal crest. 1947 dated a crest in the ideal pattern.

Dewey, 1950-G. pp. 4, 9. (Figure)

1133

A 6-year rhythmic cycle in Jones and Laughlin Steel Corporation Sales, U.S.A., 1926–1945, is alleged.

Jones and Laughlin Steel Corporation sales, as gauged by total dollar sales for the period from 1926 through 1945, followed a 6-year cyclical pattern. Typical amplitude averaged 11% above trend at time of an ideal crest. A crest in the ideal pattern occurred at 1947.

Dewey, 1950-G. pp. 4, 9. (Figure)

1134

A later article illustrated that the 6-year cycle in total dollar sales of Jones and Laughlin Steel Corporation had continued to follow an ideal 6-year pattern through 1951.

Dewey, 1952-M. (Figure)

1135

A 6-year rhythmic cycle in Republic Steel Corporation Production, U.S.A., 1933–1945, is alleged.

Net ton ingot production of Republic Steel Corporation for the period from 1933 through 1945 appeared to move in a 6-year rhythmic cycle. Typical amplitude at time of an ideal crest averaged 26% above trend. The year 1942 dated a crest in the ideal pattern.

Dewey, 1950-G. pp. 4, 12. (Figure)

1136

A 6-year rhythmic cycle in Steel Production, U.S.A., 1867–1954, is alleged.

Steel production in the United States as gauged by ingot and casting production appeared to follow a 6-year cyclic pattern during the period under observation. Typical amplitude of this 6-year cycle measured 9.6% above trend at time of an ideal crest and 8.8% below trend at time of an ideal trough.

Dewey, 1955-U. (Figure)

1137

The 6-year rhythmic cycle in steel production alleged by Dewey continued to assert itself through the third quarter of 1960. A crest in the actual as well as in the ideal pattern occurred at the end of 1959.

Dewey, 1961-A. (Figure)

1138

A 6-year rhythmic cycle in Youngstown Sheet and Tube Company Sales, U.S.A., 1926—1945, is alleged.

1948 dated a crest in the ideal pattern of a 6-year cycle which was present in the dollar sales of Youngstown Sheet and Tube Company from 1926 through 1945. Typical amplitude of this 6-year cycle was found to be approximately 29% above trend at time of an ideal crest.

Dewey, 1950-G. pp. 5, 13. (Figure)

1139

Further study of the 6-year cycle in dollar sales of Youngstown Sheet and Tube Company with data brought through 1954 revealed a change in the typical timing of that cycle. Revised timing placed a crest in the ideal pattern midway between 1953 and 1954. Typical amplitude was also revised to about 23% above and below trend at time of ideal turnings.

Dewey, 1955-N. (Figure)

1140

An 8-year rhythmic cycle in Steel-Ingot Production, U.S.A., 1867—1955, is alleged.

From 1867 through 1955, steel-ingot production in the United States appeared to follow an 8-year cyclical pattern. 1952.0 dated a crest in the ideal pattern.

Dewey, 1956-I. p. 272.

TEXTILES

Cotton

1141

A 15—18-month rhythmic cycle in Cotton Textile Production, U.S.A., no dates given, is alleged.

Mack, 1958.

1142

An 18-month rhythmic cycle in Cotton Textile Production, U.S.A., no dates given, is alleged.

A "subcycle" which measured approximately 18 months was found to be present in cotton textile production in the United States.

Chambers, 1961.

1143

A 22—26-month rhythmic cycle in Textile Production Per Capita, U.S.A., no dates given, is alleged.

Roos, 1955. p. 367.

1144

A 23-month (1.92-year) rhythmic cycle in Cotton Consumption, U.S.A., 1910—1938, is alleged.

One of the components in the movement of cotton consumption in the United States from 1910 through 1938 appeared to be a 23-month cycle.

Bassie, 1958. p. 63. (Figure)

1145

A 23 3/4-month (1.98-year) rhythmic cycle in Cotton Consumption, U.S.A., no dates given, is alleged.

The 23 3/4-month repetitive wave which appeared to characterize cotton consumption in the United States displayed a low in the ideal pattern at February 1960.

Seager, 1962.

1146

In addition to a seasonal cycle, cotton consumption in the United States from 1924 through 1958 appeared to be characterized by a cycle which measured 23.75 months long. Typical strength of this 23.75-month cycle was 11% above trend at time of an ideal crest. A crest in the ideal pattern occurred at February 1959.

Shirk, 1959-H. (Figure)

1147

The 23.75-year cycle in cotton consumption in the United States continued to follow the ideal pattern through June 1962.

Shirk, 1962-S. (Figure)

1148

A 24-month (2-year) rhythmic cycle in Cotton Consumption, U.S.A., is alleged.

Cotton consumption at mills in the United States (and, perhaps, most semi-durable manufactures) appeared to move in a 2-year rhythmic pattern during the period from 1945 through 1950. Although the period under observation was extremely short, peaks were dated at 1946 and 1948; troughs, at 1945, 1947, and 1949.

Controllership Foundation, 1950. p. 69.

1149

Davis noted that cotton consumption in the United States for the period from 1921 through 1954 appeared to move in 2-year waves.

Davis, 1958.

1150

Newbury reported that cotton consumption in the United States appeared to be characterized by 2-year waves.

Newbury, 1938. Section I; p. 1.

1151

For the period from 1913 through 1940, West alleged that cotton consumption in the United States moved in fluctuations which measured approximately 2 years in length.

West, 1941. pp. 102—107. (Figure)

1152

A 24-month (2-year) rhythmic cycle in Cotton Consumption, Great Britain, 1920—1940, is alleged.

West, 1941. pp. 102—107. (Figure)

1153

A 24-month (2-year) rhythmic cycle in Cotton Consumption, Netherlands, 1922—1938, is alleged.

Tinbergen and Polak, 1950. p. 96. (Figure)

1154

A 24-month (2-year) rhythmic cycle in Cotton Textile Output, U.S.A., 1919—1941 and 1945—1956, is alleged.

During the 30 peacetime years since World War I, 13 1/2 cycles have been evident which have typically measured about 2 years.

Stanback, 1958. p. 174. (Figure; data)

1155

A 24-month (2-year) rhythmic cycle in Cotton Textile Production, U.S.A., 1830—1937, is alleged.

Newbury, 1952. p. 136.

1156

A 3.33-year (40-month) rhythmic cycle in Cotton Consumption, U.S.A., 1910—1938, is alleged.

One of the components in the fluctuations of cotton consumption in the United States for the period under observation measured approximately 40 months.

Bassie, 1958. p. 63. (Figure)

1157

A 7—10-year rhythmic cycle in Cotton Consumption, U.S.A., 1910—1938, is

alleged.

A 7—10-year cycle, along with a 23-month and a 40-month cycle, appeared to influence cotton consumption in the United States from 1910 through 1938.

Bassie, 1958. p. 63. (Figure)

1158

A 54-year rhythmic cycle in Cotton Consumption, U.S.A., 1839—1952, is alleged.

Cotton consumed in manufacturing in the United States, measured in bales, from 1839 through 1952 appeared to move in waves approximately 54 years long. This 54-year cycle was studied to confirm the 50—60-year cycle in manufacturing production.

Dewey, 1953-J.

1159

A 54-year rhythmic cycle in Cotton Goods Manufactured, U.S.A., 1839—1952, is alleged.

One of the series studied for the confirmation of a 50—60-year cycle in manufacturing production was the amount of cotton goods manufactured measured in dollars, adjusted for prices.

Dewey, 1953-J.

General Textile Activity

1160

A 23-month (1.92-year) rhythmic cycle in Textile Manufacturing, U.S.A., no dates given, is alleged.

Newbury, 1952. p. 147.

1161

A 23-month (1.92-year) rhythmic cycle in Textile Production, U.S.A., 1919—1938, is alleged.

The textile industry has been characterized by alternate periods of expansion and construction that have averaged 23 months in duration when measured from peak to peak.

Pearson, Myers, and Brandow, 1939. p. 2695. (Figure)

1162

A 23-month (1.92-year) rhythmic cycle in Total Fabric Production, U.S.A., no dates given, is alleged.

Newbury, 1952. p. 147.

1163

A 24-month (2-year) rhythmic cycle in Apparel-Type Fiber Consumption at

Mills, U.S.A., 1921—1954, is alleged.

Davis, 1958. p. 16. (Figure; data)

1164

A 24-month (2-year) rhythmic cycle in Ladies Hosiery Output, U.S.A., 1919—1941 and 1945—1956, is alleged.

Stanback, 1958. p. 174.

1165

A 24-month (2-year) rhythmic cycle in Retailers' Sales of Clothing, U.S.A., 1935—1956, is alleged.

Davis, 1958. p. 39. (Figure; data)

1166

A 24-month (2-year) rhythmic cycle in Textile Consumption, U.S.A., is alleged.

A thorough analysis of textile consumption in the United States from 1921 through 1954 revealed the tendency for such consumption to move in waves having the duration of approximately 2 years. Major apparel fiber consumption included cotton, wool, rayon and acetate, and silk. Peaks were reported to occur in odd years while troughs occurred in even years. Amplitude was reported to average 6% in good times; 8 to 9% in recessions; 9 to 14% in deep depressions.

Davis, 1958. (Figure)

1167

A 2-year rhythmic cycle in textile-mill consumption in the United States was reported by Wells.

Wells, 1951.

1168

A 24-month (2-year) rhythmic cycle in Textile Production and Consumption, U.S.A., no dates given, is alleged.

Hunt, 1951.

1169

A 24-month (2-year) rhythmic cycle in Textile Production, U.S.A., is alleged.

Production of manufactured textiles in the United States moved in a 2-year rhythmic pattern.

Abramson and Mack, 1956. pp. 64—66.

1170

According to Bratt, "short-term movements" in textile production in the United States demonstrated a 2-year cycle.

Bratt, 1958. p. 234.

1171

American textile production appeared to be characterized by a 2-year cycle.

Haney, 1931. p. 160.

1172

From 1919 through 1936, textile production in the United States moved in a 2-year cyclic pattern.

Pearson, Myers, and Lorie, 1945. p. 3747.

1173

Textile production in the United States followed a 2-year rhythmic cycle during the period from 1919 through 1936.

Warren and Pearson, 1937. p. 158. (Figure)

1174

A 2–3-year rhythmic cycle in Textile Production, U.S.A., 1919–1941 and 1945–1956, is alleged.

"Well developed cycles" which measure between 2 and 3 years in duration have appeared in textile production in the United States during the 30 peacetime years since World War I.

Stanback, 1958. p. 183.

Rayon and Related Materials

1175

A 24-month (2-year) rhythmic cycle in Rayon and Acetate Consumption, U.S.A., 1921–1954, is alleged.

Davis, 1958.

1176

A 24-month (2-year) rhythmic cycle in Non-Acetate Rayon Deliveries, U.S.A., 1923–1936, is alleged.

Non-acetate rayon deliveries in the United States for the period from 1923 through 1936 exhibited a tendency to move in a 2-year cycle. A crest in the ideal pattern of this 24-month cycle is dated at May 1923.

Croxton and Cowden, 1939. p. 555.

1177

A 24-month (2-year) rhythmic cycle in Rayon Cloth Production, U.S.A., 1919–1941 and 1945–1956, is alleged.

Stanback, 1958. p. 174.

1178

A 24-month (2-year) rhythmic cycle in Rayon Production, U.S.A., is alleged.

A 2-year rhythmic cycle appears to have characterized rayon (viscose filament yarn) production in the United States from 1911 through 1948. The average amplitude of this 2-year cycle was about 3.8% above trend at time of an ideal crest for the period from 1912 through 1939; after 1939, the typical amplitude averaged 4.35% above trend at time of an ideal crest. A crest in the ideal pattern occurred at 1923.

Dewey, 1949-A. (Figure; data)
Dewey, 1952-C. (Figure)

1179

A later article pertaining to viscose filament yarn production in the United States showed that this cycle had continued to conform to the ideal pattern through 1952.

Dewey, 1953-H.

1180

A 33-month (2.75-year) rhythmic cycle in Rayon Production, U.S.A., 1911—1948, is alleged.

One of the cyclic patterns which appeared to characterize rayon (viscose filament yarn) production in the United States from 1911 through 1948 measured approximately 2.75 years in length. A crest in the ideal pattern of this 33-month cycle occurred at 1939.

Dewey, 1949-A. (Figure; data)

1181

The continuance of the 33-month cycle pattern in rayon production in the United States through 1952 was reported in a later article.

Dewey, 1953-H.

1182

A 3.42-year (41-month) rhythmic cycle in Rayon Production, U.S.A., 1911—1948, is alleged.

Dewey reported that this 41-month wave that was found in viscose filament yarn production in the United States from 1911 through 1948 had an over-all amplitude of approximately 6.5% of trend. A crest in the ideal pattern occurred at 1937.

Dewey, 1949-A. (Figure; data)

1183

Subsequent articles reported that the 41-month cycle in rayon production in the United States had continued to follow the ideal pattern through 1952. Dewey reported that this 41-month wave could be the well-established 41-month cycle which has been characteristic of American industry.

Dewey, 1952-C and 1953-H. (Figure)

1184

A 6-year rhythmic cycle in American Viscose Corporation Shipments, U.S.A., 1915—1945, is alleged.

Shipments of American Viscose Corporation from 1915 through 1945 appeared to move in a 6-year cyclic pattern. Typical amplitude of this 6-year cycle measured approximately 8% above trend at time of an ideal crest. The year 1941 dated such an ideal crest.

Dewey, 1950-G. pp. 4, 8. (Figure)

1185

An article indicating that the 6-year cycle in shipments of American Viscose Corporation had continued through 1951 was published.

Dewey, 1953-M. (Figure)

1186

A 6-year rhythmic cycle in Rayon Production, U.S.A., 1911—1948, is alleged.

A 6-year cyclic pattern appeared to characterize rayon (viscose filament yarn) production in the United States from 1911 through 1948. Typical over-all wave amplitude of this cycle was reported to average about 4% of trend. A crest in the ideal pattern occurred in 1935.

Dewey, 1949-A. (Figure; data)

1187

A later article showed that the 6-year cycle in rayon production in the United States had continued to assert itself through 1952.

Dewey, 1953-H.

Silk

1188

A 24-month (2-year) rhythmic cycle in Raw Silk Consumption, U.S.A., 1921—1954, is alleged.

Davis, 1958.

1189

A 24-month (2-year) rhythmic cycle in Silk Cloth Production, U.S.A., 1919—1941 and 1945—1956, is alleged.

Stanback, 1958. p. 174.

Wool

1190

A 24-month (2-year) rhythmic cycle in Wool Consumption, U.S.A., 1921—1945, is alleged.

Davis, 1958.

1191

A 24-month (2-year) rhythmic cycle in Woolen Cloth Production, U.S.A., 1919–1941 and 1945–1956, is alleged.

Stanback, 1958. p. 174.

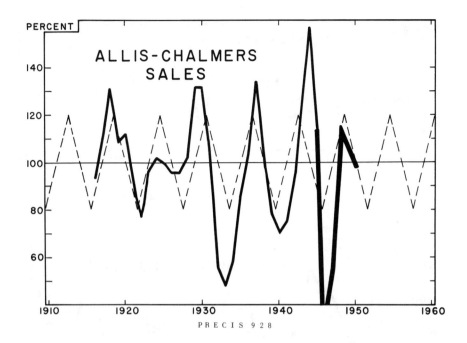

PERCENT

ALLIS-CHALMERS
SALES

PRECIS 9 2 8

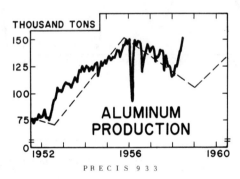

THOUSAND TONS

ALUMINUM
PRODUCTION

PRECIS 9 3 3

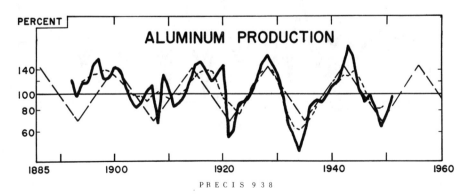

PERCENT

ALUMINUM   PRODUCTION

PRECIS 9 3 8

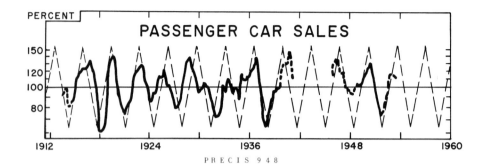

PRECIS 948

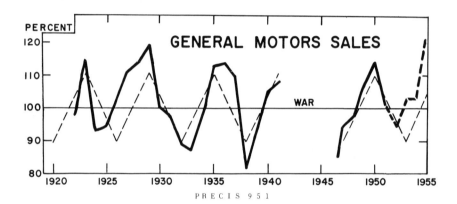

PRECIS 951

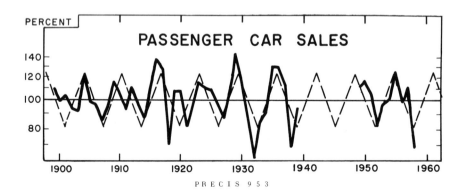

PRECIS 953

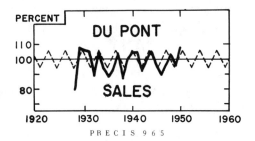

PRECIS 9 6 5

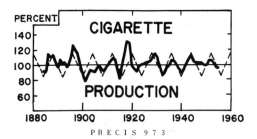

PRECIS 9 7 3

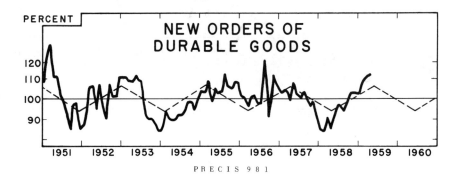

PRECIS 9 8 1

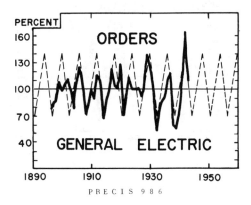

PRECIS 9 8 6

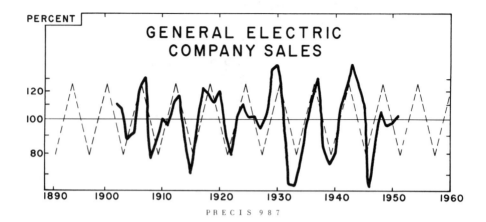

GENERAL ELECTRIC
COMPANY SALES

PRECIS 987

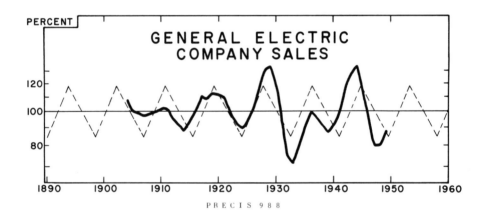

GENERAL ELECTRIC
COMPANY SALES

PRECIS 988

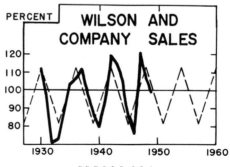

WILSON AND
COMPANY SALES

PRECIS 994

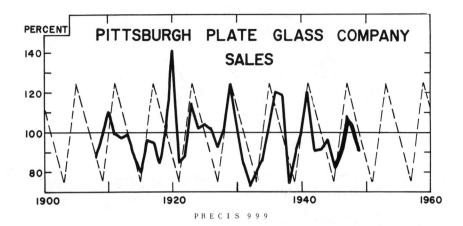

PRECIS 999

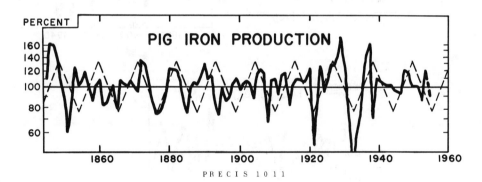

PRECIS 1011

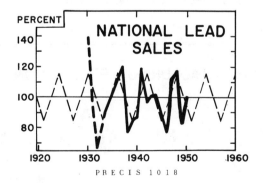

PRECIS 1018

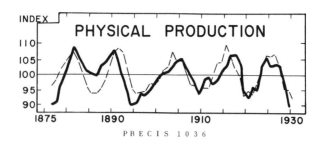

PRECIS 1036

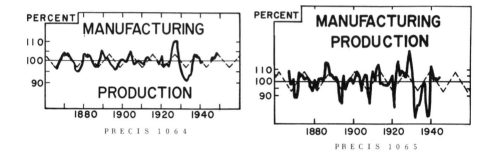

PRECIS 1064

PRECIS 1065

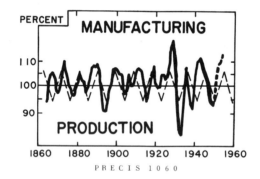

PRECIS 1060

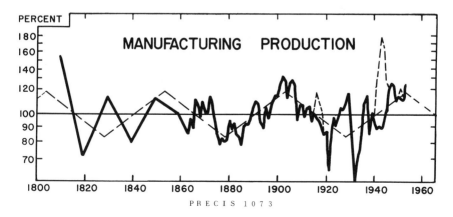

PRECIS 1073

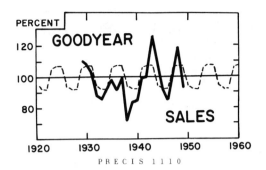

PRECIS 1110

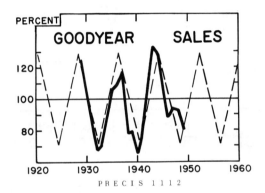

PRECIS 1112

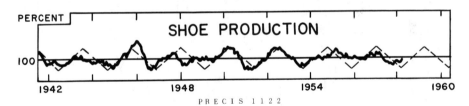

PRECIS 1122

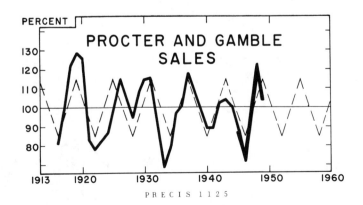

PRECIS 1125

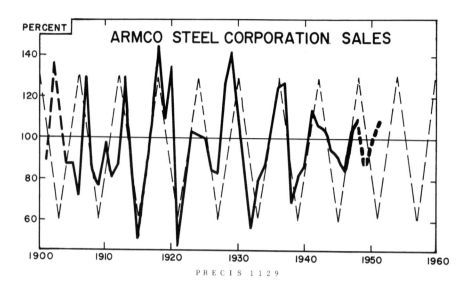

ARMCO STEEL CORPORATION SALES

PRECIS 1129

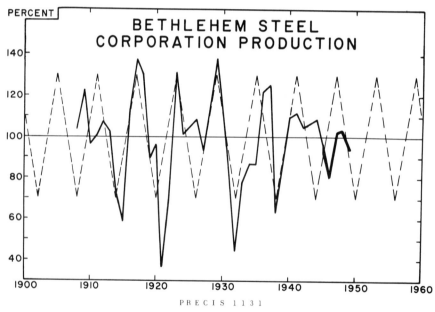

BETHLEHEM STEEL
CORPORATION PRODUCTION

PRECIS 1131

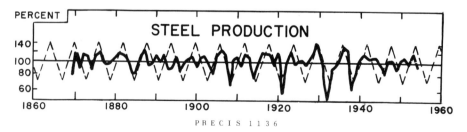

STEEL PRODUCTION

PRECIS 1136

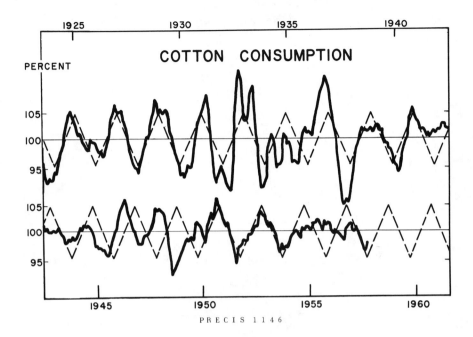

COTTON CONSUMPTION

PRECIS 1146

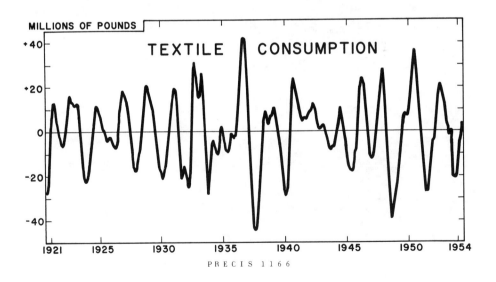

TEXTILE CONSUMPTION

PRECIS 1166

SERVICES

SERVICES

ADVERTISING

1192

Various rhythmic cycles (shortest length: 19 months) in Advertising Effectiveness, U.S.A., 1906–1951, are suggested.

In addition to a major 22-year cycle, minor cycles with lengths of about 19 months, 49 months, 53 months, 59 months, 67 months, 72 months, 122 months, and 234 months were suggested as being characteristic of the advertising effectiveness of the Lydia E. Pinkham Medicine Company during the period from 1906 through 1951.

Pinkham, 1952. (Figure)

1193

A 3.42-year (41-month) rhythmic cycle in Magazine Advertising, U.S.A., 1918–1933, is alleged.

Using Wesley C. Mitchell's method of studying business cycles and employing data from Thorp's *Business Annals*, Croxton and Cowden determined that the duration of the dominant cycle in magazine advertising in the United States from 1918 through 1933 averaged 41 months.

Croxton and Cowden, 1941. pp. 568–570. (Figures; data)

1194

A 22-year rhythmic cycle in Advertising Effectiveness, U.S.A., 1888–1950, is alleged.

Advertising effectiveness, as measured by the advertising efficiency index of the Lydia E. Pinkham Medicine Company, appeared to have moved in waves approximately 22 years long. Crests were reported in 1896, 1918, and 1940; troughs, in 1885, 1907, 1929, and 1951. Typical amplitude averaged 17 1/2% above trend at time of an ideal crest.

Pinkham, as reported by Dewey, 1951-A. p. 234. (Figure)

RETAIL SALES

1195

A 2–3-year rhythmic cycle in Department Store Sales, U.S.A., no dates given, is alleged.

Newbury, 1952. p. 147.

1196

A 3.33-year (40-month) rhythmic cycle in R. M. Macy and Company Sales, U.S.A., 1891—1940, is alleged.

The percent of change from preceding years in the annual sales of R. M. Macy and Company has shown a definite tendency to move in minor cycles averaging 3.33 years in length. A correlation with weather patterns was suggested.

Smith, 1959. pp. 114, 120. (Figure)

1197

A 4.92-year (59.1-month) rhythmic cycle in Department Store Sales, Pittsburgh, 1919—1945, is alleged.

Neff and Weifenbach, 1949.

1198

A 5.11-year (61.3-month) rhythmic cycle in Department Store Sales, Cleveland, 1921—1945, is alleged.

Neff and Weifenbach, 1949.

1199

A 6-year rhythmic cycle in Montgomery Ward and Company Sales, U.S.A., 1924—1945, is alleged.

Net dollar sales of Montgomery Ward and Company for the period 1924 through 1945 evidenced a 6-year cycle. A crest in the ideal pattern of this 6-year cycle occurred at 1947. Typical wave amplitude averaged 11% above trend at time of an ideal crest.

Dewey, 1950-G. pp. 4, 10. (Figure)

1200

A later article reported that the timing of this cycle had been revised; an ideal crest was placed at the end of 1947. Typical amplitude was also revised to 15% above trend at time of an ideal crest.

Dewey, 1955-L. (Figure)

1201

A 6-year rhythmic cycle in Sears Roebuck and Company Sales, U.S.A., 1910—1945, is alleged.

Net sales of Sears Roebuck and Company appeared to move in a 6-year cyclic pattern for the period from 1910 through 1945. Typical amplitude was reported to average 5% above trend at time of an ideal crest. Such a crest occurred at 1943.

Dewey, 1950-G. pp. 4, 13. (Figure)

1202

A later article verified the continuance of the 6-year cycle in net sales of

Sears Roebuck and Company through 1953.

Dewey, 1954-Q. (Figure)

1203

A 6.42-year (77.0-month) rhythmic cycle in Department Store Sales, Detroit, 1923–1945, is alleged.

Neff and Weifenbach, 1949.

1204

A 6.92-year (83-month) rhythmic cycle in Department Store Sales, Chicago, 1923–1945, is alleged.

Neff and Weifenbach, 1949.

1205

A 7.94-year (95.3-month) rhythmic cycle in Department Store Sales, Los Angeles, 1919–1945, is alleged.

Neff and Weifenbach, 1949.

1206

An 8.62-year (103.5-month) rhythmic cycle in Department Store Sales, San Francisco, 1919–1945, is alleged.

Neff and Weifenbach, 1949.

1207

A 10-year rhythmic pattern in R. M. Macy and Company Sales, U.S.A., 1891–1940, is alleged.

During the five decades under observation, 1891–1940, the percent of change from preceding years in the annual sales of R. M. Macy and Company followed a Decennial Pattern. Smith used rainfall data from Bern, Switzerland, in order to show a possible correlation of department store sales with cyclic weather behavior.

Smith, 1959. pp. 114, 120. (Figure)

TRADE ACTIVITY

1208

A 3 1/3-year (40-month) rhythmic cycle in Trade Activity, U.S.A. and Great Britain, 1890–1922, is alleged.

Trade activity in the United States and in Great Britain has displayed a tendency to move in a cyclic pattern, the waves of which measure about 40 months in length when measured from crest to crest. (This cycle is often referred to as the "Kitchin" cycle.)

Kitchin, 1923.

1209

A 3.41-year (41-month) rhythmic cycle in Trade Activity, U.S.A., no dates given, is alleged.

Garcia-Mata reported that H. S. Jevons was the first to discover a 41-month cycle in trade activity in the United States.

Jevons, as reported by Garcia-Mata, 1952.

1210

A 7- (or 10-) year rhythmic cycle in Trade Activity, England, no dates given, is alleged.

"The heat emitted by the sun varies in cycles of 3 1/2 years, every third fluctuation being emphasized. These cycles generate crop cycles. The impulse from the harvests comes every 3 1/2 years, so that trade fluctuations must fit into the nearest multiple of 3 1/2 years. It requires further research to decide fully the respective shares of the economic and meteorological causes in determining whether the trade cycle shall last seven or ten years."

Jevons, H. S., 1909, as reported by Williams, 1959. p. 46.

1211

An 8-year rhythmic cycle in Trade Activity, Europe, 1858—1908, is alleged.

Lavington, 1944. p. 14.

1212

A 9-year rhythmic cycle in Trade Fluctuations, France, no dates given, is alleged.

Juglar alleged that trade fluctuations in France followed a 9-year cyclical pattern and that periods of prosperity, crises, and liquidation followed each other rhythmically. (This 9-year cycle is often referred to as the "Juglar" cycle.)

Juglar, 1860, as reported by Williams, 1959. p. 40.

1213

A 9—12-year rhythmic cycle in Trade Activity, Great Britain, no dates given, is alleged.

"... trade reached a maximum of activity in or about the years 1701, 1711, 1732, 1742, 1753, 1763, 1772, 1784, 1793, 1805, 1815, 1825, 1837, 1847, 1857, 1866. These years ... are ... corresponding years and the intervals vary from nine to twelve years."

Jevons, W. S., as quoted by Davis, 1941. pp. 550—551.

1214

A 10-year rhythmic cycle in Trade and Commerce, Great Britain, 1816—1877, is alleged.

Halbert, in summarizing the results of 20 years of investigation, reported a

10-year (decennial) pattern as having been characteristic of British Trade
and Finance. This cyclic pattern was derived from general statistics available at that time for the seven decades ending with 1877.

Halbert, 1878, as reported by Smith, 1954. pp. 18—22. (Figure)

1215

A 50-year rhythmic cycle in Trade Activity, Great Britain, no dates given,
is alleged.

Trade activity followed the pattern found in the yields of consols in Great
Britain and displayed a 20—30-year upward movement.

Brown and Ozga, 1955.

1216

A 50—60-year rhythmic cycle in Foreign Trade, England, 1810—1925, is alleged.

Kondratieff, 1926. (Figure)

1217

A 50—60-year rhythmic cycle in Total Foreign Trade, France, 1830—1925,
is alleged.

Kondratieff, 1926. (Figure)

TRANSPORTATION

1218

A 9.18-month (39.91-week) rhythmic cycle in Canadian Pacific Railway
Freight Traffic, Canada, July 1903—December 1949, is alleged.

A 9.18-month cyclic pattern was discovered in the Canadian Pacific ton-
miles during the period under observation. Typical wave amplitude at time
of an ideal crest averaged 12.7% above trend.

Rountree, 1951. (Figure)

1219

A 32.86-month (2.74-year) rhythmic cycle in Canadian Pacific Railway
Freight Traffic, Canada, 1909—1947, is alleged.

Crests in a 32.86-month rhythmic pattern which characterized the ton-miles
of freight traffic of Canadian Pacific Railway from 1909 through 1947 were
dated at December 1906 and every 32.86 months thereafter. Typical over-
all amplitude of this 32.86-month cycle has averaged 18% of trend; 9.4%
above trend at time of an ideal crest and 8.6% below trend at time of an
ideal trough. This cycle in ton-miles of Canadian Pacific Railway is the
revised length of the 33-month cycle alleged by Rountree in 1948.

Dewey, 1951-U. pp. 49—52. (Figure)

1220

A 33-month (2.75-year) rhythmic cycle in Canadian Pacific Railway Freight Traffic, Canada, 1909–1947, is alleged.

Rountree, 1948. (Figure)

1221

A 3.33-year (40-month) rhythmic cycle in Rate of Change in Total Car Loadings, U.S.A., no dates given, is alleged.

Newbury, 1952. pp. 182–183.

1222

A 5.2-year (62.4-month) rhythmic cycle in Canadian Pacific Railway Freight Traffic, Canada, 1884–1941, is alleged.

Rountree, 1948. p. 4.

1223

An article by Dewey showed that the 5.2-year cycle in ton-miles of freight traffic of Canadian Pacific Railway through 1957 had not continued to follow the ideal pattern.

Dewey, 1958-A. (Figure)

1224

A 5 1/2-year (66-month) rhythmic cycle in Airplane Traffic, U.S.A., 1930–1955, is alleged.

Airplane traffic in the United States from 1930 through 1955, measured in passenger miles, showed a tendency to follow a 5 1/2-year rhythmic pattern. Typical strength of this 5 1/2-year cycle measured approximately 15.5% above trend at time of an ideal crest and 13.4% below trend at time of an ideal trough. 1957 dated a crest in the ideal pattern.

Dewey, 1956-C. (Figure)

1225

A 6-year rhythmic cycle in Seaboard Air Line Operating Revenue, U.S.A., 1901–1947, is alleged.

Gross operating revenue of the Seaboard Air Line from 1901 through 1947 appeared to follow a 6-year rhythmic pattern. Typical amplitude of this 6-year cycle averaged 9% above trend at time of an ideal crest. The year 1949 dated a crest in the ideal pattern.

Dewey, 1950-G. pp. 5, 16. (Figure)

1226

A 7.5-year (90-month) rhythmic cycle in Canadian Pacific Railway Freight Traffic, Canada, 1909–1947, is alleged.

Rountree, 1948. p. 4.

1227

A later article by Dewey showed that the 7.5-year cycle in ton-miles of
freight traffic of Canadian Pacific Railway through 1957 had continued to
follow the ideal pattern after discovery. A follow-up on this article indicated that a crest in the ideal pattern of this 7.5-year cycle occurred at
1958. Typical wave amplitude measured 5% above trend at time of an ideal
crest.

> Dewey, 1958-A. (Figure)
> Dewey, 1959-B. (Figure)

1228

A 9-year rhythmic cycle in Canadian Pacific Railway Freight Traffic,
Canada, 1918—1940, is alleged.

> Rountree, 1948. p. 4.

1229

An 18-year rhythmic cycle in Railroad Expenditures, Great Britain, 1870—
1914, is alleged.

The estimated capital expenditures of all British railways from 1870 through
1914 appeared to move in a cycle which measured approximately 18 years
when measured from crest to crest. This cycle seemed to be closely related
to the building cycle.

> Warren and Pearson, 1937. p. 134. (Figure)

1230

An 18-year rhythmic cycle in Railroad Freight Revenue, Germany, 1885—
1915, is alleged.

> Warren and Pearson, 1937. p. 133. (Figure)

1231

An 18-year rhythmic cycle in Railroad Freight Revenue, Sweden, 1890—1936,
is alleged.

Ton-kilometers of freight per kilometer of railroad in Sweden from 1890
through 1936 appeared to move in the same general pattern as the building
activity cycle.

> Warren and Pearson, 1937. pp. 132—133. (Figure)

1232

An 18-year rhythmic cycle in Railroad Receiverships, U.S.A., 1877—1935, is
alleged.

Warren and Pearson noted that the miles of railroads in receivership from
1877 through 1935 appeared to be closely related to the building activity
cycle.

> Warren and Pearson, 1937. p. 148. (Figure)

1233

An 18 1/3-year rhythmic cycle in Canadian Pacific Railway Freight Traffic,
Canada, 1909—1947, is alleged.

Revenue ton-miles of Canadian Pacific Railway from 1909 through 1947 appeared to be characterized by an 18 1/3-year repetitive pattern which closely
resembled the cyclic pattern found in general building activity in the United
States.

Rountree, 1948. p. 4.

1234

A 20-year rhythmic cycle in Capital Formation by Steam Railroads, U.S.A.,
1860—1900, is alleged.

According to Ulmer, capital formation by steam railroads in the United States
during the last half of the 19th century appeared to follow "20-year swings."
Troughs were noted in the mid 1870's and mid 1890's; a peak appeared in the
1880's.

Ulmer, 1954. p. 3.

UTILITIES

1235

A 30-month (2.5-year) rhythmic cycle in Electric Power Demand, Indiana,
1936—1957, is alleged.

The annual growth of peak power demands of the Public Service Company of
Indiana from 1936 through 1957 appeared to move in a cycle which had a
duration of 2.5 years when measured from peak to peak. With the exception
of the period encompassing World War II, the electric power demand of the
Public Service Company of Indiana followed the ideal 2.5-year cycle with
remarkable regularity. A crest in the ideal pattern of this cycle was dated at
1958.

Chapman, 1957. (Figure)

1236

A 30-month (2.5-year) rhythmic cycle in Electric Power Demand, U.S.A.,
1936—1957, is alleged.

Using data from Edison Electric Institute on power demand for the eight
Federal Power Commission regions in the United States, Chapman found a
2.5-year cycle which he felt was characteristic of the industry for the period from 1936 through 1957.

Chapman, 1957. (Figure)

1237

A 4.87-year (58.4-month) rhythmic cycle in Industrial and Commercial Power
Sales, Detroit, 1921—1945, is alleged.

Neff and Weifenbach, 1949.

1238

A 5.01-year (60.1-month) rhythmic cycle in Industrial and Commercial Power Sales, Chicago, 1921—1945, is alleged.

Neff and Weifenbach, 1949.

1239

A 6.68-year (80.2-month) rhythmic cycle in Industrial and Commercial Power Sales, San Francisco, 1921—1945, is alleged.

Neff and Weifenbach, 1949.

1240

A 7 1/2-year (90-month) rhythmic cycle in the Sales of a Public Utility Company, U.S.A., 1883—1939, is alleged.

Dewey and Dakin, 1947. pp. 172—180. (Figure)

1241

An 18 1/3-year rhythmic cycle in the Sales of a Public Utility Company, U.S.A., 1883—1939, is alleged.

Dewey and Dakin, 1947. pp. 172—180. (Figure)

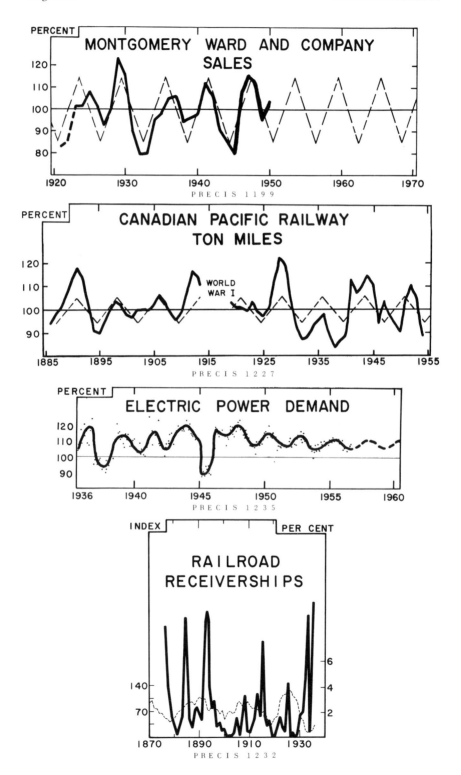

PERCENT

MONTGOMERY WARD AND COMPANY
SALES

PRECIS 1199

PERCENT

CANADIAN PACIFIC RAILWAY
TON MILES

WORLD
WAR I

PRECIS 1227

PERCENT

ELECTRIC POWER DEMAND

PRECIS 1235

INDEX   PER CENT

RAILROAD
RECEIVERSHIPS

PRECIS 1232

MISCELLANEOUS ECONOMIC ACTIVITY

MISCELLANEOUS ECONOMIC ACTIVITY

CRISES, PANICS, RECESSIONS, AND DEPRESSIONS

1242

A 3 1/3-year (40-month) rhythmic cycle in Business Recessions, U.S.A., 1796–1923, is alleged.

In a study of business recessions in the United States during a period from 1796 through 1923, Mitchell found "... an average length of not quite four years," which, according to Smith, is "not in variance with the 40-month or 3 1/3-year cycle found in other phenomena."

Mitchell, 1927, as reported by Smith, 1939. pp. 17–18.

1243

A 3.9–7.75-year rhythmic cycle in Prosperity, U.S.A., 1860–1939, is alleged.

Langham, 1954.

1244

A 4-year rhythmic cycle in Recessions, U.S.A., no dates given, is alleged.

A rhythm which repeated about every four years was found in recessions in the United States by Woytinsky and Woytinsky. They considered this extremely dangerous since, they said, there is a 2-year rhythm present in congressional efficiency.

Woytinsky and Woytinsky, 1959. p. 6.

1245

A 5–7-year rhythmic cycle in Prosperity and Depression, Great Britain, 1764–1834, is alleged.

"The commercial cycle is ordinarily completed in five to seven years, within which terms it will be found, by reference to our commercial history during the last 70 years, alternate periods of prosperity and depression have been experienced."

Wade, 1834. p. 211.

1246

A 5- or 5 1/2-year rhythmic cycle in Dow Chemical Company Plant Expansions, worldwide, no dates given, is alleged.

A crest in the ideal 5- or 5 1/2-year cycle which appeared to characterize the movement of Dow Chemical Company plant expansions was dated as the fiscal year 1957—1958.

Brinewell, 1958. p. 5.

1247

A 5.6-year (67.2-month) rhythmic cycle in Commercial Crises, Great Britain, 1558—1720, is alleged.

Scott, 1912. p. 470.

1248

A 6-year average cycle in International Crises, Europe and U.S.A., 1814—1907, is suggested.

Although Hull denied that depressions are periodic, he noted 17 industrial crises from 1814 through 1907 which measured from one to eleven years in length and which averaged slightly less than 6 years.

Hull, 1911. pp. 50—51, 54—57.

1249

A 6 2/3-year rhythmic cycle in Business Depressions, U.S.A., 1808—1921, is alleged.

Lightner stated, according to Thorp, that business depressions in the United States for the period under observation fluctuated in waves which measured from 3 to 12 years and which averaged approximately 6 2/3 years.

Lightner, 1922, as reported by Thorp, 1926. p. 39.

1250

An 8 1/2-year rhythmic cycle in Commercial Crises, Europe, 1870—1910, is alleged.

Crisis years in Europe, according to Cassel, fell in 1873, 1882, 1890, 1900, and 1907. Fluctuations averaged 8 1/2 years although the waves stretched from 4 to 11 years in duration.

Cassel, 1924. p. 508.

1251

An 8 1/2-year rhythmic cycle in Commercial Crises, U.S.A., 1870—1910, is alleged.

Commercial crises in the United States from 1870 through 1910 showed a tendency to fluctuate in waves which measured from 4 to 11 years in duration and which averaged 8 1/2 years. Peaks occurred in 1873, 1882, 1893, 1903, and 1907.

Cassel, 1924. p. 508.

1252

A 9.6-year rhythmic cycle in Financial Crises, Great Britain, c. 1820—1900, is alleged.

"The average interval from one British crisis to another, or from one peak of trade to another, is 9.6 years."

Burton, 1902, as reported by Huntington, 1945. p. 488.

1253

A 10-year rhythmic cycle in Commercial Crises, Europe, no dates given, is alleged.

Hyndman, according to Schumpeter, alleged a 10-year rhythmic cycle in European commercial crises (actually the figures were for western and central Europe and for the United States). Peaks occurred in 1815, 1825, 1836—1839, 1847, 1857, 1866, 1873, 1882, and 1890.

Hyndman, 1892, as reported by Schumpeter, 1939. p. 168.

1254

A 10-year rhythmic cycle in Commercial Crises, no locale cited, no dates given, is alleged.

Commercial crises tend to fall into waves which measure 9 to 11 years in duration with a "tendency toward a normal period of about 10 years."

Bouniatian, 1922. p. 42.

1255

A 10-year rhythmic cycle in Commercial Panics, U.S.A., no dates given, is alleged.

The Massachusetts Railroad Commission pointed out in 1895 that a panic occurred approximately every 10 years.

Massachusetts Railroad Commission, 1895, as reported by Dorfman, 1949.

1256

At a Hearing on "Depressions in Labor and Business" at the House of Representatives on August 23, 1878, George Walker "held to the usual view of a panic occurring every 10 years."
Walker, 1878, as reported by Dorfman, 1949.

1257

A 10-year rhythmic cycle in Depressions, U.S.A., no dates given, is alleged.

Otto T. Mallery, governmental administrator, contended that depressions, "occurring as they did every ten years," could be alleviated by governmental action.
Mallery, 1919. p. 57.

1258

Shillady, who was secretary of the New York City Mayors Committee on Un-

employment in 1916 declared that "periodic trade disturbances" are fundamental and occur approximately every 10 years.

Shillady, 1916, pp. 189—190, as reported by Dorfman, 1949.

1259

A 10-year rhythmic cycle in Economic Crises and Depressions, Great Britain,
1680—1840, is alleged.

Bouniatian, 1908.

1260

A 10-year rhythmic cycle in Financial Crises, England, no dates given, is
alleged.

The *London Times* on the first of January in 1857 noted a 10-year cycle in
financial crises in England. Peaks were dated at 1825, 1837, 1847, and a
peak crisis year was forecast for 1857.

Davis, Hughes and McDougall, 1961.

1261

A 10.44-year rhythmic cycle in Business Crises, England, 1701—1883, is alleged.

For the period from 1701 through 1883, Jevons refined his findings (see precis below) and reported that the business crises move in a 10.43—10.45-year
cycle.

Jevons, W. S., 1909, as reported by King, 1958. pp. 22—23.

1262

A 10.466-year rhythmic cycle in Business Crises, England, 1701—1880, is
alleged.

"I can entertain no doubt whatever that the principal commercial crises do
fall into a series having the average period of about 10.466 years."

Jevons, W. S., as reported by Proctor, 1880. p. 173.

1263

An 11-year rhythmic cycle in Business Panics, U.S.A., 1877-1878—1933-
1934, is alleged.

Within the 56-year period under observation, there were five cyclic waves
which averaged 11 years in length in the series of business panics in the
United States. A correlation between sunspot activity and business panics
was suggested.

McGrath, 1936. p. 58.

1264

An 11-year rhythmic cycle in Commercial Crises, France and England, 1793–1847, is alleged.

Dewey reported that Dr. Hyde Clarke in 1847 alleged an 11-year cycle in commercial crises in France and England for the period from 1793 through 1847. Peaks occurred in 1793, 1804, 1815, 1837, and 1847. The 54-year period, therefore, displayed five intervals about 11 years long. The fifth wave appeared to be more pronounced than the first four.

Clarke, 1847, as reported by Dewey, 1957-B. pp. 13–15.

1265

An 11-year rhythmic cycle in Economic Prosperity and International Crises, worldwide, no dates given, is alleged.

A correlation between sunspot activity and world-wide economic prosperity and international crises was suggested.

Andrews, 1936.

1266

An 11 2/3-year rhythmic cycle in Depressions, U.S.A., 1860–1939, is alleged.

Langham, 1954.

1267

An 18-, 20-, and 16-year (and repeat) rhythmic pattern in Financial Crises, U.S.A., 1819–1873, is alleged.

"Commencing with the commercial revolution of 1819, we find it was 18 years to the crisis of 1837, 20 years to the crisis of 1857, and 16 years to the crisis of 1873 – making the order of cycles sixteen, eighteen, and twenty years and repeat. It takes panics 54 years in their order to make a revolution, or to return to the same order."

Benner, 1875. (Figure)

1268

An 18-year rhythmic cycle in Major Panics, U.S.A., 1830–1936, is alleged.

A correlation between the movements of major panics and the movements of the building industry was suggested.

Warren and Pearson, 1937. pp. 150–151. (Figure)

1269

A 20-year rhythmic cycle in Crises, England and U.S.A., 1700–1958, is alleged.

Babson reports that a "complete rotation" occurred once in about every twenty years in the number of crises in England and the United States from 1700 forward.

Babson, 1959. pp. 180—181.

1270

A 20-year rhythmic cycle in Economic Depressions, U.S.A., no dates given, is alleged.

Long severe depressions in the United States, according to Newbury, have occurred about 20 years apart because the troughs of the building cycle occur approximately at that interval.

Newbury, 1952. p. 136.

1271

A 20-year rhythmic cycle in Economic Growth, U.S.A., 1810—1865, is alleged.

Harris pointed to the long swings in the rate of growth in American economy which measured approximately 20 years when measured from trough to trough. Troughs were dated at 1819, 1839, and 1858.

Harris, 1961. pp. 173—174.

1272

A 20-year rhythmic cycle in Economic Growth, varying locales, is alleged.

"These long swings...are a pervasive element of the American economy and those other economies such as the British, for which we have sufficient data to observe them." The authors noted that data were for the period from 1869 through 1948.

Davis, Hughes, and McDougall, 1961. p. 75.

1273

According to the authors, Professor Brinley Thomas indicated that the same type of movement found in the American series (a 20-year cycle) also existed in the economic growth of western European countries and Canada and Australia although the cycles appeared to move in the opposite direction.

Davis, Hughes, and McDougall, 1961. p. 75.

1274

A 20—30-year* rhythmic cycle in Depressions and Prosperity, Western Europe, 1820—1925, is alleged.

According to Von Haberler, Spiethoff noted a "20—30-year" cycle in the regularity of depressions and prosperity in Western Europe. He dated 1822—1842 as a period of depression; 1843—1873 as a period of prosperousness; 1874—1894 as a period of depression; and 1895—1913 as a period of prosperity.

Spiethoff, 1902 and 1925, as quoted by Von Haberler, 1958. p. 272.

----

* Although the cycle length was given as 20—30 years, it is actually 40—60 years long.

1275

A 27-year rhythmic cycle in Depressions, U.S.A., 1872—1948, is alleged.

Peaks in depressions have appeared to move in 27-year cycles. A correlation with the eruptions of Vesuvius with a lag of one year was suggested.

Wiesenberger, 1949.

1276

A 33-year rhythmic cycle in Economic Conditions, U.S.A., 1760—1959, is alleged.

Dennon, 1960. (Figure)

1277

A 54-year rhythmic cycle in Famines and Panics, worldwide, 1793—1847, is alleged.

Clark, 1847, as reported by Jevons, 1878. pp. 222—223.

1278

A 108-year rhythmic cycle in Crises and Panics, U.S.A., 1795—1906, is alleged.

A cycle which measured 108 years in length and which was composed of three minor cycles which measured 38, 36, and 34 years, respectively, was reported to characterize the behavior pattern of crises and panics in the U.S.

Foster, 1907. p. 6. (Figure)

GENERAL ECONOMIC PHENOMENA

1279

A 13.5-day (1.9-week) rhythmic cycle in Failures of Underground Cables, 1955—1960, is alleged.

A 13.5-day repetitive pattern was discovered by Williams in underground cable failures (K-index) on the 2300 to 13800- v. system of the Consolidated Edison Company during the period from 1955 through 1960. This corresponds, says Williams, with a cycle of similar length in geomagnetic activity.

Williams, 1962. (Figure)

1280

A 3.33-year (40-month) rhythmic cycle in General Economic Phenomena, no dates given, is alleged.

Schumpeter reported that the 40-month cycle, first discovered by Kitchin, is one of the three basic cycles in economic phenomena. It was suggested that the 9—10-year cycle and the 50—60-year cycle may be multiples of this 40-month cycle.

Schumpeter, 1939. p. 165.

1281

A 3.33-year (40-month) rhythmic cycle in Marginal Propensity to Consume, U.S.A., no dates given, is alleged.

Hubbard, 1942. p. 199.

1282

A 5—6-year rhythmic cycle in Economic Growth, U.S.A., 1849—1950, is alleged.

Woytinsky and Associates, 1953. p. 61.

1283

A 6-year rhythmic cycle in Economic Affairs, U.S.A., no dates given, is alleged.

The 6-year cycle in economic affairs was first discovered in 1937 by Hoskins.

Dewey, 1953-A. p. 215.

1284

An 8-year rhythmic cycle in General Economic Activity, England and Czechoslovakia, varying dates, is alleged.

General economic activity in Czechoslovakia as well as in England appeared to be characterized by an 8-year rhythmic pattern during the periods under observation.

Hrase, 1938. pp. 4—5.

1285

An 8-year rhythmic cycle in General Economic Phenomena, no locale cited, 1857—..., is alleged.

Aftalion, as reported by Moore, 1923. p. 34.

1286

A 9—10-year rhythmic cycle in General Economic Phenomena, U.S.A., no dates given, is alleged.

According to Schumpeter, one of the three basic cycles in economic phenomena measures approximately 9—10 years in length. This cycle is often referred to as the "Juglar" cycle.

Schumpeter, 1939. pp. 162—163, 170—171.

1287

A 10-year rhythmic cycle in General Economic Phenomena, no dates given, is alleged.

According to Smith who alleged a 10-year (Decennial) pattern as being characteristic of the behavior of general economic phenomena, many others had found this cyclic pattern. W. S. Jevons reported a 10-year recurring pattern in economic phenomena in Great Britain in 1878; John Mills had noted in 1868 that general economic phenomena displayed a tendency to move in a 10-year cyclic pattern; MacLeod reported that crises tended to move in repetitive 10-year waves.

Smith, 1939. p. 17. (Figure)

1288

A 10-year rhythmic cycle in Industrial Capital, no locale cited, no dates given, is alleged.

Whittaker quotes Engels as translating Marx as measuring the "average life of industrial capital at 10 years."

Whittaker, 1960. p. 343.

1289

A 17—18-year rhythmic cycle in Transport-Building, U.S.A., 1825—1933, is alleged.

Isard, 1942-B. pp. 149—158.

1290

An 18—20-year rhythmic cycle in Economic Activity, U.S.A., 1815—1860, is alleged.

A periodicity of 18—20 years duration was "strikingly evident after 1815" in economic activity in the United States, particularly in connection with capital investments of relatively long gestation periods such as transportation and construction.

North, 1961.

1291

A 35-year rhythmic cycle in General Economic Phenomena, U.S.A., no dates given, is alleged.

Hasbrouck, 1941.

1292

A 50-year rhythmic cycle in General Economic Activity, U.S.A., is alleged.

A cyclic pattern which measured about one-half of a century appeared to characterize American economy.

Kirkbride, 1939. p. 7.

1293

Kuznets, quoting Kondratieff, said that movements of general economic phenomena are rhythmical and that the waves measure approximately 50 years in length.

Kondratieff, 1922, as reported by Kuznets, 1930.

1294

For the period from 1787 through 1941, general economic activity in the U.S. moved in a cyclic pattern which measured 50 years.

Rose, 1941.

1295

A 50–60-year rhythmic cycle in General Economic Phenomena, worldwide, no dates given, is alleged.

Kondratieff, 1926. pp. 573–609. (Figure)

1296

A 130-year rhythmic cycle in Economy and Waste, worldwide, 1535–1950, is alleged.

A long cycle approximately 130 years in length appears to have been present in the movements of economy and waste in the period from 1535 through 1950. Periods of great waste showed highs occurring at 1535, 1660, 1790, and 1920. Peaks in the periods of economy were reported at 1560, 1690, 1820, and 1950.

Petrie, 1948.

EXPORTS AND IMPORTS

1297

A 24-month (2-year) rhythmic cycle in Import of Raw Cotton, Netherlands, 1922–1938, is alleged.

Tinbergen and Polak, 1950. p. 96. (Figure)

1298

A 3.2-year (38.4-month) rhythmic cycle in Exports, U.S.A., 1879...1959, is alleged.

The period under observation was divided into three distinct intervals: 1879–1913, 1921–1938 (excluding 1929–1937), and 1945–1959. American exports during that period displayed an average 3.2-year wave.

Mintz, 1961. pp. 15, 66.

1299

A 3.3-year (39.56-month) rhythmic cycle in Exports, U.S.A., 1879–1913, is alleged.

During the period from 1879 through 1913, exports of the United States showed ten and a half cycles of about two to five years' duration. The average export cycle during this period lasted approximately 3.3 years.

Mintz, 1961. pp. 13–15. (Figure, data)

1300

A 3–4-year rhythmic cycle in Exports, New Zealand, 1856–1911, is alleged.

Exports from New Zealand for the years from 1856 through 1911 ranged in duration from 2 to 9 years and averaged from 3 to 4 years.

Simkin, 1951. pp. 27, 39.

1301

A 5.3-year (63.6-month) rhythmic cycle in Imports, New Zealand, 1856–1909, is alleged.

Imports to New Zealand during the period from 1856 through 1909 ranged in duration from 3 to 8 years and averaged approximately 5.3 years.

Simkin, 1951. p. 58.

1302

A 6.9-year (82.8-month) average cycle in Export of Consumer Goods, United Kingdom, 1870–1914, is suggested.

Tinbergen, 1951. p. 126.

1303

A 9-year average cycle in Capital Exports, United Kingdom, 1870–1914, is suggested.

Tinbergen, 1951. p. 124.

1304

An 18-year rhythmic cycle in Quantity of Fir Timber Imported, Great Britain, 1788–1841, is alleged.

Cairncross and Weber, 1956.

1305

A 50–60-year rhythmic cycle in Exports, France, 1848–1925, is alleged.

Kondratieff, 1922.

1306

A 50–60-year rhythmic cycle in Imports, France, 1848–1925, is alleged.

Kondratieff, 1922.

1307

A 54-year rhythmic cycle in Imports of Domestic Copper and Copper Manufactures, U.S.A., 1810–1952, is alleged.

This 54-year cyclic pattern in the dollar amount, adjusted for price, of exports of domestic copper and copper manufactures was one of the series studied for confirmation of a 50–60-year cycle in manufacturing production.

Dewey, 1953-J. p. 300.

1308

A 54-year rhythmic cycle in Exports of Iron and Steel Manufactures, U.S.A., 1800–1952, is alleged.

Dewey, 1953-J. p. 300.

1309

A 54-year rhythmic cycle in Total Exports of Manufactured Goods, U.S.A., 1821–1952, is alleged.

Total exports of manufactured goods from the United States, measured in dollars adjusted for price from 1821 through 1952, appeared to move in a 54-year rhythmic pattern.

Dewey, 1953-J. p. 300.

INVENTORY

1310

A 23.3-month (1.94-year) rhythmic cycle in the Stocks of Case, Unsold Condensed Milk, U.S.A., April 1924–February 1930, is alleged.

Three waves which averaged approximately 23.3 months long appeared to characterize the quantity of stocks of case, unsold condensed milk at the mills which was in the hands of the producers in the United States during the period from April 1924 through February 1930. This cycle displayed an average over-all amplitude of 51.1%.

Blodgett, 1935. p. 67.

1311

A 31-month (2.58-year) rhythmic cycle in the Stocks of Raw Sugar, U.S.A., April 1922–January 1930, is alleged.

The quantity of stocks of raw sugar at refiners and importers in the hands of the industrial consumer during the period from April 1922 through January 1930 moved in cycles which measured approximately 31.0 months and displayed an over-all amplitude of approximately 77.8%.

Blodgett, 1935. p. 40.

1312

A 31-month (2.58-year) rhythmic cycle in the Stocks of Tin, U.S.A., July 1919–November 1929, is alleged.

During the period under observation, four 31.0-month cycles were noted in the quantity of stocks of tin at warehouses in the hands of the industrial consumer which displayed an over-all amplitude of 40.3%.

Blodgett, 1935. p. 40.

1313

A 34.0-month (2.83-year) rhythmic cycle in the Stocks of Unsold Steel Sheets, U.S.A., May 1919–September 1930, is alleged.

A total over-all amplitude of 124.2% was reported in the 34.0-month cycle which appeared to characterize the movement of the quantity of stocks of unsold steel sheets at the mills in the hands of producers in the United States for the period under observation.

Blodgett, 1935. p. 67.

1314

A 35.0-month (2.92-year) rhythmic cycle in the Stocks of Newsprint Paper,
U.S.A., April 1921—January 1930, is alleged.

During the period under observation, Blodgett reported a 35.0-month cycle
in the quantity of stocks of newsprint paper at publishers in the hands of
the industrial consumer. The typical over-all amplitude of the cycle measured 37.0%.

Blodgett, 1935. p. 41.

1315

A 35.3-month (2.94-year) rhythmic cycle in the Stocks of Book Paper, U.S.A.,
October 1920—July 1932, is alleged.

A total over-all amplitude of 37.8% was reported by Blodgett in the 35.3-
month cycle which appeared to characterize the movement of the quantity of
stocks of book paper at the mills which was in the hands of producers in the
United States for the period from October 1920 through July 1932.

Blodgett, 1935. p. 84.

1316

A 35.3-month (2.94-year) rhythmic cycle in the Stocks of Refined Sugar,
U.S.A., July 1922—May 1931, is alleged.

During the period under observation, three waves which averaged 35.3
months in duration were evident in the quantity of stocks of refined sugar at
two ports in the hands of the producers in the United States. According to
Blodgett, this cycle in stock numbers displayed a typical over-all amplitude
of 64.9%.

Blodgett, 1935. p. 84.

1317

A 35.5-month (2.96-year) rhythmic cycle in Stocks of Wheat Flour, U.S.A.,
September 1920—July 1932, is alleged.

The total number of wheat flour stocks in the hands of producers in the
United States displayed four 35.5-month waves during the period under
observation and had a typical over-all amplitude of approximately 10.9%
according to Blodgett.

Blodgett, 1935. p. 84.

1318

A 3-year rhythmic cycle in the Stocks of Chemical Wood Pulp, U.S.A., May
1921—May 1930, is alleged.

During the period under observation, the quantity of stocks of chemical
wood pulp at the mills in the hands of the industrial consumer evidenced
three 36-month cycles which displayed an over-all amplitude of 38.5%.

Blodgett, 1935. p. 40.

1319

A 3.02-year (36.3-month) rhythmic cycle in the Stocks of Hides and Skins, U.S.A., May 1922—June 1931, is alleged.

According to Blodgett, the movement of the quantity of stocks of hides and skins (total) in the hands of the industrial consumer during the period from May 1922 through June 1931 evidenced a cycle which measured 36.3 months in duration. Typical over-all amplitude measured approximately 23.9%.

Blodgett, 1935. p. 41.

1320

A 3.08-year (37-month) rhythmic cycle in the Stocks of Cotton Hosiery, U.S.A., April 1924—June 1930, is alleged.

The movement of the quantity of stocks of cotton hosiery at mills in the hands of producers in the United States during the period from April 1924 through June 1930 followed a 37.0-month rhythmic pattern and displayed an over-all amplitude of about 28.1%.

Blodgett, 1935. p. 66.

1321

A 3.08-year (37-month) rhythmic cycle in the Stocks of Zinc, U.S.A., July 1921—October 1930, is alleged.

The quantity of stocks of zinc at refineries in the hands of producers in the United States from July 1921 through October 1930 appeared to move in a cyclic pattern which measured 37.0 months in duration and displayed an over-all amplitude of approximately 165.1%.

Blodgett, 1935. p. 66.

1322

A 3.12-year (37.5-month) rhythmic cycle in Stocks of Steel Sheets, U.S.A., October 1919—April 1932, is alleged.

The quantity of steel sheet (total mill) stocks in the hands of the producers in the United States during the period from October 1919 through April 1932 appeared to move in waves which measured approximately 37.5 months in duration. According to Blodgett, these waves had a typical over-all amplitude of about 43.0%.

Blodgett, 1935. p. 84.

1323

A 3.17-year (38-month) rhythmic cycle in the Stocks of Department Stores, U.S.A., 1919—1932, is alleged.

The quantity of stock in department stores in the United States during the period from 1919 through 1932 appeared to be characterized by a cycle which measured approximately 38 months in duration. The total over-all amplitude of this cycle was reported by Blodgett to be about 43%.

Blodgett, 1935. p. 103.

1324

A 3.23-year (38.8-month) rhythmic cycle in the Stocks of Iron Ore, U.S.A.,
May 1919—April 1932, is alleged.

The quantity of iron ore at furnaces in the hands of the industrial consumer
moved in four 38.8-month cycles during the period from May 1919 through
April 1932, according to Blodgett. This cycle displayed an over-all amplitude of approximately 18.1%.

Blodgett, 1935. p. 41.

1325

A 3.33-year (40-month) rhythmic cycle in the Stocks of Solid and Cushion
Tires, U.S.A., June 1922—June 1932, is alleged.

According to Blodgett, the quantity of manufacturers stocks in the hands of
the producers of solid and cushion tires in the United States moved in a cyclic pattern which measured approximately 40.0 months in duration. This cycle showed an average over-all amplitude of 44.2%.

Blodgett, 1935. p. 85.

1326

A 3.46-year (41.5-month) rhythmic cycle in the Stocks of Bulk, Unsold Condensed Milk, U.S.A., January 1924—December 1930, is alleged.

The quantity of stocks of bulk, unsold condensed milk at the mills in the
hands of producers in the United States during the period from January 1924
through December 1930 appeared to move in cycles which were approximately 41.5 months in duration and which displayed an average over-all amplitude of 101.3%.

Blodgett, 1935. p. 67.

1327

A 3.52-year (42.3-month) rhythmic cycle in the Stocks of Crude Petroleum,
U.S.A., October 1918—May 1929, is alleged.

The typical over-all amplitude of the 42.3-month cycle which appeared to be
present in the movement of the quantity of stocks of crude petroleum at refineries in the hands of the industrial consumer measured approximately 51%.

Blodgett, 1935. p. 40.

1328

A 3.58-year (43-month) rhythmic cycle in the Stocks of Newsprint Paper,
U.S.A., March 1921—December 1931, is alleged.

The quantity of stocks of newsprint paper in the hands of producers appeared to move in a cycle which measured approximately 43.0 months in
duration. This cycle displayed an over-all amplitude of 74.4%.

Blodgett, 1935. p. 66.

1329

A 3.64-year (43.7-month) rhythmic cycle in the Stocks of Innertubes, U.S.A., July 1921–June 1932, is alleged.

During the period under observation, the quantity of manufacturers stocks in the hands of the producers of innertubes in the United States appeared to move in a cycle which measured 43.7 months in duration and which displayed an over-all amplitude of approximately 51.9%.

Blodgett, 1935. p. 85.

1330

A 3.69-year (44.3-month) rhythmic cycle in the Stocks of Crude Cottonseed Oil, U.S.A., June 1921–July 1932, is alleged.

A total over-all amplitude of 95.6% was reported in the 44.3-month cycle which appeared to characterize the movement of the quantity of stocks of total crude cottonseed oil in the hands of the industrial consumer during the period from June 1921 through July 1932.

Blodgett, 1935. p. 40.

1331

A 3.75-year (45-month) rhythmic cycle in Finished Cotton Goods, U.S.A., April 1921–July 1932, is alleged.

A cycle which measured approximately 45.0 months long appeared to characterize the quantity of stocks of finished cotton goods at finishers in the hands of producers during the period under observation. This cycle displayed an over-all amplitude of about 28.4%.

Blodgett, 1935. p. 84.

1332

A 3.77-year (45.3-month) rhythmic cycle in the Stocks of Enameled Baths, U.S.A., May 1919–September 1930, is alleged.

An over-all amplitude of 164.9% was reported in the 45.3-month cycle in the quantity of stocks of enameled baths at manufacturers in the hands of producers during the period from May 1919 through September 1930.

Blodgett, 1935. p. 66.

1333

A 4-year (48.0-month) rhythmic cycle in the Stocks of Refined Cottonseed Oil, U.S.A., September 1920–September 1932, is alleged.

The typical over-all amplitude of the 48.0-month cycle which appeared to be present in the quantity of stocks of refined cottonseed oil (total) in the hands of producers in the United States during the period under observation appeared to measure approximately 86.9%.

Blodgett, 1935. p. 67.

1334

A 4.14-year (49.7-month) rhythmic cycle in the Stocks of the Visible Supply
of Wheat, U.S.A., February 1919—July 1931, is alleged.

An over-all amplitude of 115.1% was evident in the 49.7-month cycle which
appeared to characterize the movement of the quantity of stocks in the visible supply of wheat in the hands of the industrial consumer in the United
States from February 1919 through July 1931.

Blodgett, 1935. p. 41.

1335

A 4.25-year (51-month) rhythmic cycle in Stocks of Cold Storage Holdings of
Pork, U.S.A., February 1922—August 1930, is alleged.

During the period from February 1922 through August 1930, the cold storage
holdings of pork stocks in the hands of producers in the United States appeared to move in waves which measured approximately 51.0 months in duration and which displayed an over-all amplitude of 55.6%.

Blodgett, 1935. p. 84.

1336

A 4.33-year (52-month) rhythmic cycle in the Stocks of Raw Cotton, U.S.A.,
July 1919—July 1932, is alleged.

During the period under observation, the quantity of stocks of raw cotton
(total) in the hands of the industrial consumer appeared to move in a 52.0-
month cyclic pattern which displayed an over-all amplitude of approximately
52.2%.

Blodgett, 1935. p. 41.

1337

A 4.33-year (52-month) rhythmic cycle in the Stocks of Upper Leather,
U.S.A., April 1922—December 1930, is alleged.

According to Blodgett, the quantity of stocks of upper leather (total) which
was in the hands of the producers in the United States showed a tendency
to move in a cyclic pattern which measured approximately 52.0 months in
duration and displayed an average over-all amplitude of 35.5%.

Blodgett, 1935. p. 67.

1338

A 4.38-year (52.5-month) rhythmic cycle in the Stocks of Raw Silk, U.S.A.,
August 1922—May 1931, is alleged.

The quantity of stocks of raw silk at manufacturing plants in the hands of
the industrial consumer appeared to move in cycles which averaged 52.5
months in duration during the period under observation. Typical over-all
amplitude measured approximately 51.9%.

Blodgett, 1935. p. 40.

1339

A 4.71-year (56.5-month) rhythmic cycle in the Stocks of Common Brick,
U.S.A., January 1921—June 1930, is alleged.

During the period from January 1921 through June 1930, the quantity of
stocks of common brick at the manufacturers in the hands of producers in
the United States appeared to move in a cyclic pattern which was approximately 56.5 months long. This cycle displayed an over-all amplitude of
75.7%.

Blodgett, 1935. p. 67.

1340

A 4.75-year (57-month) rhythmic cycle in the Stocks of Oak Flooring, U.S.A.,
December 1920—June 1930, is alleged.

A total over-all amplitude of 84.4% was reported in the 57-month cycle which
appeared to characterize the movement of the quantity of stocks of oak flooring at mills in the hands of producers in the United States during the period
from December 1920 through June 1930.

Blodgett, 1935. p. 66.

1341

A 5.33-year (64-month) rhythmic cycle in the Stocks of Ethyl Alcohol, U.S.A.,
December 1924—April 1930, is alleged.

A cycle with the length of approximately 64.0 months may have been present
in the quantity of stocks of ethyl alcohol at the warehouses which was in
the hands of the producers during the period under observation. The over-all
amplitude of this cycle appeared to measure approximately 74.7%.

Blodgett, 1935. p. 84.

1342

A 5.58-year (67.0-month) rhythmic cycle in the Stocks of Cement, U.S.A.,
August 1919—October 1930, is alleged.

Blodgett alleged that two 67.0-month cycles were present in the quantity of
stocks in the hands of producers of cement at mills during the period from
August 1919 through October 1930. An over-all amplitude of 83.6% was reported.

Blodgett, 1935. p. 66.

1343

A 5.87-year (70.5-month) rhythmic cycle in the Stocks of Gasoline, U.S.A.,
September 1920—June 1932, is alleged.

A total over-all amplitude of 83.1% was reported in the 70.5-month cycle
which appeared to characterize the movement of the quantity of stocks in
the hands of producers of gasoline at refineries during the period from
September 1920 through June 1932.

Blodgett, 1935. p. 85.

1344

A 5.92-year (71-month) rhythmic cycle in Stocks of Knit Underwear, U.S.A., July 1925—July 1931, is alleged.

The quantity of stocks in the hands of the producers of knit underwear at mills during the period under observation appeared to move in a 71.0-month cyclic pattern. An over-all amplitude of 48.2% was reported.

Blodgett, 1935. p. 85.

MINERAL PRODUCTION
Coal and Coke

1345

A 3.55-year (42.6-month) rhythmic cycle in Coke Production, U.S.A., 1914—1932, is alleged.

Short ton production of coke in the United States from 1914 through 1932 appeared to move in waves averaging 42.6 months in duration. The amplitude of the rise and fall combined measured 119.9%.

Burns and Mitchell, 1946. pp. 26—36. (Figure; data)

1346

During the period from 1914 through 1932, coke production in the United States appeared to move in waves which measured approximately 42.6 months in duration.

Dauten, 1954. p. 154.

1347

A 3.77-year (45.2-month) rhythmic cycle in Bituminous Coal Production, U.S.A., 1907—1938, is alleged.

Typical amplitude of the rise and fall combined of the 45.2-month rhythmic cycle present in bituminous coal production in the United States for the period under observation averaged 77.2%.

Burns and Mitchell, 1946. pp. 59, 128—135. (Figure; data)

1348

A 5.2-year (62.4-month) rhythmic cycle in Bituminous Coal Production, U.S.A., 1840—1924, is alleged.

Kuznets, 1930. p. 297. (Data)

1349

An 8-year rhythmic cycle in Coal Production, U.S.A., no dates given, is alleged.

Moore, 1923. p. 32.

1350

A 17 3/4-year rhythmic cycle in Bituminous Coal Production, U.S.A., 1800–1961, is alleged.

An assymmetrical 17 3/4-year wave appeared to be present in soft coal production in the United States during the period from 1800 through 1961. The wave appeared to rise for about 10 years during each cycle and a crest in the ideal pattern occurred at 1960. Typical amplitude at time of an ideal crest averaged 10.7% above trend; typical amplitude at time of an ideal trough, 9.6% below trend.

Wilson, 1962-B. (Figure)

1351

An 18-year rhythmic cycle in Coal Production and Consumption, U.S.A., no dates given, is alleged.

Newbury, 1952. p. 139.

1352

A 50–60-year rhythmic cycle in Coal Production, U.S.A., is alleged.

Kondratieff found a 50–60-year cycle present in coal production in the United States during the period from 1893 through 1925. A crest in the ideal pattern occurred at 1893.

Kondratieff, 1926. (Figure)

1353

Coal production in the United States with data extended backward to 1814 and forward through 1952 showed a definite tendency to follow the 50–60-year cyclic pattern alleged by Kondratieff, according to a study performed by Dewey.

Dewey, 1953-J. p. 300.

1354

A 50–60-year rhythmic cycle in Coal Production, England and Germany, varying dates, is alleged.

Coal production in England from 1850 through 1925 and in Germany from 1873 through 1925 showed a tendency to move in 50–60-year cycles. 1873 dated a crest in the ideal pattern for both countries.

Kondratieff, 1926. (Figure)

1355

A 50–60-year rhythmic cycle in Coal Production, worldwide, 1873–1925, is is alleged.

World-wide coal production, following the same pattern as coal production in the United States, England, and Germany, appeared to move in waves measuring 50–60 years from crest to crest for the period from 1873 through 1925.

Kondratieff, 1926. (Figure)

1356

A 50-60-year rhythmic cycle in Coal Consumption, France, 1830–1925, is alleged.

Coal consumption in France from 1830 through 1925 moved in a cyclical pattern which measured approximately 50–60 years in length. 1873 dated a crest in the ideal pattern.

Kondratieff, 1926. (Figure)

General

1357

An 11-year rhythmic cycle in the Physical Production of Minerals, U.S.A., 1878–1926, is alleged.

Garcia-Mata and Shaffner, 1934. pp. 16–18. (Figure)

Salt

1358

A 5.3-year (63.6-month) rhythmic cycle in Salt Production, U.S.A., 1880 – 1924, is alleged.

Kuznets, 1930. p. 297. (Data)

PATENTS ISSUED

1359

An 8.3-year rhythmic cycle in Patents Issued, U.S.A., is alleged.

The total number of patents issued in the United States from 1838 through 1957 appeared to be characterized by an 8.3-year rhythmic cycle. Typical amplitude of this 8.3-year cycle averaged 11.9% above trend at time of an ideal crest and 10.7% below trend at time of an ideal trough. A crest in the ideal pattern occurred at 1958.3.

Dewey, 1958-G. (Figure; data)

1360

The 8.3-year rhythmic cycle in patents issued in the United States was charted in combination with the 9.17-year cycle and trend. The movement of patents as a percent of trend followed the ideal pattern of the combined cycles and trend through 1960.

Shirk, 1962-R. (Figure)

1361

A 9.17-year rhythmic cycle in Patents Issued, U.S.A., is alleged.

Also characteristic of the total number of patents issued in the United States for the period under observation was a 9.17-year cyclic pattern.

Typical amplitude of this cycle averaged 8.4% above trend at time of an ideal crest and 7.7% below trend at time of an ideal trough.

Dewey, 1958-G. (Figure; data)

1362

The 9.17-year rhythmic cycle in patents issued in the United States along with an 8.3-year cycle and trend were charted as a combined cycle. The actual patents as a percent of trend followed the ideal pattern through 1960.

Shirk, 1962-R. (Figure)

1363

A 22-year rhythmic cycle in Patents Issued, U.S.A., 1838–1957, is alleged.

Dewey, 1958-G. (Figure; data)

WAGE EARNER ACTIVITY

1364

A 23-month (1.92-year) rhythmic cycle in Employment in the Production of Men's Shirts and Collars, U.S.A., no dates given, is alleged.

Newbury, 1952. p. 147.

1365

A 23.6-month (1.97-year) rhythmic cycle in Layoffs in Manufacturing, U.S.A., 1930–1961, is alleged.

One of the cycles which appeared to influence layoffs in manufacturing in the United States during the period from 1930 through 1961 measured about 23.6 months in duration. An ideal trough occurred in October of 1962 and the typical amplitude at the time of an ideal crest measured 22% above trend.

Shirk, 1962-O. (Figure)

1366

A 26-month (2.17-year) rhythmic cycle in Hours Worked per Week, U.S.A., January 1946–June 1960, is alleged.

According to figures supplied by the Bureau of Labor Statistics, hours worked per week in all manufacturing industries in the United States appeared to move in waves approximately 26 months in length when measured from crest to crest. A trough in the ideal pattern of this 26-month cycle was dated for September 1960.

Dewey, 1960-C. (Figure)

1367

The 26-month cycle in average weekly hours worked in all manufacturing in the United States which was first observed in September of 1960 continued to work after discovery through 1961.

Shirk, 1962-C. (Figure)

1368

A 4-year rhythmic cycle in Employment in Nonagricultural Establishments, U.S.A., 1944–1958, is alleged.

Peaks of the 4-year cycle in employment in nonagricultural establishments were dated at 1949, 1954, and 1958 for the period under observation.

Woytinsky and Woytinsky, 1959. p. 43. (Figure)

1369

A 4.09-year (49.1-month) rhythmic cycle in Industrial Employment, Detroit, 1920–1945, is alleged.

Neff and Weifenbach, 1949.

1370

A 4.75-year (57-month) rhythmic cycle in Industrial Employment, Cleveland, 1921–1945, is alleged.

Neff and Weifenbach, 1949.

1371

A 4.96-year (59.5-month) rhythmic cycle in Industrial Employment, Pittsburgh, 1923–1945, is alleged.

Neff and Weifenbach, 1949.

1372

A 5.07-year (60.8-month) rhythmic cycle in Industrial Employment, Chicago, 1923–1945, is alleged.

Neff and Weifenbach, 1949.

1373

A 10-year rhythmic cycle in Income High-Points, U.S.A., no dates given, is alleged.

According to Davies, Franklyn Hobbs, a Chicago economist, alleged a 10-year rhythmic cycle in income high-point in a series of figures covering over 100 years.

Davies, 1938.

1374

A 14 2/3- or 14 3/4-year rhythmic cycle in the Number of Strikes U.S.A., 1881–1951, is alleged.

A repetitive pattern which showed waves of about 14 2/3 or 14 3/4 years long was observed in the annual number of strikes in the United States from 1881 through 1951. A crest in the ideal pattern of this cycle was recorded at 1903.

Dewey, 1952-D. (Figure; data)

1375

A later article compared the behavior of the actual cycle and the ideal 14 2/3-year cycle in the number of strikes and lock-outs in the United States from 1881 through 1954.

Dewey, 1955-E. (Figure)

1376

An 18–25-year rhythmic cycle in Employment, U.S.A., no dates given, is alleged.

Downs, 1959. Chapter IV.

1377

A 20-year rhythmic cycle in Migration of Labor and Capital from Europe to the U.S.A., no dates given, is alleged.

Thomas, 1954, as cited by Gordon, 1961. p. 242.

1378

A 50–60-year rhythmic cycle in Wages of Coal Miners, France, no dates given, is alleged.

Kondratieff, 1926. p. 110.

1379

A 50–60-year rhythmic cycle in Weekly Wages of Workers, England, varying dates, is alleged.

The weekly wages of workers in the English cotton textile industry from 1806 through 1918 and of English agricultural laborers from 1789 through 1918 were studied by Kondratieff. He postulated that "long waves are undoubtedly present in the movement of wages, the periods of which correspond fairly well with those in commodity prices and interest rates."

Kondratieff, 1926. p. 108. (Figure)

1380

A 54-year rhythmic cycle in the Number of Wage Earners in Manufacturing, U.S.A., 1849–1952, is alleged.

The number of wage earners in manufacturing in the United States from 1849 through 1952 was one of the series of economic data employed in the study of a possible 50–60-year cycle in manufacturing production.

Dewey, 1953-J.

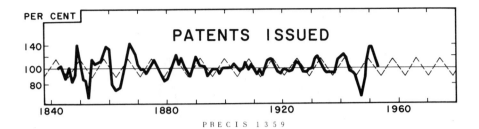

PER CENT

PATENTS ISSUED

140
100
80

1840   1880   1920   1960

PRECIS 1359

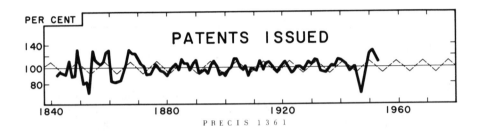

PER CENT

PATENTS ISSUED

140
100
80

1840   1880   1920   1960

PRECIS 1361

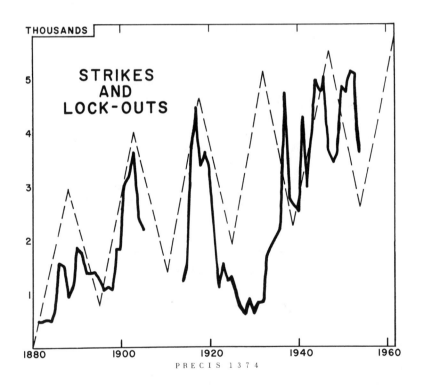

THOUSANDS

STRIKES
AND
LOCK-OUTS

5
4
3
2
1

1880   1900   1920   1940   1960

PRECIS 1374

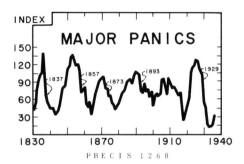

PRECIS 1268

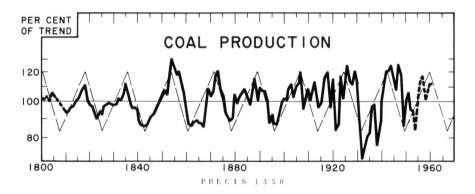

PRECIS 1350

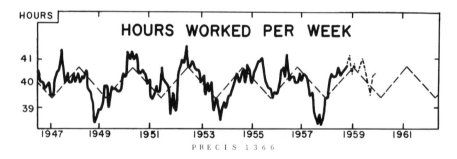

PRECIS 1366

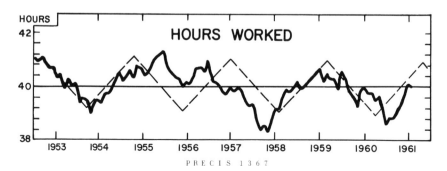

PRECIS 1367

BIBLIOGRAPHY

ABEL, MARTIN E. 1962. "Harmonic Analysis of Seasonal Variations," *Journal of the American Statistical Association.* Vol. 57; No. 299; September.

ABRAMOVICH, MOSES. 1956. *Resource and Output Trends in the United States Since 1870.* Occasional Paper 52. New York: National Bureau of Economic Research, Inc.

ABRAMSON, ADOLPH G. and RUSSELL H. MACK. 1956. *Business Forecasting in Practice: Principles and Cases.* New York: John Wiley and Sons, Inc.

ACHINSTEIN, ASHER. 1950. *Introduction to Business Cycles.* New York: Thomas Y. Crowell Company.

ADELMAN, IRMA. 1960. "Business Cycles — Endogenous or Stochastic?" *The Economic Journal.* Vol. LXX. pp. 783–796.

AFTALION, ALBERT. 1913. *Les Crises Periodiques de Surproduction.* Vol. ii. Paris: M. Riviere et Cie. pp. 41–42. As reported by MOORE, HENRY L., 1923. *Generating Economic Cycles.* New York: The Macmillan Company. p. 34.

ALLEN, W. and E. C. HOPE. 1937. *The Farm Outlook for Saskatchewan, 1937.* p. 7. As quoted in WARREN, GEORGE F. and FRANK A. PEARSON, 1937. *World Prices and the Building Industry.* New York: John Wiley and Sons, Inc.

ANDREWS, LORING B. 1936. "The Earth, the Sun and Sunspots," *Harvard Alumni Bulletin.* Vol. 38; No. 28; May 1. pp. 928–934.

ANONYMOUS. 1960. "A Cycle Analysis of Standard and Poor's Index of Copper Share Prices," *Cycles.* Vol. XI; No. 12. pp. 265–268.

APPEL, JOSEPH. 1950. *The Coming Crash in Wholesale Commodity Prices.* St. Louis: Joseph Appel.

ARMSTRONG, C. E. 1936. "The Short-Term Business Cycle: Its Average Form and Period as Observed in the Axe-Houghton Index of Business Activity," *Review of Economic Statistics.* May.

AYRES, LEONARD P. 1939. *Turning Points in Business Cycles.* New York: The Macmillan Company. As quoted in KING, HUGH P. 1958. "Cycles in Financial Data," *Journal of Cycle Research.* Vol. 7; No. 1; January. pp. 3–8.

BABSON, ROGER W. 1932. *Fighting Business Depressions.* New York: Harper & Brothers Publishers.

_____. 1948. *Looking Ahead Fifty Years.* New York: Harper & Brothers Publishers.

_____. 1959. *Business Barometers for Profits — Security — Income.* New York: Harper & Brothers Publishers.

BARBOUR, PERCY E. 1937. "Startling Results of 10-12 Cent Copper Producer's Opening Many Mines," *The Annalist*. August 6. As quoted in KING, WILLFORD I. 1939. *The Causes of Economic Fluctuations*. New York: Ronald Press Co.

BARGER, HAROLD. 1962. *Money, Banking and Public Policy*. Chicago: Rand McNally & Company.

BARTLETT, EDWIN B. 1947. *Cycles and Rhythms: A 50-year Comparison with Dow-Jones Industrial Average*. Milwaukee: Edwin B. Bartlett.

BASSIE, V. LEWIS. 1958. *Economic Forecasting*. New York: McGraw-Hill Book Company, Inc.

BEAN, L. H. 1928. "Major and Minor Hog-Price Cycles," *The Agriculture Situation*. Vol. 12; No. 7; July. As quoted in HADORN, ERWIN T. 1949. *Cycles in Economic Data: A Digest*. Riverside, Connecticut: Foundation for the Study of Cycles.

BENJAMIN, EARL W., HOWARD C. PIERCE, and WILLIAM D. TERMOHLEN. 1949. *Marketing Poultry Products*. New York: John Wiley and Sons, Inc.

BENNER, SAMUEL. 1875. *Benner's Prophecies of Future Ups and Downs in Prices*. Cincinnati: Chase and Hall. Reprinted in *Journal of Cycle Research*. 1959. Vol. 8; No. 1; January.

BENNETT, K. R. 1941. See PEARSON, F. A., J. V. CASSETTA, and K. R. BENNETT. 1941.

BERNSTEIN, E. M. 1940. "War and Business Cycles," *American Economic Review*. Vol. XXX; No. 3; September. pp. 524–535.

BERRY, THOMAS SENIOR. 1943. *Western Prices Before 1861: A Study of the Cincinnati Market*. Harvard Economic Studies – Vol. LXXIV. Cambridge: Harvard University Press.

BEVERIDGE, WILLIAM H. 1921. "Weather and Harvest Cycles," *Economic Journal*. London. Vol. 31. pp. 429–452.

————. 1922. "Wheat Prices and Rainfall in Western Europe," *Journal of the Royal Statistical Society*. London. Vol. 85. pp. 412–459. As quoted in HADORN, ERWIN T. 1949. *Cycles in Economic Data: A Digest*. Riverside, Connecticut: Foundation for the Study of Cycles.

————. 1944. *Full Employment in a Free Society*. London: Oxford University Press.

BJORKA, KNUTE. 1927. *Some Statistical Characterizations of the Hog Market*. Iowa State Agricultural Experimental Station Research Bulletin 102. May. pp. 6–7. As quoted in HADORN, ERWIN T. 1949. *Cycles in Economic Data: A Digest*. Riverside, Connecticut: Foundation for the Study of Cycles.

BLACKETT, OLIN W. and WINIFRED P. WILSON. 1936–38. "A Method of Isolating Sinusoidal Components in Economic Time Series," *Michigan Business Studies*. 8:358–365. As quoted in KING, HUGH P. 1958. "Cycles in Financial Data," *Journal of Cycle Research*. Vol. 7; No. 1; January.

BLANK, DAVID. 1956. See GREBLER, LEO, DAVID BLANK and LOUIS WINNICK. 1956.

BLAU, L. W. 1962. "LETTERS: The Stock Market," *Cycles*. Vol. XIII; No. 6; June. p. 168.

BLODGETT, RALPH H. 1935. *Cyclical Fluctuations in Commodity Stocks*. Philadelphia: University of Pennsylvania Press.

BODFISH, MORTON and HOMER HOYT. 1951. "The Real Estate Cycle," *Savings and Home Ownership*. April. Chicago: First Federal Savings and Loan Association of Chicago.

BOND, M. C. 1946. *Livestock—Trends, Cycles, Outlook*. New York State College of Agriculture. A. E. 571; October. p. 12.

BOUNIATIAN, MENTOR. 1908. *Studien zur Theorie und Geschichte der Wirschaftskrisen, II Geschicte der Handelskrisen in England 1640–1840*. Munich: E. Reinhardt.

————. *Les Crises Economiques*. Munich: E. Reinhardt.

BOWERMAN, WALTER G. 1944. "Residential Mortgage Loans and Sunspot Numbers," *Popular Astronomy*. Vol. 52; No. 3; May.

————. 1945. "Three Correlations: A Statistical Survey," *American Astronomy*. January.

BRADLEY, P. D., JR., and W. L. CRUM. 1937. "Periodicity as an Explanation of Variation in Hog Production," *Econometrica*. Vol. 7; No. 3; July.

BRANDOW, GEORGE E. 1939. "Cycles in Industry and Prices," an unpublished doctorate thesis dated June 1939 and on file in the library at Cornell University, Ithaca, New York. As quoted by NEWBURY, FRANK D. 1952. *Business Forecasting: Principles and Practice*. New York: McGraw-Hill Book Company, Inc.

BRATT, ELMER C. 1937. *Business Cycles and Forecasting*. Chicago: Business Publications, Inc.

————. 1958. *Business Forecasting*. New York: McGraw-Hill Book Company, Inc.

BRESSLER, RAYMOND G. 1962. See FRENCH, BEN C. and RAYMOND G. BRESSLER. 1962.

BRESSMAN, EARL N. 1947. See WALLACE, HENRY A. and EARL N. BRESSMAN. 1947.

BRINEWELL. 1958. Midland, Michigan: The Dow-Chemical Company. Vol. 16; No. 16.

BROWN, E. H. PHELPS and S. A. OZGA. 1955. "Economic Growth and the Price Level," *Economic Journal.* Vol. LXV; No. 6; March. p. 1.

BURNS, ARTHUR EDWARD, ALFRED C. NEAL and D. S. WATSON. 1953. *Modern Economics.* New York: Harcourt, Brace and Company.

BURNS, ARTHUR F. and WESLEY C. MITCHELL. 1946. *Measuring Business Cycles.* New York: National Bureau of Economic Research.

BURTON, T. E. 1902. *Financial Crises and Periods of Industrial and Commercial Depressions.* New York: D. Appleton. As reported by HUNTINGTON, ELLSWORTH. 1945. *Mainsprings of Civilization.* New York: John Wiley and Sons, Inc.

BUSINESS WEEK. 1958. "What History Teaches about Boom-and-Bust Cycles," *Business Week.* No. 1480; January 11.

_____. 1963. "Is the Long Cycle Why We Don't Grow?" *Business Week.* February 16. pp. 78–80.

CAIRNCROSS, A. K. 1934. "Linings," *The Review of Economic Studies.* 2:15–16. As quoted in WARREN, GEORGE F. and FRANK A. PEARSON. 1937. *World Prices and the Building Industry.* New York: John Wiley and Sons, Inc.

_____. 1953. *Home and Foreign Investment.* Cambridge. As reported by SAUL, S. B. 1962. "House Building in England, 1890–1914." *The Economic History Review; Second Series.* Vol. XV; No. 1; August.

CAIRNCROSS, A. K. and B. WEBER. 1956. "Fluctuations in Building in Great Britain, 1785–1849," *The Economic History Review; Second Series.* Vol. 9; No. 2; December.

CAMPBELL, CARLOS E. 1932. *Factors Affecting the Price of Rice.* U.S.D.A. Technical Bulletin 297. April. pp. 3–4. As quoted in HADORN, ERWIN T. 1949. *Cycles in Economic Data: A Digest.* Riverside, Connecticut: Foundation for the Study of Cycles.

CARD, DANA G. 1928-A. *Marketing Kentucky Eggs.* Kentucky Agriculture Experimental Station Bulletin 283; January. p. 31. As quoted in HADORN, ERWIN T. 1949. *Cycles in Economic Data: A Digest.* Riverside, Connecticut: Foundation for the Study of Cycles.

_____. 1928-B. *Marketing Kentucky Poultry.* Kentucky Agriculture Experimental Station Bulletin 285; June. p. 143. As quoted in HADORN, ERWIN T. 1949. *Cycles in Economic Data: A Digest.* Riverside, Connecticut: Foundation for the Study of Cycles.

CARDOZO, J. N. 1857. "Supply and Consumption of Cotton, Present and Prospective," *De Bow's Review*. Vol. XXII; April.

CASSELL, GUSTAV. 1924. *The Theory of Social Economy*. Translated by McCABE, JOSEPH. New York: Harcourt, Brace and Company.

CASSETTA, J. V. 1941. See PEARSON, F. A., J. V. CASSETTA, and K. R. BENNETT. 1941.

CASTLE, D. S. 1959. "The 17.12-week Stock Cycle," *Cycles*. Vol. X; No. 8; August. p. 181.

CHAMBERS, EDWARD J. 1961. *Economic Fluctuations and Forecasting*. Englewood Cliffs, New Jersey: Prentice-Hall, Inc.

CHAPMAN, C. R. 1957. "A 2 1/2-year Demand Growth Cycle," *Electrical Engineering*. August.

CLARK, HYDE. 1847. "Physical Economy — A Preliminary Inquiry into the Physical Laws Governing the Periods of Famines and Panics," *Railway Register*. London.

CLEMENT, M. O. 1962. "Automatic Stabilizers and Business Cycle Mechanisms," *The Southern Economic Journal*. Vol. XXVIII; No. 3; January. pp. 246–250.

CLOUGH, H. W. 1933. "The 11-year Sunspot Period, Secular Periods of Solar Activity, and Synchronous Variations in Terrestrial Phenomena," *Monthly Weather Review*. Vol. 61; April. pp. 99–108.

————. 1939. "The Effect of Climatic Changes Upon the Price of Wheat," *Bulletin of the American Meteorological Society*. Vol. 20. pp. 399–400.

————. 1942. "On the Interpretation of the Results of Periodogram Analysis and of Self-Correlation," *Bulletin American Meteorological Society*. Vol. 23. p. 293.

CLOUGH, SHEPARD BANCRAFT and CHARLES WOOLSEY COLE. 1952. *Economic History of Europe*. Boston: D. C. Heath and Company.

COCHRANE, WILLARD W. 1958. *Farm Prices: Myth and Reality*. Minneapolis: University of Minnesota Press.

COLE, CHARLES WOOLSEY. 1952. See CLOUGH, SHEPARD BANCRAFT and CHARLES WOOLSEY COLE. 1952.

COLEAN, MILES L., ERNEST M. FISHER and M. MASON GAFFNEY. 1960. *House and Home*.

COLLINS, CHARLES J. 1947. "Master Market Cycles," *Commercial and Financial Chronicle*. New York. May 22. As quoted in KING, HUGH P. 1958. "Cycles in Financial Data," *Journal of Cycle Research*. Vol. 7; No. 1; January. pp. 15–16.

COMMONS, JOHN ROGERS. 1893. "Economic Reform," *The Voice*. September 14.

CONTROLLERSHIP FOUNDATION, INC. 1950. *Business Forecasting: A Survey of Business Practices and Methods*. New York: Controllership Foundation, Inc.

COOLEY, DONALD G. 1944-A. "Cycles Predict the Future," *Mechanix Illustrated*. Vol. 33; March.

————. 1944-B. "Cycles Predict the Future," *Mechanix Illustrated*. Vol. 33; September.

COPPOCK, D. J. 1962. "Business Cycles – Endogenous or Stochastic? – A Comment," *The Economic Journal*. Vol. LXXII; No. 286; June. pp. 458–468.

COPPOCK, E. S. C. 1951. As reported by DEWEY, EDWARD R. 1951-E. "Cycles in the Stock Market," *Cycles*. Vol. II; No. 3; March. pp. 83–85.

COWDEN, DUDLEY J. 1941. See CROXTON, FREDERICK E. and DUDLEY J. COWDON, 1941.

COX, GARFIELD V. 1928. See HARDY, CHARLES O. and GARFIELD V. COX. 1928.

CRANE, BURTON. 1959. *The Sophisticated Investor – A Guide to Stock Market Profits*. New York: Simon and Schuster.

CROXTON, FREDERICK E. and DUDLEY J. COWDEN. 1941. *Applied General Statistics*. New York: Prentice-Hall, Inc.

CRUM, W. L. 1923. "Cycles of Rates on Commercial Paper," *The Review of Economic Statistics*. January. pp. 17–29. Also quoted in DEWEY, EDWARD R. 1951-H. "The 41-month Cycle in Industrial Common Stock Prices," *Cycles*. Vol. II; No. 9; November. pp. 327–335.

————. 1937. See BRADLEY, P. D., JR., and W. L. CRUM. 1937.

CURTISS, W. M. 1940. See PEARSON, F. A., W. I. MYERS and W. M. CURTISS. 1940.

DAKIN, EDWIN F. 1947. See DEWEY, EDWARD R. and EDWIN F. DAKIN. 1947.

DANIELS, FRED B. 1955. "Existence of Periods in the Stock Market," *Science*. Vol. 121; No. 3136; February 4. pp. 151–154.

DANSON, J. F. 1959. "An Idea About the 54-Year Cycle," *Cycles*. Vol. X; No. 11; November. p. 252.

DAUTEN, CARL A. 1954. *Business Fluctuations and Forecasting*. Cincinnati: South-Western Publishing Company.

DAVIES, JULIAN G. 1938. "Cycles of Business and Commodity Prices," printed copy of a lecture read at Toronto University, Toronto, Canada, on October 13, 1938.

DAVIS, HAROLD T. 1936. "Significant Tests for Periodogram Analysis with Application to Prices of Common Stocks," *Abstracts of Papers Presented at the Research Conference on Economics and Statistics Held by the Cowles Commission for Research in Economics, 1936.* Colorado College: General Series Number 208. pp. 102–103.

_____. 1941. *The Analysis of Economic Time Series.* Bloomington, Indiana: The Principia Press, Inc.

DAVIS, LANCE E., JONATHON R. T. HUGHES and DUNCAN M. McDOUG-ALL. 1961. *American Economic History (The Development of a National Economy).* Homewood, Illinois: Richard D. Irwin, Inc.

DAVIS, THOMAS JEFFERSON. 1958. *Cycles and Trends in Textiles.* Washington: U. S. Department of Commerce. As quoted by SHIRK, GERTRUDE. 1959. "The 2-year Cycle in Textiles," *Cycles.* Vol. X; No. 7; July. pp. 155–158.

DEGRAFF, H. 1952. See PEARSON, F. A., W. I. MYERS, DON PAARL-BERG, and H. DEGRAFF. 1952.

DE LURY, RALPH E. 1938. "Sunspot Influences," *Journal of the Royal Astronomical Society of Canada.* March–April.

DENNON, JAMES. 1960. *United States Economic Cycles: 1760–1972,* U. S. A.: James Dennon.

DERKSON, J. B. D. 1940. "Long Cycles in Residential Building: An Explanation," *Econometrica.* pp. 97–116.

DEWEY, EDWARD R. and EDWIN F. DAKIN. 1947. *Cycles: The Science of Prediction.* New York: Henry Holt and Company.

DEWEY, EDWARD R. 1949-A. "Cycles in Industrial Production: Viscose Rayon Filament Yarn Production: The 2-year Rhythm, The 2 3/4-year Rhythm, The 3 1/2-year Rhythm, The 6-year Rhythm, and the Trend, 1911–1948," *Foundation Report No. 1.* Riverside, Connecticut: Foundation for the Study of Cycles.

_____. 1949-B. "Cycles in Wholesale Prices: Cotton (a) War and Post-War Behavior (b) The 6-year Rhythm, 1731– 32 to 1947–48," *Foundation Report No. 2.* Riverside, Connecticut: Foundation for the Study of Cycles.

_____. 1949-C. "Cycles in Industrial Production: General Electric Company: The 6-Year Rhythm in Orders Received, 1893–1946," *Foundation Report No. 3.* Riverside, Connecticut: Foundation for the Study of Cycles.

_____ . 1950-A. "Cycles in Automobile Sales: The 6-year Rhythm, 1893–1949," *Cycles*. Vol. I; No. 3; October. pp. 5–9.

_____ . 1950-B. "Cycles in Cigarette Production: The 8-year Rhythm, 1880–1949," *Cycles*. Vol. I; No. 3; October. pp. 18–22.

_____ . 1950-C. "Cycles in General Business: The 3- to 3 1/2-year Waves, 1790–1946," *Cycles*. Vol. I; No. 4; November. pp. 4–14.

_____ . 1950-D. "Cycles in Sunspots: The 22 1/5-year Cycle in Relative Sunspot Numbers with Alternate Cycles Reversed, 1749–1949," *Cycles*. Vol. I; No. 1; June. pp. 8–11.

_____ . 1950-E. "Long Cycles in Cotton Prices," *Cycles*. Vol. I; No. 4; November. pp. 17–19.

_____ . 1950-F. "Multiple Harmonic Analysis: Applied to Cotton Prices, 1731-32–1939-40," *Cycles*. Vol. I; No. 4; November. pp. 20–26.

_____ . 1950-G. "The 6-year Cycle,"*Cycles*. Vol. I; No. 5; December. pp. 3–17.

_____ . 1951-A. "Construction of the Charles H. Pinkham Index of Advertising Efficiency," *Cycles*. Vol. II; No. 6; June. p. 234.

_____ . 1951-B. "Cycles in the Prices of Malleable Iron Pipe Fittings," *Cycles*. Vol. II; No. 10; December. pp. 362–366.

_____ . 1951-C. "Cycles in Residential Building Construction: The 17 1/3-year Cycle," *Cycles*. Vol. II; No. 5; May. pp. 171–173.

_____ . 1951-D. "Cycles in the Sales of Company G," *Cycles*. Vol. II; No. 4; April. pp. 130–134.

_____ . 1951-E. "Cycles in the Stock Market," *Cycles*. Vol. II; No. 3; March. pp. 83–88.

_____ . 1951-F. "The Director's Letter," *Cycles*. Vol. II; No. 6; June. pp. 201–203.

_____ . 1951-G. "An Economic Cycle: The 17 2/3-year Rhythm in Liabilities of Commercial and Industrial Failures in the U.S., 1857–1950," *Journal of Cycle Research*. Vol. 1; No. 1; Autumn. pp. 2–5.

_____ . 1951-H. "The 41-month Cycle in Industrial Common Stock Prices," *Cycles*. Vol. II; No. 9; November. pp. 327–335.

_____ . 1951-I. "The 41-month Cycle in the Price of Common Stock – Continued," *Cycles*. Vol. II; No. 10; December. pp. 371–377.

_____ . 1951-J. "Harmonic Analysis of Cotton Prices – Continued," *Cycles*. Vol. II; No. 4; April. pp. 141–142.

————. 1951-K. "Long Cycles in Cotton Prices — Continued," *Cycles*. Vol. II; No. 4; April. p. 140.

————. 1951-L. "The 9.2-year Cycle in Common Stocks," *Cycles*. Vol. II; No. 6; June. pp. 204—207.

————. 1951-M. "The 19.4-year Cycle in Railroad Stock Prices," *Cycles*. Vol. II; No. 7; September. pp. 255—260.

————. 1951-N. "Techniques Involved in the Determination of Four Cycles in the Prices of Malleable Iron Pipe Fittings," *Cycles*. Vol. II; No. 10; December. pp. 378—379.

————. 1951-O. "Techniques Involved in the Determination of the 9.2-year Cycle in Industrial Common Stock Prices," *Cycles*. Vol. II; No. 6; June. p. 233.

————. 1951-P. "Techniques Involved in the Determination of the 19.4-year Cycle in Railroad Stock Prices," *Cycles*. Vol. II; No. 7; September. p. 263.

————. 1951-Q. "Techniques Involved in the Determination of the 22.7-month Cycle in the Sales of Company G," *Cycles*. Vol. II; No. 1; January. p. 13.

————. 1951-R. "Techniques Involved in the Synthesis of Ten Possible Long Cycles in Stock Prices," *Cycles*. Vol. II; No. 7; September. pp. 261—263.

————. 1951-S. "The 37-year Cycle," *Cycles*. Vol. II; No. 8; October. pp. 277—278.

————. 1951-T. "The 33-month Cycle in Building Construction," *Cycles*. Vol. II; No. 4; April. pp. 138—139.

————. 1951-U. "The 33-month Cycle in the Sales of Company G," *Cycles*. Vol. II; No. 2; February. pp. 49—52.

————. 1951-V. "The Synthesis of Long Cycles in Stock Prices," *Cycles*. Vol. II; No. 7; September. pp. 245—252.

————. 1951-W. "The 22.7-month Cycle in the Sales of Company G," *Cycles*. Vol. II; No. 1; January. pp. 10—11.

————. 1951-X. "The 9.6-year Cycle in the Acreage of Wheat," *Cycles*. Vol. II; No. 5; May. pp. 175—177.

————. 1952-A. "Cycles in Pig Iron Prices," *Cycles*. Vol. III; No. 2; February. pp. 50—52.

————. 1952-B. "The 8-year Cycle in Cigarette Production," *Cycles*. Vol. III; No. 9; November. p. 330.

————. 1952-C. "The 8-year Cycle in Industrial Common Stocks," *Cycles*. Vol. III; No. 1; January. pp. 5–8.

————. 1952-D. "The 14 2/3-year Cycle in the Number of Strikes in the United States," *Journal of Cycle Research*. Vol. 1; No. 5; Fall.

————. 1952-E. "Is There a 17 1/3-year Pattern in Stocks?" *Cycles*. Vol. III; No. 6; June. pp. 205–206.

————. 1952-F. "More About the 46-month Cycle in Stock Prices," *Cycles*. Vol. III; No. 9; November. pp. 297–299.

————. 1952-G. "Possible Cycles in Industrial Stock Prices, 1871–1950," *Cycles*. Vol. III; No. 5; May. pp. 166–179.

————. 1952-H. "Possible Cycles in Pig Iron Prices, 1784–1951," *Cycles*. Vol. III; No. 6; June. pp. 207–209.

————. 1952-I. "Possible Cycles in Railroad Stock Prices, 1831–1950," *Cycles*. Vol. III; No. 4; April. pp. 123–129.

————. 1952-J. "The 17 3/4-year Cycle in Pig Iron Prices, 1784–1951," *Journal of Cycle Research*. Vol. 1; No. 3; Spring. pp. 76–86.

————. 1952-K. "The 6-year Cycle in Allis-Chalmers," *Cycles*. Vol. III; No. 10; December. pp. 342–343.

————. 1952-L. "The 6-year Cycle in the Sales of Armour and Company," *Cycles*. Vol. III; No. 8; October. p. 282.

————. 1952-M. "The 6-year Cycle in Jones and Laughlin," *Cycles*. Vol. III; No. 10; December. pp. 344–345.

————. 1952-N. "The 6-year Cycle in the Sales of the Pittsburgh Plate Glass Company," *Cycles*. Vol. III; No. 8; October. p. 283.

————. 1952-O. "A Stock Market Forecast Made in 1912," *Cycles*. Vol. III; No. 6; June. pp. 197–200.

————. 1952-P. "Techniques Involved in the Construction of the Periodogram of Railroad Stock Prices, 1831–1950," *Cycles*. Vol. III; No. 4; April. p. 140.

————. 1952-Q. "Techniques Involved in the Determination of the 12.6-year Cycle in the Sales of Company G," *Cycles*. Vol. III; No. 3; March. pp. 99–109.

————. 1952-R. "The 13-year Cycle in Automobile Sales," *Cycles*. Vol. III; No. 8; October. pp. 271–276.

————. 1952-S. "The 33-month Cycle in the Sales of Company G," *Cycles*. Vol. III; No. 7; September. pp. 242–243.

————. 1952-T. "The 12.6-month Cycle in the Sales of Company G," *Cycles*. Vol. III; No. 3; March. pp. 94—96.

————. 1952-U. "War Cycles and the 6-year Cycle in Cotton Prices, 1731—1949," *Journal of Cycle Research*. Vol. 1; No. 2; Winter 1951—1952.

————. 1952-V. "What Made the Benner Forecast Tick?" *Cycles*. Vol. III; No. 3; March. pp. 90—93.

————. 1952-W. "Will Dunbar's Cycle Stand Up?" *Cycles*. Vol. III; No. 8; October. pp. 267—270.

————. 1952-X. "Cycles in Pig Iron Prices," *Cycles*. Vol. III; No. 2; February. pp. 50—52.

————. 1952-Y. "Possible Cycles in Railroad Stock Prices, 1831—1950," *Cycles*. Vol. III; No. 4; April. pp. 123—129.

————. 1953-A. "Bethlehem Steel Corporation: 6-year Cycle in Production," *Cycles*. Vol. IV; No. 7; September. pp. 215—218.

————. 1953-B. "Business Failures: Liabilities of Commercial and Industrial Failures in the United States, 1857—1953: Cycles, Trend, and Forecast," *Cycles*. Vol. IV; No. 8; October. pp. 255—272.

————. 1953-C. "Continental Oil Company: Cycles, Trend, and Forecast," *Cycles*. Vol. IV; No. 6; June—July. pp. 171—175.

————. 1953-D. "Cycles in Manufacturing Production — Continued," *Cycles*. Vol. IV; No. 10; December. pp. 333—335.

————. 1953-E. "The Director's Letter," *Cycles*. Vol. IV; No. 4; April. pp. 103—104.

————. 1953-F. "Editor's Notes," *Cycles*. Vol. IV; No. 5; May. pp 158—162.

————. 1953-G. "The 8-year Cycle," *Cycles*. Vol. IV; No. 5; May. pp. 142—144.

————. 1953-H. "A Forecast of Viscose Rayon Filament Yarn Production," *Cycles*. Vol. IV; No. 2; February. pp. 61—62.

————. 1953-I. "45 6/7-day Cycle in a Common Stock" *Cycles*. Vol.IV; No. 6; June—July. pp. 178—181.

————. 1953-J. "Manufacturing Production (Physical Production: 1810—1953)," *Cycles*. Vol. IV; No. 9; November. pp. 296—306.

————. 1953-K. "The 9.3-year Cycle in Wheat Prices," *Cycles*. Vol.IV; No. 5; May. pp. 139—141.

————. 1953-L. "The 9.2- and 8.5-year Cycles in Pig Iron Prices," *Journal of Cycle Research*. Vol. 2; No. 4; Fall. pp. 79–89.

————. 1953-M. "The 6-year Cycle – In American Viscose – In Armour – In Du Pont – In Mansanto Chemical – In Montgomery Ward – In National Lead," *Cycles*. Vol. IV; No. 1; January. pp. 21–33.

————. 1953-N. "The 6-year Cycle in Armco Steel," *Cycles*. Vol. IV; No. 4; April. pp. 115–116.

————. 1953-O. "The 6-year Cycle in Cotton Production," *Cycles*. Vol. IV; No. 1; January. pp. 9–13.

————. 1953-P. "The 6-year Cycle in Proctor and Gamble Sales," *Cycles*. Vol. IV; No. 9; November. pp. 307–308.

————. 1953-Q. "The 6-year Cycle in Wilson and Company Sales," *Cycles*. Vol. IV; No. 6; June–July. pp. 191–192.

————. 1953-R. "The 6.41-month Cycle in Stock Prices," *Cycles*. Vol. IV; No. 7; September. p. 228.

————. 1953-S. "The 6.33-month Cycle in Stock Prices," *Cycles*. Vol. IV; No. 10; December. p. 342.

————. 1953-T. "What's Ahead for Wheat Prices?" *Cycles*. Vol. IV; No. 6; June–July. pp. 182–188.

————. 1953-U. "What's Ahead for Wheat Prices?" *Cycles*. Vol. IV; No. 7; September. pp. 222–227.

————. 1953-V. "Cycles in the Prices of Malleable Iron Pipe Fittings," *Cycles*. Vol. IV; No. 1; January. p. 34.

————. 1953-W. "A Letter from Massachusetts," *Cycles*. Vol. IV; No. 7; September. p. 230.

————. 1954-A. "Continental Oil Company: Cycles, Trend, and Forecast," *Cycles*. Vol. V; No. 6; June–July. pp. 227–232.

————. 1954-B. "Cycles in Automobile Sales – Continued," *Cycles*. Vol. V; No. 8; October. pp. 286–291.

————. 1954-C. "Cycles in Automobile Sales – Continued: The 36-month Cycle," *Cycles*. Vol. V; No. 9; November. pp. 321–323.

————. 1954-D. "Cycles in Automobile Sales – Continued: The 23 2/3-month Cycle," *Cycles*. Vol. V; No. 10; December. pp. 347–351.

————. 1954-E. "Cycles in Manufacturing Production – Continued: The Basic Structure," *Cycles*. Vol. V; No. 1; January. pp. 5–7.

————. 1954-F. "Cycles in Manufacturing Production: The Basic Structure – Continued," *Cycles*. Vol. V; No. 2; February. pp. 45–53.

————. 1954-G. "Cycles in the Sales of Du Pont," *Cycles*. Vol. V; No. 6; June—July. pp. 205—214.

————. 1954-H. "The 8-year and 6-year Cycles in Goodyear Tire and Rubber Company Sales," *Cycles*. Vol. V; No. 1; January. pp. 8—12.

————. 1954-I. "The 41-month Cycle in Stock Prices," *Cycles*. Vol. V; No. 5; May. pp. 176—179.

————. 1954-J. "My Stock Market Forecast of 1944," *Cycles*. Vol. V; No. 6; June—July. pp. 215—226.

————. 1954-K. "The 9.3- and 8.6-year Cycles in Copper Prices," *Journal of Cycle Research*. Vol. 3; No. 4; Fall. pp. 99—107.

————. 1954-L. "The 9.2- and 8.5-year Cycle in Pig Iron Prices," *Cycles*. Vol. V; No. 3; March. pp. 86—95.

————. 1954-M. "1954 Postscript to Chapter VIII," *Cycles*. Vol. V; No. 3; March. pp. 108—118.

————. 1954-N. "1954 Postscript to Chapter VII," *Cycles*. Vol. V; No. 1; January. pp. 32—39.

————. 1954-O. "1954 Postscript: Samuel Benner's Forecast of 1875," *Cycles*. Vol. V; No. 2; February. pp. 76—78.

————. 1954-P. "The 6-year Cycle in Pittsburgh Plate Glass Company Sales," *Cycles*. Vol. V; No. 1; January. pp. 13—16.

————. 1954-Q. "The 6-year Cycle in Sears, Roebuck," *Cycles*. Vol. V; No. 5; May. pp. 180—182.

————. 1954-R. "Three Minor Stock Market Cycles," *Cycles*. Vol. V; No. 2; February. pp. 54—55.

————. 1954-S. "The 3.4-year Cycle in Automobile Sales," *Cycles*. Vol. V; No. 7; August—September. pp. 245—247.

————. 1954-T. "The 6-year Cycle — In Swift and Company — In Mansanto Chemical — In National Lead — In Standard Oil of California," *Cycles*. Vol. V; No. 10; December. pp. 353—361.

————. 1954-U. "The 9.6-year Cycle in the Acreage of Wheat," *Cycles*. Vol. V; No. 9; November. p. 320.

————. 1955-A. "The Director's Letter," *Cycles*. Vol. VI; No. 5; May. pp. 135—138.

————. 1955-B. "The 15 1/7-year Cycle in Black Pepper Prices, 1819—1953," *Cycles*. Vol. VI; No. 6; June—July. pp. 184—185.

————. 1955-C. "The 5 1/2-year Cycle in Corn Prices," *Cycles*. Vol. VI; No. 2; February. pp. 43—47. Also Vol. VI; No. 3; March. pp. 77—81.

————. 1955-D. "The 4-year Cycle in the Consumption of Cheese, 1867–1953," *Cycles*. Vol. VI; No. 6; June–July. pp. 188–189.

————. 1955-E. "The 14 2/3-year Cycle in the Number of Strikes in the United States," *Cycles*. Vol. VI; No. 1; January. pp. 12–13.

————. 1955-F. "The Long Cycle in Stock Prices," *Cycles*. Vol. VI; No. 1; January. pp. 10–11.

————. 1955-G. "The 17 3/4- and 18 1/5-year Cycles in Various Phenomena," *Journal of Cycle Research*. Vol. 4; No. 2; April. pp. 35–60.

————. 1955-H. "The 17 3/4-year Cycle in Cotton Prices, 1731-32–1953-54," *Cycles*. Vol. VI; No. 1; January. pp. 14–17.

————. 1955-I. "The 17.2-year Cycle in Stock Prices, 1831–1954," *Cycles*. Vol. VI; No. 5; May. pp. 149–151.

————. 1955-J. "The 6-year Cycle in Allis-Chalmers Sales," *Cycles*. Vol. VI; No. 3; March. pp. 94–95.

————. 1955-K. "The 6-year Cycle in General Motor Sales," *Cycles*. Vol. VI; No. 8; October. pp. 236–238.

————. 1955-L. "The 6-year Cycle in Montgomery Ward and Company Sales," *Cycles*. Vol. VI; No. 2; February. pp. 54–55.

————. 1955-M. "The 6-year Cycle in Swift and Company Sales," *Cycles*. Vol. VI; No. 6; June-July. pp. 192–193.

————. 1955-N. "The 6-year Cycle in Youngstown Sheet and Tube Company Sales," *Cycles*. Vol. VI; No. 2; February. pp. 52–53.

————. 1955-O. "The 6-year and the 8 1/3-year Cycles in General Electric Sales," *Cycles*. Vol. VI; No. 7; August-September. pp. 201–208.

————. 1955-P. "The 16- or 16 2/3-year Cycle in Coffee Prices, 1854-1954," *Cycles*. Vol. VI; No. 6; June–July. pp. 180–183.

————. 1955-Q. "The 16 2/3-year Cycle in Wrought Iron Prices in England, 1277–1918," *Cycles*. Vol. VI; No. 5; May. pp. 141–147.

————. 1955-R. "The 3.49-year Cycle in Corn Prices," *Cycles*. Vol. VI; No. 9; November. pp. 273–280.

————. 1955-S. "The 3 1/2- to 3 3/4-year Cycles in Corn Prices, 1720–1954," *Cycles*. Vol. VI; No. 8; October. pp. 239–248.

————. 1955-T. "The 3 1/2-year Cycle in General Business," *Cycles*. Vol. VI; No. 9; November. pp. 261–266.

————. 1955-U. "The 6-year Cycle in Steel Production, 1867–1954," *Cycles*. Vol. VI; No. 6; June–July. pp. 169–174.

————. 1956-A. "Axe-Houghton Stock Prices Index," *Cycles*. Vol. VII; No. 11; November. pp. 314–315.

————. 1956-B. "The 8-year Cycle in Cigarette Production, 1880–1955," *Cycles*. Vol. VII; No. 10; October. pp. 275–277.

————. 1956-C. "The 5 1/2-year Cycle in Airplane Traffic, U.S.A., 1930–1955," *Cycles*. Vol. VII; No. 12; December. pp. 334–335.

————. 1956-D. "The 46-month Cycles in Stock Prices," *Cycles*. Vol. VII; No. 8; August. pp. 221–227.

————. 1956-E. "The 9.18-year Cycle in Common Stock Prices," *Cycles*. Vol. VII; No. 6; June. pp. 157–166. Vol. VII; July. pp. 185–188.

————. 1956-F. "The 9.18-year Cycle in Railroad Stock Prices, 1831–1955, and the Techniques Used in its Definitization," *Journal of Cycle Research*. Vol. 5; No. 3; July. pp. 63–84.

————. 1956-G. "1956 Postscript: Samuel Benner's Forecast of 1875," *Cycles*. Vol. VII; No. 7; July. pp. 208–210.

————. 1956-H. "The 1956 Postscript to Cycles: *The Science of Prediction*. Part V: The 9-year Cycle Continued," *Cycles*. Vol. VII; No. 5; May. pp. 145–153.

————. 1956-I. "The 1956 Postscript to *Cycles*: *The Science of Prediction*. Part IX: The 8-year Cycle," *Cycles*. Vol. VII; No. 10; October. pp. 271–274.

————. 1956-J. "The 7.94- and the 8.39-year Cycles in Railroad Stock Prices, 1831–1955," *Cycles*. Vol. VII; No. 11; November. pp. 289–294.

————. 1957-A. "The Combination of 11 Stock Market Cycles and Trend," *Cycles*. Vol. VIII; No. 7; July. p. 176.

————. 1957-B. "The 11-year Cycle Discovered by Dr. Hyde Clarke in 1847," *Cycles*. Vol. VIII; No. 1; January. pp. 13–15.

————. 1957-C. "The 54-year Cycle in Copper Prices," *Cycles*. Vol. VIII; No. 9; September. pp. 238–239.

————. 1957-D. "The 5.91- or 5.92-year Cycle in Stock Prices," *Cycles*. Vol. VIII; No. 4; April. pp. 93–98.

————. 1957-E. "The 5.92-year Cycle in Railroad Stock Prices, 1831–1956, and the Techniques Used in its Definitization," *Journal of Cycle Research*. Vol. 6; No. 1; January. pp. 16–31.

————. 1957-F. "The 1957 Postscript to *Cycles*: *The Science of Prediction*. Part XI: The 5.91-year Cycle," *Cycles*. Vol. VIII; No. 1; January. pp. 17–21.

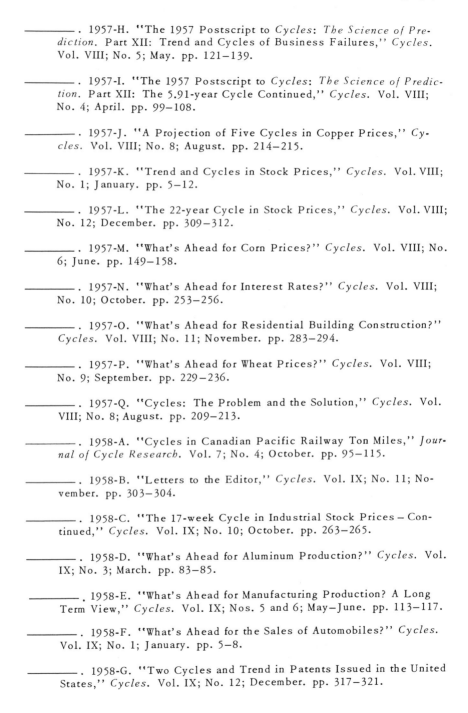

————. 1957-H. "The 1957 Postscript to *Cycles: The Science of Prediction*. Part XII: Trend and Cycles of Business Failures," *Cycles*. Vol. VIII; No. 5; May. pp. 121–139.

————. 1957-I. "The 1957 Postscript to *Cycles: The Science of Prediction*. Part XII: The 5.91-year Cycle Continued," *Cycles*. Vol. VIII; No. 4; April. pp. 99–108.

————. 1957-J. "A Projection of Five Cycles in Copper Prices," *Cycles*. Vol. VIII; No. 8; August. pp. 214–215.

————. 1957-K. "Trend and Cycles in Stock Prices," *Cycles*. Vol. VIII; No. 1; January. pp. 5–12.

————. 1957-L. "The 22-year Cycle in Stock Prices," *Cycles*. Vol. VIII; No. 12; December. pp. 309–312.

————. 1957-M. "What's Ahead for Corn Prices?" *Cycles*. Vol. VIII; No. 6; June. pp. 149–158.

————. 1957-N. "What's Ahead for Interest Rates?" *Cycles*. Vol. VIII; No. 10; October. pp. 253–256.

————. 1957-O. "What's Ahead for Residential Building Construction?" *Cycles*. Vol. VIII; No. 11; November. pp. 283–294.

————. 1957-P. "What's Ahead for Wheat Prices?" *Cycles*. Vol. VIII; No. 9; September. pp. 229–236.

————. 1957-Q. "Cycles: The Problem and the Solution," *Cycles*. Vol. VIII; No. 8; August. pp. 209–213.

————. 1958-A. "Cycles in Canadian Pacific Railway Ton Miles," *Journal of Cycle Research*. Vol. 7; No. 4; October. pp. 95–115.

————. 1958-B. "Letters to the Editor," *Cycles*. Vol. IX; No. 11; November. pp. 303–304.

————. 1958-C. "The 17-week Cycle in Industrial Stock Prices — Continued," *Cycles*. Vol. IX; No. 10; October. pp. 263–265.

————. 1958-D. "What's Ahead for Aluminum Production?" *Cycles*. Vol. IX; No. 3; March. pp. 83–85.

————. 1958-E. "What's Ahead for Manufacturing Production? A Long Term View," *Cycles*. Vol. IX; Nos. 5 and 6; May–June. pp. 113–117.

————. 1958-F. "What's Ahead for the Sales of Automobiles?" *Cycles*. Vol. IX; No. 1; January. pp. 5–8.

————. 1958-G. "Two Cycles and Trend in Patents Issued in the United States," *Cycles*. Vol. IX; No. 12; December. pp. 317–321.

———. 1959-A. "Steel Production," *Cycles.* Vol. X; No. 7; July. p. 165.

———. 1959-B. "The 7 1/2-year Cycle in Ton Miles of the Canadian Pacific Railway," *Cycles.* Vol. X; No. 2; February. pp. 32–33.

———. 1959-C. "The 17.75-year Cycle in Stock Prices," *Cycles.* Vol. X; No. 3; March. pp. 53–55.

———. 1959-D. "The 17-week Cycle in Industrial Stocks," *Cycles.* Vol. X; No. 11; November. pp. 247–248.

———. 1959-E. "Copper Prices," *Cycles.* Vol. X; No. 12; December. p. 279.

———. 1960-A. "Current Status of the 9.18-year Cycle," *Cycles.* Vol. XI; No. 11; November. p. 247.

———. 1960-B. "My Stock Market Forecasts and How They Came Out," *Cycles.* Vol. XI; No. 1; January. pp. 9–11.

———. 1960-C. "A Possible Cycle in Hours Worked: Its Timing and Effect," *Cycles.* Vol. XI; No. 9; September. pp. 193–194.

———. 1960-D. "The 17.166-week Cycle in the Dow-Jones Industrial Stock Price Averages, January 9, 1897–February 13, 1960," *Journal of Cycle Research.* Vol. 9; No. 3; July. pp. 87–116.

———. 1960-E. "The 17-week Cycle in Stocks: Findings of New Research," *Cycles.* Vol. XI; No. 7; July. pp. 152–153.

———. 1961-A. "Steel Production Matches 6-year Cycle Peak," *Cycles.* Vol. XII; No. 1; January. p. 13.

———. 1962-A. "Is There a Pattern? The 8-year Cycle in Cigarette Production," *Tobacco: The International Weekly of Industry and Science.* Vol. 155; No. 2; July 13. pp. 12–14. Also published in *Cycles.* Vol. XIII; No. 4; April. pp. 90–92.

———. 1962-B. "The 8 1/2-year Pig Iron Price Cycle Turns Up," *Cycles.* Vol. XIII; No. 6; June. pp. 150–152.

———. 1962-C. "The Director's Letter," *Cycles.* Vol. XIII; No. 10; October. p. 277.

———. 1962-D. "More Evidence on the 36-year Cycle," *Cycles.* Vol. XIII; No. 10; October. p. 287.

———. 1962-E. "The 54-year Cycle in European Wheat Prices," *Cycles.* Vol. XIII; No. 12; December. pp. 310–311.

———. 1963-A. "The 6.4-year Cycle in Aluminum Production," *Cycles.* Vol. XIV; No. 1; January. pp. 9–13.

DEWOLF. 1924. "Der Lebendige Marxismus," *Properitats und Depressions-periodene.* Jena. pp. 30ff. As quoted by WAGEMANN, ERNST. 1930. *Economic Rhythm: A Theory of Business Cycles.* New York: McGraw-Hill Book Company, Inc.

DOANE, WILLIAM S. 1962. "LETTERS: The Stock Market," *Cycles.* Vol. XIII; No. 8; August. p. 232.

DODD, JAMES HARVEY, JOHN W. KENNEDY and ARTHUR R. OLSEN. 1962. *Applied Economics: Introductory Principles Applied to Every-day Problems.* Cincinnati, Ohio: South Western Publishing Company.

DORFMAN, JOSEPH. 1949. *The Economic Mind in American Civilization, 1865–1918.* Vol. III. New York: The Viking Press.

————. 1959. *The Economic Mind in American Civilization, 1918–1933.* Vols. IV and V. New York: The Viking Press.

DORLAND, JACK A. 1962-A. "The 5 1/2-year Cycle in Soft Coal Stocks," *Cycles.* Vol. XIII; No. 7; July. pp. 181–183.

————. 1962-B. "The 5.91-year Cycle in Coal Stocks," *Cycles.* Vol. XIII; No. 10; October. pp. 279–281.

DOUAI, ADOLPH. 1878. *Testimony at the Hearings on "Depression in Labor and Business."* House of Representatives. August 23, 1878.

DOWNS, JAMES C., JR. 1959. *Principles of Real Estate Management.* Chicago: Institute of Real Estate Management.

DUNBAR, VERYL L. 1952. "The Bull Market: A 46-month Cycle Indicator Sees Its End This Year," *Barrons.* June 30. pp. 11–12.

————. 1956. "A Correction by Veryl Dunbar," *Cycles.* Vol. VII; No. 11; November. p. 315.

————. 1959. "The 46-month Cycle in Common Stock Prices, 1834–1959; Table I." As quoted by SHIRK, GERTRUDE. 1959. "Dunbar's 46-month Stock Price Cycle," *Cycles.* Vol. X; No. 6; June. pp. 130–131.

EATON, PHILLIP. 1941. *History Repeating.* Detroit, Michigan: Jackson and Lawson. As quoted in KING, HUGH P. 1958. "Cycles in Financial Data," *Journal of Cycle Research.* Vol. 7; No. 1; January. p. 21.

EINARSEN, JOHAN. 1938. *Reinvestment Cycles and their Manifestation in the Norwegian Shipping Industry.* Oslo: University Institute of Economics. pp. 99, 133–135, 144–146.

ELLIOTT, F. F. 1927. *Adjusting Hog Production to Market Demand.* Illinois Agriculture Experimental Station Bulletin No. 293. May. pp. 506–507.

ENCYCLOPEDIC DICTIONARY OF BUSINESS. 1952. Prentice-Hall, Inc.

ENSMINGER, M. E. 1960. *Beef Cattle Science (Animal Agriculture Series)*. Danville, Illinois: The Interstate Printers and Publishers.

ERNST, HARRY. 1957. "Cyclical Diffusion and Better Forecasting." A press release by the Institute for Economic Research dated December 22, 1957.

ESTEY, JAMES ARTHUR. 1941. *Business Cycles: Their Nature, Cause, and Control*. New York: Prentice-Hall, Inc.

EZEKIEL, MORDECAI. 1926. See HAAS, G. C. and M. EZEKIEL. 1926.

————. 1938. "The Cobweb Theorum," *Quarterly Journal of Economics*. Vol. 52; February. pp. 255–280.

FARM ECONOMICS. 1937. Ithaca, N.Y.: Cornell University. No. 100; March. p. 2442. As quoted in KING, WILLFORD I. 1938. *The Causes of Economic Fluctuations*. New York: Ronald Press Co.

FEIG, J. and W. MEVES. 1911. *Unsere Wohnungsproducktion und ihre Regelung*. p. 44. As quoted in WARREN, GEORGE F. AND FRANK A. PEARSON. 1937. *World Prices and the Building Industry*. New York: John Wiley and Sons, Inc.

FELLNER, WILLIAM. 1956. *Trends and Cycles in Economic Activity*. New York: Henry Holt and Company.

————. 1960. *Emergence and Content of Modern Economic Analysis*. New York: McGraw-Hill Book Company, Inc.

FELS, RENDIGS. 1952. "The Theory of Business Cycles," *The Quarterly Journal of Economics*. Vol. LXVI; No. 1; February. pp. 25–42.

FINANCIAL REPORTS, INC. 1951. "Cycles in the Market," *Financial Reports, Inc.* August.

FISHER, ERNEST M. 1960. See COLEAN, MILES L., ERNEST M. FISHER, and M. MASON GAFFNEY. 1960.

FISHMAN, BETTY G. and LEO. 1962. *The American Economy*. Princeton, New Jersey: D. Van Nostrand Company, Inc.

FISHMAN, LEO. 1962. See FISHMAN, BETTY G. and LEO. 1962.

FLOOD, MERRILL M. 1940. "Recursive Methods in Business Cycle Analysis," *Econometrica*. Vol. 8; No. 4; October.

FOSTER, HERBERT. 1907. "Trade Cycles: The Periodic Rise and Fall in Prices, Wages, Etc.," *Iron Age*. October 24.

FRENCH, BEN C. and RAYMOND G. BRESSLER. 1962. "The Lemon Cycle," *Journal of Farm Economics*. Vol. XLIV; No. 4; November.

FRICKEY, EDWIN. 1942. *Economic Fluctuations in the United States:, A Systematic Analysis of Long-Run Trends and Business Cycles, 1866– 1914.* Cambridge: Harvard University Press.

FRIEDMAN, MILTON. 1959. "Money and Banking," *The Study of Economic Growth: Thirty-ninth Annual Report.* New York: National Bureau of Economic Research, Inc. May. pp. 52–53.

FRITZ, WILBERT G. 1934. *Contributions to Business-Cycle Theory: A Collection, Classification and Reference Manual.* Ann Arbor: Edwards Brothers, Inc.

FRUECHTE, RICHARD. 1953. Personal letter from the author to Edward R. Dewey dated March 20, 1953.

FUNK, E. M. 1931. *The Feed Purchasing Power of Eggs.* Pennsylvania State College Bulletin 262; February. p. 13.

GAFFNEY, M. MASON. 1960. See COLEAN, MILES L., ERNEST M. FISHER, and M. MASON GAFFNEY. 1960.

GARCIA-MATA, CARLOS. 1952. "First Reference to 41-month Cycle," *Cycles.* Vol. III; No. 4; April. p. 152.

GARCIA-MATA, CARLOS and FELIX SHAFFNER. 1934. "Solar and Economic Relationships: A Preliminary Report," *Quarterly Journal of Economics.* Vol. XLIX; November. pp. 1–51.

GAUBIS, ANTHONY. 1961. "My Thirty Years' Study of Stock Market Cycles," *Cycles.* Vol. XII; No. 2; February. pp. 31–41.

————. 1962-A. "What are the Timing Cycle Indications for 1962? A Talk Given December 12, 1961 to the New York Chapter of the Foundation for the Study of Cycles," *Cycles.* Vol. XIII; No. 2; February. pp. 41–46.

————. 1962-B. "Postscript to: 'What are the Timing Cycle Indications for 1962?'" *Cycles.* Vol. XIII; No. 9; September. pp. 248–250.

GERTLER, SIDNEY. 1946. "Construction and Business Cycles," *Survey of Current Business.* November.

GILBOY, ELIZABETH W. 1934. "Time Series and the Derivation of Demand and Supply Curves. A Study of Coffee and Tea, 1850–1930," *Quarterly Journal of Economics.* Vol. XLVIII. pp. 667–685.

GITLOW, ABRAHAM L. 1962. *Economics.* New York: Oxford University Press.

GODINHO, VITORINO MAGALHAES. 1955. *Prix et Monnaies au Portugal, 1750–1850.* Paris: Centre de Recherches Historiques.

GORDON, ROBERT AARON. 1961. *Business Fluctuations.* New York: Harper & Brothers Publishers.

GRAND. 1953. See WILLARD W. GRANT. 1953.

GRANGER, CLIVE W. J. 1960. "First Report of the Time Series Project,"
    Econometric Research Program, Research Memorandum Number 12.
    February 3.

GRANGER, CLIVE W. J. and OSKAR MORGENSTERN. 1963. "Spectral Anal-
    ysis of New York Stock Market Prices," *KYKLOS.* Vol. XVI; Fasc. 1.

GRANT, WILLARD W. (Pseudonym — Mr. GRAND). 1953. "45 6/7-day Cycle
    in a Common Stock," *Cycles.* Vol. IV; No. 6; June—July. pp. 178—181.

GRASSMAN, as reported by NISHIOKA, HIDEO. 1957. *Long Warm Weather
    Cycle Ahead — History of Cold and Warmth.* New York: International
    Economic Research Bureau.

GREBLER, LEO, DAVID BLANK, and LOUIS WINNICK. 1956. *Capital For-
    mation in Residential Real Estate.* Princeton, New Jersey: Princeton
    University Press.

GREEN, R. M. and H. HOWE. 1926. *Year-to-Year and Seasonal Fluctuations
    in Hog Prices.* Kansas State Agricultural Experiment Station Circular
    No. 132; December. p. 3.

GREENSTEIN, BENJAMIN. 1935. "Periodogram Analysis with Special Ap-
    plication to Failures in the United States, 1867—1932," *Econometrica.*
    Vol. 3. pp. 170—198.

GUTTENTAG, JACK M. 1961. "The Short Cycle in Residential Construction,
    1946—1959," *The American Economic Review.* Vol. LI; No. 3, June.

HAAS, G. C. and M. EZEKIEL. 1926. *Factors Affecting the Price of Hogs.*
    U.S.D.A. Bulletin 1440; November. p. 25. As quoted in HADORN,
    ERWIN T. 1949. *Cycles in Economic Data: A Digest.* Riverside,
    Connecticut: Foundation for the Study of Cycles.

HABERLER, GOTTFRIED. 1958. See VON HABERLER, GOTTFRIED. 1958.

HADORN, ERWIN T. 1947. "Trends in Cattle Numbers and Prices," *The
    Farm Outlook.* Columbia, Missouri: University of Missouri College of
    Agriculture and the United States Department of Agriculture, Cooper-
    ating. March 24.

_____ . 1948. *Research in Cycles in Agricultural Prices.* Not published.
    Department of Agricultural Economics, University of Missouri.

_____ . 1949-A. *Cycles in Economic Data: A Digest.* Riverside, Connect-
    icut: Foundation for the Study of Cycles.

_____ . 1949-B. *Research in Cycles in Agricultural Prices.* Not published.
    Department of Agricultural Economics, University of Missouri.

HAINES, WALTER W. 1961. *Money, Prices, and Policy*. New York: McGraw-Hill Book Company, Inc.

HALBERT, WILLIAM MORTON. 1878. *An Exploration of Economics and Financial Science Based Upon a Cycle of the Seasons in Each Decade.* London. As quoted in SMITH, EDGAR LAWRENCE. 1954. *When to Hold Common Stock and When to Reduce Holdings.* Darien, Connecticut.

HALD, EARL C. 1954. *Business Cycles.* Boston: Houghton Mifflin Company.

HALM, GEORGE N. 1961. *Economics of Money and Banking.* Homewood, Illinois: Richard D. Irwin, Inc.

HAMBERG, D. 1951. *Business Cycles.* New York: The Macmillan Company.

HAMILTON, DAVID. 1962. *The Consumer in Our Economy.* Boston: Houghton Mifflin Company.

HANAN, A., as quoted by HRASE, JOSEF. 1938. "Cycles Economiques en Tchecoslovaquie," *Societe Belge d'Etudes & d'Expansion.* No. 100.65.

HANAU, A. 1927. "Die Prognose der Schweenpreise," *Vierteljahreshefte zur Konjunkturforschung.* Sonderheft 2. As quoted by TINGERGEN, JAN and J. J. POLAK. 1950. *The Dynamics of Business Cycles: A Study in Economic Fluctuations.* Chicago: The University of Chicago Press.

HANLEY, LEWIS H. 1931. *Business Forecasting: The Principles and Practice of Forecasting Business and Stock Market Trends with Special Reference to Business Cycles.* New York: Ginn and Company.

HANSEN, A. H. 1941. *Fiscal Policy and Business Cycles.* New York: W. W. Norton and Company, Inc. p. 19. As reported by ACHINSTEIN, ASHER. 1950. *Introduction to Business Cycles.* New York: Thomas Y. Crowell Company.

HARDY, CHARLES O. and GARFIELD V. COX. 1928. *Forecasting Business Conditions.* New York: The Macmillan Company.

HARLOW, ARTHUR A. 1960. "The Hog Cycle and the Cobweb Theorum," *Journal of Farm Economics.* Vol. XLII; November. pp. 842–853.

HARRIS, SEYMOUR. 1961. *American Economic History.* New York: McGraw-Hill Book Company, Inc.

HARTKEMEIER, HARRY PELLE. 1943 "Review on Variability in Wheat Yields and Outputs," *Journal of Political Economy.* Vol. LI; No. 4; August.

HARVEY, JOHN. 1958. "The 9.25-year Cycle in the Dow-Jones Industrial Average," *Cycles.* Vol. IX; No. 11; November. pp. 298–301.

HASBROUCK, M. and L. 1941. "Certain Practical Conclusions Drawn from the Hasbrouck Research in Time Cycles," *The Hasbrouck Letters.* January 28.

HAWTREY, R. G. 1913. *Currency and Credit.* London: Longmans, Green and Co.

————. 1927. "The Monetary Theory of the Trade Cycle and Its Statistical Tests," *The Quarterly Journal of Economics.* May.

HAYS, LOUIS B. 1937. *Financial Time Table.* Mimeographed paper. Pittsburgh.

HEDGES, HAROLD. 1928. *Economic Aspects of the Cattle Industry of the Nebraska Sand Hills.* University of Nebraska College of Agriculture Experimental Station Bulletin 231; December. pp. 41–42. As quoted in HADORN, ERWIN T. 1949. *Cycles in Economic Data: A Digest.* Riverside, Connecticut: Foundation for the Study of Cycles.

HERSCHEL, WILLIAM, SIR. 1801. *Observations of the Sun.* London: Phil. Trans. Royal Society. As quoted in WILLIAMS, DAVID. 1961. "Sunspot Cycle Correlations," *Annals of the New York Academy of Sciences.* Vol. 95; No. 1; October 5. pp. 78–88.

HOPE, E. C. 1937. See ALLEN, W. and E. C. HOPE. 1937.

HOPKINS, JOHN A., JR. 1926. *A Statistical Study of the Prices and Production of Beef Cattle.* Iowa Agriculture Experimental Station Research Bulletin 101; December. As quoted in HADORN, ERWIN T. 1949. *Cycles in Economic Data: A Digest.* Riverside, Connecticut: Foundation for the Study of Cycles.

HORTON, BYRNE J. 1948. *Dictionary of Modern Economics.* Washington, D.C.: Public Affairs Press.

HOSKEN, FRANKLIN. 1953. *Bright Horizons.* May.

HOSKINS, CHAPIN. 1938. "Pig Iron Production," *Bus. Con. 69 – Harvard Business School.* Reprinted 1941.

————. 1939. Private communication with Edward R. Dewey.

HOWE, H. 1926. See GREEN, R. M. and H. HOWE. 1926.

HOYT, HOMER. 1933. *One Hundred Years of Land Values in Chicago.* Chicago: University of Chicago Press. pp. 382, 410, 474, 483. As quoted in WARREN, GEORGE F. and FRANK A. PEARSON. 1937. *World Prices and the Building Industry.* New York: John Wiley and Sons, Inc.

————. 1951. See BODFISH, MORTON and HOMER HOYT. 1951.

HRASE, JOSEF. 1938. "Cycles Economiques en Tchecoslovaquie," *Societe Belge d'Etudes & d'Expansion.* No. 100.65.

HUBBARD, JOSHUA C. 1942. "A Model of the Forty-Month or Trade Cycle," *The Journal of Political Economy*. Vol. L; No. 2; April.

HUGHES, E. M. 1940-A. "The Beef Cattle Cycle," *Illinois Farm Economics*. Vol. 59. pp. 333–334. As quoted in HADORN, ERWIN T. 1949. *Cycles in Economic Data: A Digest*. Riverside, Connecticut: Foundation for the Study of Cycles.

—————. 1940-B. "The Sheep Cycle," *Illinois Farm Economics*. Vol. 65. p. 415. As quoted in HADORN, ERWIN T. 1949. *Cycles in Economic Data: A Digest*. Riverside, Connecticut: Foundation for the Study of Cycles.

HUGHES, JONATHON R. T. 1961. See DAVIS, LANCE E., JONATHON R. T. HUGHES and DUNCAN M. McDOUGALL. 1961.

HUGHEY, VEDDER. 1956. (Also see pseudonym: PREDIX.) "A Cycle Analysis of General Motor Sales," *Cycles*. Vol. VII; No. 3; March. pp. 59–65.

HULL, GEORGE H. 1911. *Industrial Depressions*. New York: Frederick A. Stokes Company.

HUNT, STANLEY B. 1951. *The Rayon Organon*. New York: Textile Economics Bureau. Vol. XXII; No. 11; December. pp. 178–180. As quoted by DAVIS, THOMAS JEFFERSON. 1958. *Cycles and Trends in Textiles*. Washington: U. S. Department of Commerce. p. 14.

HUNTINGTON, ELLSWORTH. 1941. "Effect of Atmosphere Electricity on Business," *The Frontier*. Chicago: Armour Research Foundation. As quoted in KING, HUGH P. 1958. "Cycles in Financial Data," *Journal of Cycle Research*. Vol. 7; No. 1; January. p. 22.

—————. 1945. *Mainsprings of Civilization*. New York: John Wiley and Sons, Inc.

HUTNER, SIMEON. 1940. "Business Activity's Complex Cyclical Pattern: The Three Component Forces, a Composite Curve Derived Therefrom, and a Composite Obtained by Substituting a Sunspot Curve for the 11.14-year Cycle," *The Annalist*. June 13.

HYNDMAN, HENRY M. 1892. *Commercial Crises in the Nineteenth Century*. London: S. Sonnenschein and Company, Limited. As quoted in SCHUMPETER, JOSEPH A. 1939. *Business Cycles*. Vol. I and II. New York: McGraw-Hill Book Company, Inc.

THE INDUSTRIAL DIGEST. 1924. "Pig Iron Prices Due to Rise." November. Reprinted in *Cycles*. 1952. Vol. III; No. 8; October. p. 277.

ISARD, WALTER. 1942-A. "Transport Development and Building Cycles," *Quarterly Journal of Economics*. November.

—————. 1942-B. "A Neglected Cycle: The Transport-Building Cycle," *Review of Economic Statistics*. November.

JEVONS, H. S. 1909. "Changes in the Sun's Heat as Causes of Fluctuations of the Activity of Trade and Unemployment," *Contemporary Review*. August. As quoted in KING, WILLFORD I. 1938. *The Causes of Economic Fluctuations*. New York: Ronald Press Co.

———. 1910. *The Causes of Unemployment, the Sun's Heat, and Trade Activity*. London.

JEVONS, WILLIAM STANLEY. 1875. "The Solar Period and the Price of Corn." Not published. As reported by WILLIAMS, DAVID. 1959. "Business Cycle Forecasting," *Journal of Cycle Research*. Vol. 8; No. 2; April. pp. 39–63.

———. 1878. "The Periodicity of Commercial Crises and Its Physical Explanation," *Investigations in Currency and Finance*. pp. 207, 214–216.

———. 1909. *Investigations in Currency and Finance*. 2nd Edition. London: The Macmillan and Co., Ltd. As quoted in KING, HUGH P. 1958. "Cycles in Financial Data," *Journal of Cycle Research*. Vol. 7; No. 1; January.

JOHNSON, ALVIN S. 1915. "Causes of Crisis," *New Republic*. Vol. II. pp. 17–19.

JOHNSON, L. P. V. 1940. "Relation of Sunspot Periodicity to Precipitation, Temperature, and Crop Yields in Alberta and Saskatchewan," *Canadian Journal of Research*. Vol. 18; March. pp. 79–91.

JORDAN, DAVID F. 1927. *Practical Business Forecasting*. Englewood Cliffs, New Jersey: Prentice-Hall, Inc.

KENDALL, MAURICE G. 1960. *The Advanced Theory of Statistics*. Vol. II. New York: Hafner Publishing Company.

KENNEDY, JOHN W. 1962. See DODD, JAMES HARVEY, JOHN W. KENNEDY and ARTHUR R. OLSEN. 1962.

KING, HUGH P. 1958. "Cycles in Financial Data," *Journal of Cycle Research*. Vol. 7; No. 1; January. pp. 3–40.

KING, WILLFORD I. 1931. "Has the Business Cycle a Definite Wave Length? — Evidence Points That Way," *The Annalist*. May 1.

———. 1938. *The Causes of Economic Fluctuations: Possibilities of Anticipation and Control*. New York: The Ronald Press Co.

KIRKBRIDE, FRANKLIN B. 1939. "Do Wars Last Forever?" *Trusts and Estates*. October.

KITCHIN, JOSEPH. 1923. "Cycles and Trends in Economic Factors," *The Review of Economic Statistics*. Cambridge, Massachusetts: Harvard Economic Service. Vol. 5; No. 1; January. pp. 10–16.

KLEMME, CARL J. 1950. "The Sales Forecast... and its Relation to Production Control" (an A.P.M.A. paper read at the Central Section meeting of the American Pharmaceutical Manufacturers Association in Chicago, February 4, 1950), *Drug and Allied Industries.* June.

KONDRATIEFF, N. D. 1922. *The World Economy and its Conjectures During and After the War.* Vologda. p. 242. As reported by KUZNETS, SIMON S. 1930. *Secular Movements in Production and Prices.* Boston: Houghton-Mifflin Company. Chapter IV.

_____. 1926. "Die langen Wellen der Konjunktur," *Archiv fur Sozialwissenschaft und Sozialpolitik.* Vol. 56. pp. 573–609. Translated by W.F. Stolper and printed under the title of "The Long Waves in Economic Life," *The Review of Economic Statistics.* Vol. 17; No. 6; November 1935. pp. 105–115. Reprinted in *Cycles.* Vol. IV; No. 10; December 1953. pp. 349–360.

KUZNETS, SIMON S. 1930. *Secular Trends in Production and Prices:* A Hart, Schaffner and Marx Prize Essay. Boston: Houghton Mifflin Company. Also as cited in "Is the Long Cycle Why We Don't Grow?" *Business Week.* February 16, 1963. p. 78.

LANE, G. T. 1954. As reported by DEWEY, EDWARD R. 1954-I. "The 41-month Cycle in Stock Prices," *Cycles.* Vol. V; No. 5; May. pp. 176–179.

LANGHAM, JAMES M. 1954. "Year in Advance Forecast," *1955 Stocks.* Santa Monica, California: James M. Langham.

LAVINGTON, F. 1944. *The Trade Cycle.* Westminster, England: P. S. King & Staples, Limited.

LIGHTNER, OTTO C. 1922. *History of Business Depressions.* As quoted by THORP, WILLARD LONG. 1926. *Business Annals.* New York: National Bureau of Economic Research, Inc.

LONDON TIMES. 1857. See DAVIS, LANCE E., JONATHON R. T. HUGHES and DUNCAN M. McDOUGALL. 1961.

LONG, CLARENCE D., JR. 1940. *Building Cycles and the Theory of Investment.* Princeton: Princeton University Press.

LORIE, JAMES H. 1947. "Causes of Annual Fluctuations in the Production of Livestock and Livestock Products," *Studies in Business Administration.* pp. 60–62. As quoted in HADORN, ERWIN T. 1949. *Cycles in Economic Data: A Digest.* Riverside, Connecticut: Foundation for the Study of Cycles.

LÖSCH, AUGUST. 1937. "Population Cycles as a Cause of Business Cycles," *Quarterly Journal of Economics.* August. pp. 649–662.

MACAULEY, FREDERICK R. 1947. "Rhythmic Cycles in the Stock Market," *The Commercial and Financial Chronicle.* Vol. 165; June 12. p. 4602.

MACK, RUTH P. 1957. "Notes on Subcycles in Theory and Practice," *American Economic Review*. Vol. 47; May. pp. 161–174.

————. 1958. "Subcycles," *Investing in Economic Knowledge*. National Bureau of Economic Research, Inc. Thirty-eighth Annual Report. May.

MACK, RUSSELL H. 1956. See ABRAMSON, ADOLPH G. and RUSSELL H. MACK. 1956.

MACLEOD. No Date. *Dictionary of Political Economy*. As reported by SMITH, EDGAR LAWRENCE. 1939. *Tides in the Affairs of Men*. New York: The Macmillan Company. p. 17.

MAISEL, SHERMAN, J. 1957. *Fluctuations, Growth and Forecasting: The Principles of Dynamic Business Economics*. New York: John Wiley and Sons.

MAKI, WILBUR R. 1962. "Decomposition of the Beef and Pork Cycles," *Journal of Farm Economics*. Vol. XLIV; No. 3; August.

MALINOWSKI, ALEXANDER. 1952. "The Three-year Cycle in Industrial Common Stock Prices," *Cycles*. Vol. III; No. 7; September. pp. 233–235.

MALLERY, OTTO T. 1919. "A National Policy – Public Works to Stabilize Employment," *The Annals of the American Academy of Political and Social Sciences*. January.

MASSACHUSETTS RAILROAD COMMISSION. 1895. *26th Annual Report of the (Massachusetts) Board of Railway Commissioners*. Boston. p. 13. As reported by DORFMAN, GEORGE. 1949. *The Economic Mind in American Civilization, 1865–1918. Volume III*. New York: The Viking Press.

MATTHEWS, R. C. O. 1959. *The Business Cycle*. Chicago: The University of Chicago Press.

MAVERICK, L. A. 1932. "Cycles in Real Estate Activity," *Journal of Land and Public Utility Economics*. Vol. 8. p. 199. As quoted in WARREN, GEORGE F. and FRANK A. PEARSON. 1937. *World Prices and the Building Industry*. New York: John Wiley and Sons, Inc.

McCABE, JOSEPH. 1924. See CASSELL, GUSTAV. 1924.

McCONNELL, CAMPBELL R. 1960. *Elementary Economics: Principles, Problems, and Policies*. New York: McGraw-Hill Book Company, Inc.

McCORMACK, GEORGE J. 1947. "The Moon's Node: An Important Cyclic Indicator," *Yearbook of A.F.A.*

McDOUGALL, E. HUGH. 1958-A. "Cycles in Consols," *Investors Chronical and Money Market Review*. London. Reprinted in *Cycles*. Vol. X; No. 1; January. pp. 11–14.

————. 1958-B. "Cycles in Ordinary Shares," *Investors Chronicle and Money Market Review.* Reprinted in *Cycles.* 1959. Vol. X; No. 3; March.

McDOUGALL, DUNCAN M. 1961. See DAVIS, LANCE E., JONATHON R. T. HUGHES, and DUNCAN M. McDOUGALL. 1961.

McGRATH, THOMAS ORRIN. 1936. *Anticipating the Future.* Los Angeles: Thomas Orrin McGrath.

MEVES, W. 1911. See FEIG, J. and W. MEVES. 1911.

MILLS, FREDERICK C. 1926. "An Hypothesis Concerning the Duration of Business Cycles," *Journal of the American Statistical Association.* Vol. XXI; December. pp. 447–457.

————. 1959. As reported by SHIRK, GERTRUDE. 1959-I. "What's Ahead for Hog Prices? A Short-Term View," *Cycles.* Vol. X; No. 10; October. pp. 221–227.

MILLS, JOHN. 1867. "On Credit Cycles and the Origin of Commercial Panics," *Transactions of the Manchester Statistical Society,* 1867–1868.

MINTZ, ILSE. 1961. *American Exports During Business Cycles, 1879–1958.* New York: National Bureau of Economic Research, Inc.

MITCHELL, WESLEY C. 1926. See THORP, W. L. and W. C. MITCHELL. 1926.

————. 1927. *Business Cycles: The Problem and Its Setting.* New York: National Bureau of Economic Research, Inc.

————. 1946. See BURNS, ARTHUR F. and WESLEY C. MITCHELL. 1946.

MOORE, HENRY L. 1923. *Generating Economic Cycles.* New York: The Macmillan Company.

MORGENSTERN, OSKAR. 1959. *International Financial Transactions and Business Cycles.* A Study by the National Bureau of Economic Research, Inc. Princeton: Princeton University Press.

————. 1963. See GRANGER, CLIVE W. J. and OSKAR MORGENSTERN. 1963.

MORRIS, WILLIAM W. 1948. *Sunspots and Crop Production.* Madison, Wisconsin: William W. Morris.

MORSE, TRUE D. 1948. "How You Can Profit by Cycles," *Farm Journal.* March. pp. 26–27.

MUSHAM, HARRY A. 1943. "The Practical Application of the Rhythmic Fluctuation of the Levels of the Great Lakes," *Journal of the Western Society of Engineers.* Vol. 48; No. 4; December. pp. 185–196.

MYERS, W. I. 1939. See PEARSON, F. A., W. I. MYERS, and G. E. BRANDOW. 1939.

———. 1941. See PEARSON, F. A. and W. I. MYERS. 1941.

———. 1952. See PEARSON, F. A., W. I. MYERS, DON PAARLBERG, and H. DEGRAFF. 1952.

NAKAME, SATOSHI, as reported by NISHIOKA, HIDEO. 1957. *Long Warm Weather Cycle Ahead: History of Cold and Warmth.* New York: International Economic Research Bureau.

NANCE, GORDON B. 1953. "A 14- to 16-year Cycle in Beef Cattle Prices," *Weekly Star Farmer.* Columbia, Missouri. May 6. Reprinted in *Cycles.* 1953. Vol. IV; No. 10; December. pp. 338–339.

NAUMANN, A. L. 1960. See SNAPP, ROSCOE R. and A. L. NAUMANN, 1960.

NEAL, ALFRED C. 1953. See BURNS, ARTHUR EDWARD, ALFRED C. NEAL and D. S. WATSON. 1953.

NEFF, PHILIP and ANNETTE WEIFENBACH. 1949. *Business Cycles in Selected Industrial Areas.* Berkeley: University of California Press.

NEWBURY, FRANK D. 1938. *The Cycle of Pittsburgh Production.* Pittsburgh: Westinghouse Electric and Manufacturing Company.

———. 1947. "A Forecast of Business Prospects," *Harvard Business Review.* Spring.

———. 1952. *Business Forecasting: Principles and Practice.* New York: McGraw-Hill Book Company, Inc.

NEWMAN, WILLIAM H. 1935. "The Building Industry," *The Journal of Business of the University of Chicago: Studies in Business Administration.* Vol. V; No. 4.

NISHIOKA, HIDEO. 1957. *Long Warm Weather Cycle Ahead: History of Cold and Warmth.* New York: International Economic Research Bureau.

NORTH, DOUGLASS C. 1961. *The Economic Growth of the United States, 1790–1860.* Englewood Cliffs, New Jersey: Prentice-Hall, Inc. pp. 11–12.

NORTON, L. J. and B. B. WILSON. 1930. *Prices of Illinois Farm Products from 1866 to 1929.* Illinois Agriculture Experimental Station Bulletin 351. pp. 537, 573.

OLSEN, ARTHUR R. 1962. See DODD, JAMES HARVEY, JOHN W. KENNEDY and ARTHUR R. OLSEN.

OZGA, S. A. 1955. See BROWN, E. H. PHELPS and S. A. OZGA. 1955.

PAARLBERG, DON. 1947. "Prices of Milk, Butter, and Beef," *Farm Economics*. No. 153. pp. 3970–3972.

————. 1952. See PEARSON, F. A., W. I. MYERS, DON PAARLBERG and H. DEGRAFF. 1952.

PEARSON, FRANK A. 1937. See WARREN, GEORGE F. and FRANK A. PEARSON. 1937.

————. 1940. *Farm Economics*. No. 118. p. 2918.

————. 1942. *Farm Economics*. No. 130. pp. 3267–3275.

————. 1954. *The Tempest in the Coffee Pot*. Agricultural Experiment Station. A. E. 960.

PEARSON, F. A., J. V. CASSETTA and K. R. BENNETT. 1941. *Pepper*. Ithaca, New York: Cornell University. p. 16.

PEARSON, F. A., and W. I. MYERS. 1955. "Potatoes," *Farm Economics*. No. 198; January. p. 5215.

————. 1957. "The Fact Finder," *Farm Economics*. No. 208; February. p. 5470.

PEARSON, F. A., W. I. MYERS and K. R. BENNETT. 1954. "Prices, Supplies and Demands for Hogs and Pork," *Farm Economics*. No. 195; June. pp. 5142–5151.

PEARSON, F. A., W. I. MYERS and G. E. BRANDOW. 1939. "Industrial Cycles and Business Activity," *Farm Economics*. No. 111; February. pp. 2687–2703.

PEARSON, F. A., W. I. MYERS, DON PAARLBERG and H. DEGRAFF. 1952. "Prices, Building, and History," *The Appraisal Journal*. Vol. XX; No. 2; April.

PEARSON, F. A., W. I. MYERS and W. M. CURTISS. 1940. "Livestock," *Farm Economics*. No. 118; April. p. 2921.

————. 1943. "Livestock," *Farm Economics*. No. 135; July. p. 3429.

————. 1944. "Livestock," *Farm Economics*. No. 140; April. p. 3566.

PEARSON, F. A., W. I. MYERS and J. H. LORIE. 1945-A. "Rents, Building Activity and Full Employment," *Farm Economics*. No. 147; October. pp. 3746–3751.

————. 1945-B. "Meat," *Farm Economics*. No. 145; April.

PEARSON, F. A., W. I. MYERS and E. E. VIAL. 1954. "Cycles in Prices, Supplies and Demands for Cattle," *Farm Economics*. No. 193; February. p. 5072.

PETRIE, SIR W. M. FLINDERS. 1948. "Cycles of Economy and Waste and Cycles of Civilization," *Nature.* Vol. 148; October 1.

PETTY, SIR WILLIAM. 1662. As cited by FRITZ, WILBERT G. 1934. *Contributions to Business-Cycle Theory: A Collection, Classification and Reference Manual.* Ann Arbor: Edwards Brothers, Inc. p. 1.

PIERCE, HOWARD C. 1949. See BENJAMIN, EARL W., HOWARD C. PIERCE and WILLIAM D. TERMOHLEN. 1949.

PIGOU, ARTHUR C. 1920. *The Economics of Welfare.* London. pp. 827–830, 841–848. As cited by MITCHELL, WESLEY C. 1927. *Business Cycles: The Problem and Its Setting.* New York: National Bureau of Economic Research, Inc.

PINKHAM, CHARLES H. 1952. "Cycles in the Sales and Advertising of the Pinkham Medicine Company," *Cycles.* Vol. III; No. 1; January.

————. 1956. "Observations on the 6-year Cycle," *Cycles.* Vol. VII; No. 5; May. pp. 129–134.

POLAK, J. J. 1950. See TINBERGEN, JAN and J. J. POLAK. 1950.

PREDIX (pseudonym for HUGHEY, VEDDER). 1951. *Cyclical Analysis: Industrial Common Stock Index, 1854–1951.* Coral Gables, Florida: Predix. *(Predix Plate I* was reprinted in *Cycles.* 1953. Vol. IV; No. 3; March. pp. 79–98. *Predix Plate I-A* was reprinted in *Cycles.* 1953. Vol. IV; No. 4; April. pp. 123–130. *Predix Plate II* was reprinted in *Cycles.* 1953. Vol. IV; No. 5; May. pp. 157–162).

PROCTOR, R. A. 1880. "Sunspots and Financial Panics," *Scribners.* Vol. 20; No. 2; June.

RADICE, E. A. 1939. "A Dynamic Scheme for the British Trade Cycle," *Econometrica.* Vol. 7; No. 1; January. pp. 477–506.

REICH, E. 1912. "Der Wohnungsmarkt in Berlin Von 1840–1910," *Staats und Sozialwissenschaftliche Forschungen.* Heft 164. pp. 139–140. As reported in WARREN, GEORGE F. and FRANK A. PEARSON. 1937. *World Prices and the Building Industry.* New York: John Wiley and Sons.

RIGGLEMAN, J. R. 1933. "Building Cycles in the United States, 1830–1935," *Journal of American Statistical Association.* Vol. 28. As reported by WARREN, GEORGE F. and FRANK A. PEARSON. 1937. *World Prices and the Building Industry.* New York: John Wiley and Sons, Inc. Also reported by LONG, CLARENCE D., JR. 1940. *Building Cycles and the Theory of Investment.* Princeton, New Jersey: Princeton University Press.

————. 1934. *Variations in Building Activity in United States Cities.* John Hopkins University Library. pp. 38–39. As reported by LONG, CLARENCE D., JR. 1940. *Building Cycles and the Theory of Investment.* Princeton, New Jersey: Princeton University Press.

RINGER, C. R. 1955. "LETTERS: A Stock Market Forecast," *Cycles*. Vol. VI; No. 1; January. pp. 18–19.

RONK, S. E. No Date. *Prices of Farm Products in New York State, 1841– 1935.* Cornell University Agricultural Experimental Station Bulletin 643. p. 34. As quoted in HADORN, ERWIN T. 1949. *Cycles in Economic Data: A Digest.* Riverside, Connecticut: Foundation for the Study of Cycles.

ROOS, CHARLES F. 1934. *Dynamic Economics.* Bloomington, Indiana.

————. 1948. *Charting the Course of Your Business.* New York: Funk and Wagnalls Company. As quoted by NEWBURY, FRANK D. 1952. *Business Forecasting: Principles and Practice.* New York: McGraw-Hill Book Company, Inc.

————. 1955. "Survey of Economic Forecasting Techniques," *Econometrica.* Vol. 23; No. 4.

ROSE, ALBERT. 1941. "Wars, Innovations and Long Cycles: A Brief Comment," *American Economic Review.* Vol. XXXI; No. 1; March. pp. 105– 107.

ROSS, ROBERT C. 1951. *An Introduction to Agricultural Economics.* New York: McGraw-Hill Book Company, Inc. pp. 144–146.

ROUNTREE, G. MEREDITH. 1948. *Study of Cyclical Fluctuations in Freight Traffic. Interim Report.* Montreal, Canada: Canadian Pacific Railway Company. November.

————. 1951. "Cycles in Canadian Pacific Railway Freight Traffic," *Journal of Cycle Research.* Vol. 1; No. 1; Autumn. pp. 6–19.

SAUL, S. B. 1962. "House Building in England, 1890–1914," *The Economic History Review; Second Series.* Vol. XV; No. 1; August. pp. 119–137.

SCHMIDT, CARL T. 1934. *German Business Cycles, 1924–1933.* New York: National Bureau of Economic Research, Inc.

SCHUMANN, C. G. W. 1938. *Structural Changes and Business Cycles in South Africa, 1806–1936.* London: Staples Press Limited.

SCHUMPETER, JOSEPH A. 1939. *Business Cycles, Vol. I and Vol. II.* New York: McGraw-Hill Book Company, Inc.

SCOTT, WILLIAM ROBERT. 1912. *Constitution and Finance of English, Scottish and Irish Joint-Stock Companies to 1720. Volume 1.* Cambridge.

SEAGER, GEORGE B. 1958. "Letters to the Editor: Short Stock Market Cycles," *Cycles.* Vol. IX; No. 3; April. p. 91.

————. 1962. "Stock Market Cycle Folklore: A Talk Given October 19, 1961, to the New York Chapter of the Foundation for the Study of Cycles," *Cycles.* Vol. XIII; No. 2; February. pp. 47–50.

SHAFFNER, FELIX. 1934. See GARCIA-MATA, CARLOS and FELIX
SHAFFNER. 1934.

SHANNON, H. A. 1934. "Bricks — A Trade Index, 1785–1849," *Economica,
New Series*. No. 3; August. pp. 300–318. As quoted in WARREN,
GEORGE F. and FRANK A. PEARSON. 1937. *World Prices and the
Building Industry*. New York: John Wiley and Sons, Inc.

SHAW, as reported by NISHIOKA, HIDEO. 1957. *Long Warm Weather Cycle
Ahead: History of Cold and Warmth*. New York: International Economic
Research Bureau.

SHEPHERD, GEOFFREY S. 1941. *Agricultural Price Analysis*. Ames, Iowa:
Iowa State College Press. pp. 58, 62–64. As reported by HADORN,
ERWIN T. 1949. *Cycles in Economic Data: A Digest*. Riverside, Con-
necticut: Foundation for the Study of Cycles.

——————. 1947. *Agricultural Price Analysis*. Ames, Iowa: Iowa State College Press.

SHILLADY, JOHN R. 1916. "Planning Public Expenditures to Compensate
for Decreased Private Employment During Business Depression," *Pro-
ceedings of the National Conference of Charities and Corrections, 43rd
Session*.

SHINOHARA, MIYOHEI. 1962. *Growth and Cycles in the Japanese Economy*.
Tokyo: Institute of Economic Research at Hitotsubashi University.

SHIRK, GERTRUDE. 1958-A. "Automobiles," *Cycles*. Vol. IX; No. 11; November. p. 309.

——————. 1958-B. "The 7-year Cycle in Railroad Stock Prices," *Cycles*.
Vol. IX; No. 11; November. pp. 285–287.

——————. 1958-C. "The 7-year Cycle in Stock Prices," *Cycles*. Vol. IX;
No. 8; August. pp. 187–190.

——————. 1958-D. "The 17-week Cycle in Industrial Stock Prices," *Cycles*.
Vol. IX; No. 7; July. pp. 149–154.

——————. 1958-E. "The 6.4-year Cycle in Primary Aluminum Production,
U.S.A., 1886–1957," *Journal of Cycle Research*. Vol. 7; No. 2; April.
pp. 49–62.

——————. 1958-F. "What's Ahead for Egg Prices?" *Cycles*. Vol. IX; No.
4; April. pp. 86–87.

——————. 1958-G. "What's Ahead for Oats Prices?" *Cycles*. Vol. IX; No.
9; September. pp. 217–220.

——————. 1959-A. "Dunbar's 46-month Stock Price Cycle," *Cycles*. Vol.
X; No. 6; June. pp. 130–131.

————. 1959-B. "The 18 1/3-year Cycle in Real Estate Activity," *Cycles.* Vol. X; No. 2; February. p. 31.

————. 1959-C. "The 11.2-year Cycle in Pig Iron Production," *Cycles.* Vol. X; No. 3; March. pp. 57–59.

————. 1959-D. "The 5.91-year Cycle in Cotton Prices," *Cycles.* Vol. X; No. 2; February. pp. 29–30.

————. 1959-E. "The Stock Market Projection: Audit of the 11-year Cycle," *Cycles.* Vol. X; No. 8; August. pp. 173–175.

————. 1959-F. "The 3.9-year Cycle in Grass Seed Production," *Cycles.* Vol. X; No. 11; November. p. 249.

————. 1959-G. "The 2-year Cycle in Textiles," *Cycles.* Vol. X; No. 7; July. pp. 155–158.

————. 1959-H. "What's Ahead for Cotton Consumption?" *Cycles.* Vol. X; No. 5; May. pp. 101–103.

————. 1959-I. "What's Ahead for Hog Prices: A Short Term View," *Cycles.* Vol. X; No. 10; October. pp. 221–227.

————. 1959-J. "Aluminum Production," *Cycles.* Vol. X; No. 5; May. p. 115.

————. 1959-K. "Cotton Prices," *Cycles.* Vol. X; No. 11; November. p. 257.

————. 1959-L. "Copper Prices," *Cycles.* Vol. X; No. 5; May. p. 111.

————. 1960-A. "Actual Wheat Prices Match a Theoretical Low," *Cycles.* Vol. XI; No. 10; October. pp. 231–232.

————. 1960-B. "The Decennial Pattern in Stock Prices," *Cycles.* Vol. XI; No. 2; February. pp. 35–36.

————. 1960-C. "Dunbar's 46-month Stock Price Cycle," *Cycles.* Vol. XI; No. 4; April. pp. 78–79.

————. 1960-D. "During 1960 Cycles in Durable Goods Orders May Cancel Out," *Cycles.* Vol. XI; No. 7; July. pp. 150–151.

————. 1960-E. "Hog Prices Climb with the Cycles," *Cycles.* Vol. XI; No. 11; November. p. 256.

————. 1960-F. "The Hutner Cycle Analysis," *Cycles.* Vol. XI; No. 3; March. p. 59.

————. 1960-G. "The Hutner Cycle Analysis," *Cycles.* Vol. XI; No. 6; June. p. 129.

————. 1960-H. "Nonresidential Building May Have Passed the Peak," *Cycles*. Vol. XI; No. 10; October. pp. 221–222.

————. 1960-I. "A Possible 4.43-year Cycle in the Price of Lead," *Cycles*. Vol. XI; No. 12; December. pp. 275–277.

————. 1960-J. "A Possible 34-week Stock Cycle," *Cycles*. Vol. XI; No. 3; March. p. 56.

————. 1960-K. "The 17-week Cycle in Stocks: How Good Is It?" *Cycles*. Vol. XI; No. 8; August. pp. 174–177.

————. 1960-L. "Shoe Production in 1960," *Cycles*. Vol. XI; No. 3; March. pp. 53–55.

————. 1960-M. "Smith's Decennial Pattern Still looks Good," *Cycles*. Vol. XI; No. 10; October. p. 233.

————. 1960-N. "Stock Prices," *Cycles*. Vol. XI; No. 9; September. pp. 206–207.

————. 1960-O. "What's Ahead for Cocoa Bean Prices: A Short Term View," *Cycles*. Vol. XI; No. 1; January. pp. 5–8.

————. 1960-P. "Egg Price Cycles Continue to Operate," *Cycles*. Vol. XI; No. 11; November. p. 255.

————. 1960-Q. "Oats Prices," *Cycles*. Vol. XI; No. 8; August. pp. 183–184.

————. 1960-R. "Who's to Blame: Writers, Publishers, Public?" *Cycles*. Vol. XI; No. 7; July. p. 154.

————. 1960-S. "Bond Yields," *Cycles*. Vol. XI; No. 2; February. p. 44.

————. 1960-T. "Corn Prices," *Cycles*. Vol. XI; No. 7; July. p. 162.

————. 1960-U. "Liabilities of Failures," *Cycles*. Vol. XI; No. 3; March. pp. 68–69.

————. 1961-A. "Aluminum Production," *Cycles*. Vol. XII; No. 6; June. p. 160.

————. 1961-B. "The 49.33-week Cycle in the Price of General Motors Common Stock," *Cycles*. Vol. XII; No. 11; November. pp. 291–295.

————. 1961-C. "How It Came Out: Benner's Pig Iron Price Forecast," *Cycles*. Vol. XII; No. 11; November. pp. 283–289.

————. 1961-D. "A Possible 17.63-week Cycle in Westinghouse Electric Stock Prices," *Cycles*. Vol. XII; No. 6; June. pp. 145–148.

————. 1961-E. "Postscript to: 'My Thirty Years' Study of Stock Market Cycles,'" *Cycles*. Vol. XII; No. 4; April. pp. 88–91.

―――――. 1961-F. "The 35.4-month Cycle in Industrial Common Stocks," *Cycles*. Vol. XII; No. 7; July. pp. 169–172.

―――――. 1961-G. "A Possible 32-week Cycle in Westinghouse Electric Stock Prices," *Cycles*. Vol. XII; No. 3; March. pp. 68–73.

―――――. 1961-H. "What's Ahead? The Cycle Outlook for Auto Sales," *Cycles*. Vol. XII; No. 10; October. pp. 249–253.

―――――. 1961-I. "Wheat Prices," *Cycles*. Vol. XII; No. 12; December. p. 328.

―――――. 1961-J. "Oats," *Cycles*. Vol. XII; No. 9; September. p. 233.

―――――. 1961-K. "Cocoa," *Cycles*. Vol. XII; No. 9; September. pp. 234–235.

―――――. 1961-L. "Average Weekly Hours Worked in Manufacturing," *Cycles*. Vol. XII; No. 10; October. p. 272.

―――――. 1961-M. "Corn Prices," *Cycles*. Vol. XII; No. 12; December.

―――――. 1961-N. "Cotton Consumption," *Cycles*. Vol. XII; No. 12; December. p. 331.

―――――. 1961-O. "Cycles in the Stock Market," *Cycles*. Vol. XII; No. 5; May. pp. 109–112.

―――――. 1961-P. "Egg Prices," *Cycles*. Vol. XII; No. 12; December. p. 328.

―――――. 1961-Q. "No Increase in Residential Construction," *Cycles*. Vol. XII; No. 1; January. p. 12.

―――――. 1961-R. "The Price of Copper Shares," *Cycles*. Vol. XII; No. 9; September. p. 237.

―――――. 1961-S. "The 17-week Cycle," *Cycles*. Vol. XII; No. 9; September. p. 237.

―――――. 1961-T. "Shoe Production," *Cycles*. Vol. XII; No. 12; December. p. 329.

―――――. 1962-A. "Cycles in the Price of Copper," *Cycles*. Vol. XIII; No. 1; January. pp. 5–11.

―――――. 1962-B. "A Review of Hog Price Cycles," *Cycles*. Vol. XIII; No. 1; January. pp. 22–23.

―――――. 1962-C. "What Is It All About?" *Cycles*. Vol. XIII; No. 3; March. pp. 61–63, 67.

―――――. 1962-D. "Bond Yields," *Cycles*. Vol. XIII; No. 3; March. p. 65.

————. 1962-E. "New Orders," *Cycles*. Vol. XIII; No. 3; March. p. 68.

————. 1962-F. "Residential Building," *Cycles*. Vol. XIII; No. 3; March. p. 69.

————. 1962-G. "Cycles in Westinghouse Stock Prices," *Cycles*. Vol. XIII; No. 3; March. p. 72.

————. 1962-H. "Shoe Production," *Cycles*. Vol. XIII; No. 3; March. p. 73.

————. 1962-I. "Cotton Consumption," *Cycles*. Vol. XIII; No. 3; March.

————. 1962-J. "Wheat Prices," *Cycles*. Vol. XIII; No. 3; March. p. 74.

————. 1962-K. "Passenger Car Factory Sales," *Cycles*. Vol. XIII; No. 3; March. p. 75.

————. 1962-L. "A Possible 12.32-week Cycle in the Price of General Motors Common Stock," *Cycles*. Vol. XIII; No. 4; April. pp. 99–101.

————. 1962-M. "Record of the Price of Chrysler Stock," *Cycles*. Vol. XIII; No. 5; May. pp. 126–127.

————. 1962-N. "A Review: Cocoa Bean Prices," *Cycles*. Vol. XIII; No. 5; May. pp. 132–133.

————. 1962-O. "The 23.6-month Cycle in Layoffs," *Cycles*. Vol. XIII; No. 6; June. pp. 162–163.

————. 1962-P. "Wheat Prices," *Cycles*. Vol. XIII; No. 8; August. p. 227.

————. 1962-Q. "Egg Prices," *Cycles*. Vol. XIII; No. 9; September. p. 257.

————. 1962-R. "Patents Issued," *Cycles*. Vol. XIII; No. 10; October. p. 290.

————. 1962-S. "Cotton Consumption," *Cycles*. Vol. XIII; No. 10; October. p. 291.

————. 1962-T. "Shoe Production," *Cycles*. Vol. XIII; No. 11; November. p. 322.

————. 1962-U. "Hog Prices," *Cycles*. Vol. XIII; No. 11; November. p. 324.

————. 1962-V. "Bond Yields," *Cycles*. Vol. XIII; No. 11; November.

————. 1963-A. "On Some Difficulties in Using Cycles," *Cycles*. Vol. XIV; No. 2; February. p. 36.

————. 1963-B. "Egg Prices: The Evolution of a Cycle Study," *Cycles*. Vol. XIV; No. 3; March. pp. 65–67.

SHISKIN, JULIUS. 1961. *Signals of Recession and Recovery*. New York: National Bureau of Economic Research, Inc.

SILBERLING, N. J. 1943. *The Dynamics of Business*. New York: McGraw-Hill Book Company. As reported in WILLIAMS, DAVID. 1961. "Sunspot Cycle Correlations," *Annals of the New York Academy of Sciences*. Vol. 95; No. 1; October 5.

SILK, LEONARD. 1948. *Sweden Plans for Better Housing*. Durham, North Carolina: Duke University Press.

SMITH, BRADFORD B. 1928. "Factors Affecting the Price of Cotton," *U.S.D.A. Technical Bulletin 50*. p. 2. As quoted in HADORN, ERWIN T. 1949. *Cycles in Economic Data: A Digest*. Riverside Connecticut: Foundation for the Study of Cycles.

SMITH, EDGAR LAWRENCE. 1939. *Tides in the Affairs of Men*. New York: The Macmillan Company.

————— . 1947. "The Decennial Pattern: A Calendar for the Business Cycle," *Brookmire Pioneer*. Vol. 36 ; No. P-2; March 21.

————— . 1948. "1949: A Battleground for Cycles," *Brookmire Pioneer*. Vol. 37; No. P-5; August 27.

————— . 1949. "Realistic View of 1950 Needed for Investor's Safety," *Brookmire Pioneer*. Vol. 37; No. P-8; December 15.

————— . 1954. *When to Hold Common Stocks and When to Reduce Holdings*. Darien, Connecticut: Edgar Lawrence Smith.

————— . 1959. *Common Stocks and Business Cycles*. New York: William-Frederick Press.

SNAPP, ROSCOE R. and A. L. NAUMANN. 1960. *Beef Cattle*. New York: John Wiley and Sons, Inc.

SPAID, J. F. 1949. "Turkey Prices," *Farm Economics*. Vol. 172; November.

SPIETHOFF, A. 1902. "Vorbemerkugen zu einer Theorie der Ueberproduktion," *Jahrbuch fur Gesetzgebung, Verwaltung und Volkswirtschaft*. Also "Krisen," *Handworterbuch der Staatswissenchaften*. 1925. As quoted by VON HABERLER, GOTTFRIED. 1928. *Prosperity and Depression: A Theoretical Analysis of Cyclical Movements*. Cambridge, Massachusetts: Harvard University Press.

————— . 1923. "Krisen," *Handworterbuch der Staatswissenchaften*. Fourth Edition. As reported in SCHUMPETER, JOSEPH A. 1939. *Business Cycles, Vol. I*. p. 164.

SPRAKE, AUSTIN. 1959. *Booms and Slumps*. New York: Pageant Press Inc.

STANBACK, T. M., JR. 1958. "The Textile Cycle: Characteristics and Contributing Factors," *The Southern Economic Journal.* Vol. XXV; No. 2; October. pp. 174–188.

STETSON, HARLAN T. 1937. *Sunspots and Their Effects.* York, Pennsylvania: Whittlesey House.

————. 1946. "Sunspots. . . . And Business Activity," *Dun's Review.* October. pp. 18–19, 62–69.

STOKES, W. E. D., JR. 1952. *Planetary Configurations and Stock Market Sentiment.* February. Lenox, Massachusetts: Golden Arrow Press.

SZATROWSKI, ZENON. 1949-A. "The Pattern of Changing Cycles in United States Steel Corporation Earnings per Share of Common Stock," *Economic Cycle Studies.* March 3.

————. 1949-B. "Common Stock Studies," *Economic Cycle Studies.* February 3, March 3, and June 3.

THERMOHLEN, WILLIAM D. 1949. See BENJAMIN, EARL W., HOWARD C. PIERCE and WILLIAM D. TERMOHLEN. 1949.

THOMAS, BRINLEY. 1954. *Migration and Economic Growth.* Cambridge. Chapter VII.

THOMSEN, FREDERICK L. 1936. *Agricultural Prices.* New York: McGraw-Hill Book Company, Inc. As quoted in HADORN, ERWIN T. 1949. *Cycles in Economic Data: A Digest.* Riverside, Connecticut: Foundation for the Study of Cycles.

THORP, WILLARD LONG and W. C. MITCHELL. 1926. *Business Annals.* New York: National Bureau of Economic Research, Inc. p. 43.

TIMOSHENKO, V. P. 1942. *Variability in Wheat Yields and Outputs, Part 1; Cycles or Random Fluctuations.* Stanford University: Food Research Institute.

TINBERGEN, JAN. 1939. *A Method and Its Application to Investment Activity.* Geneva: League of Nations.

————. 1951. *Business Cycles in the United Kingdom, 1870–1914.* Amsterdam: North-Holland Publishing Company.

TINBERGEN, JAN and J. J. POLAK. 1950. *The Dynamics of Business Cycles: A Study in Economic Fluctuations.* Chicago: The University of of Chicago Press. Based on TINBERGEN's *Economische Bewegingsleer.* 1942. Amsterdam: North Holland Publishing Company.

TINTNER, GERHARD. 1935. *Prices in the Trade Cycle.* Vienna. pp. 46–47.

TRIPP, CHESTER D. 1948. *A New Method of Projecting Cyclical Patterns in the Fluctuations of Common Stock Prices.* Chicago: Chester D. Tripp.

TUGAN-BARANOVSKI, M. 1913. *Les Crisis Industrielles en Angleterre.* Paris. First published in Russian in 1894.

ULMER, MELVILLE J. 1954. "Trends and Cycles in Capital Formation by United States Railroads, 1870–1950," *National Bureau of Economic Research, Inc. Occasional Paper 43.*

U.S.D.A. 1930. "Prices of Farm Products Graphically Presented," *U.S.D.A. Yearbook of Agriculture,* 1930. As reported by HADORN, ERWIN T. 1949. *Cycles in Economic Data:* A Digest. Riverside, Connecticut: Foundation for the Study of Cycles.

VIAL, E. E. 1937. "Purchasing Power Per Capita," *Farm Economics.* No. 101; May. As quoted in WARREN, GEORGE F. and FRANK A. PEARSON. 1937. *World Prices and the Building Industry.* New York: John Wiley and Sons, Inc.

VIELE, A. C. 1962. "LETTERS: The Stock Market," *Cycles.* Vol. XIII; No. 6; June. p. 169.

VOITINSKII, V. S. and E. S. VOITINSKII. 1959. See WOYTINSKY, W. S. and E. S. WOYTINSKY. 1959.

VON HABERLER, GOTTFRIED. 1958. *Prosperity and Depression: A Theoretical Analysis of Cyclical Movements.* Cambridge, Massachusetts: Harvard University Press.

WADE, JOHN. 1934. *History of the Middle and Working Classes.* London.

WAGEMANN, ERNST. 1930. *Economic Rhythm: A Theory of Business Cycles.* New York: McGraw-Hill Book Company, Inc.

————. 1940. *Konjunkturlehre.* p. 70. As cited by BERNSTEIN, E. M. 1940. "War and Business Cycles," *American Economic Review.* Vol. XXX; No. 3; September. pp. 524–535.

WALKER, GEORGE. 1878."Testimony at the Hearings on 'Depression in Labor and Business,'" *House of Representatives.* August 23.

WALLACE, HENRY A. 1934. *New Frontiers.* New York: Reynal and Hitchcock.

WALLACE, HENRY A. and EARL N. BRESSMAN. 1937. *Corn and Corn Growing.* New York: John Wiley and Sons, Inc.

WARDWELL, CHARLES A. R. 1927. *An Investigation of Economic Data for Major Cycles.* Philadelphia: Westbrook Publishing Co. pp. 9, 71–75. As quoted in KING, HUGH P. 1958. "Cycles in Financial Data," *Journal of Cycle Research.* Vol. 7; No. 1; January. pp. 34–39.

WARREN, GEORGE F. 1913. *Farm Management.* New York: The Macmillan Company. As reported by PEARSON, F. A. and W. I. MYERS. 1957. "The Fact Finder," *Farm Economics.* No. 208; February.

WARREN, GEORGE F. and FRANK A. PEARSON. 1937. *World Prices and the Building Industry*. New York: John Wiley and Sons, Inc.

————. 1938. *Farm Economics*. No. 106. p. 2577. As reported by HADORN, ERWIN T. 1949. *Cycles in Economic Data: A Digest*. Riverside, Connecticut: Foundation for the Study of Cycles.

WATSON, D. S. 1953. See BURNS, ARTHUR EDWARD, ALFRED C. NEAL and D. S. WATSON. 1953.

WEBER, B. 1956. See CAIRNCROSS, A. K. and B. WEBER. 1956.

WEIFENBACH, ANNETTE. 1949. See NEFF, PHILIP and ANNETTE WEIFENBACH. 1949.

WEIGEL, CARL R. 1948. *Investment Timer*. Salem, Oregon.

WELLS, RICHARD D. 1951. *Position of the Textile Industry in Relation to Research and Development* — a paper presented at the 22nd annual meeting of the Textile Research Institute. As quoted by DAVIS, THOMAS JEFFERSON. 1958. *Cycles and Trends in Textiles*. Washington: U. S. Department of Commerce. p. 14.

WENZLICK, R. 1932–1934-A. *The Real Estate Analyst*. July 1932. p. 44. *The Real Estate Analyst*. May 1934. p. 264. As quoted in WARREN, GEORGE F. and FRANK A. PEARSON. 1937. *World Prices and the Building Industry*. New York: John Wiley and Sons, Inc.

————. 1932–1934-B. *The Real Estate Analyst*. June 1932. p. 34. Also *The Real Estate Analyst*. April 1934. pp. 254–256. As reported by WARREN, GEORGE F. and FRANK A. PEARSON. 1937. *World Prices and the Building Industry*. New York: John Wiley and Sons, Inc.

————. 1932–1934-C. *The Real Estate Analyst*. July 1932. p. 44. Also *The Real Estate Analyst*. January 1934. p. 244. As reported by WARREN, GEORGE F. and FRANK A. PEARSON. 1937. *World Prices and the Building Industry*. New York: John Wiley and Sons, Inc.

————. 1932–1934-D. *The Real Estate Analyst*. April 1932. p. 15. Also *The Real Estate Analyst*. January 1934. p. 224. As reported by WARREN, GEORGE F. and FRANK A. PEARSON. 1937. *World Prices and the Building Industry*. New York: John Wiley and Sons, Inc.

————. 1933. "The Problem of Analyzing Local Real Estate Cycles," *Journal of the American Statistical Association*. Vol. 27; No. 181a; March Supplement.

————. 1934. *The Real Estate Analyst*. January 1934. p. 224. Also *The Real Estate Analyst*. May 1934. p. 264. As reported by WARREN, GEORGE F. and FRANK A. PEARSON. 1937. *World Prices and the Building Industry*. New York: John Wiley and Sons, Inc.

——————. 1936-A. "Preliminary Study of National Cycles of Real Estate Activity," *The Real Estate Analyst.* October. p. 622. As reported by WARREN, GEORGE F. and FRANK A. PEARSON. 1937. *World Prices and the Building Industry.* New York: John Wiley and Sons, Inc.

——————. 1936-B. "National Cycles of Real Estate Activity," *The Real Estate Analyst.* April. p. 537. As reported by WARREN, GEORGE F. and FRANK A. PEARSON. 1937. *World Prices and the Building Industry.* New York: John Wiley and Sons, Inc.

——————. 1936-C. *The Real Estate Analyst.* April 1936. As reported by WARREN, GEORGE F. and FRANK A. PEARSON. 1937. *World Prices and the Building Industry.* New York: John Wiley and Sons, Inc.

WEST, ROBERT JAMES. 1941. *The Relationship Between Business Cycles in Great Britain and the United States as Indicated by Ratios of Moving Averages.* An unpublished doctorate thesis: University of Pittsburgh.

WESTENDORF, HANS C. 1948. *Cycles in the Stock Market.* New York: Hans C. Westendorf.

WHELDON, C. H., JR. 1937. "Concurrent Long and Short Cycles in Industrial Stock Prices, 1872–1936," *The Annalist.* January 1. p. 6. As quoted in KING, HUGH P. 1958. "Cycles in Financial Data," *Journal of Cycle Research.* Vol. 7; No. 1; January. p. 39.

WHITE, HORACE. 1878. "Testimony at the Hearings on Depression in Labor and Business," *House of Representatives.* August 23.

WHITTAKER, EDMUND. 1960. *Schools and Streams of Economic Thought.* Chicago: Rand McNally & Company.

WIESENBERGER, ARTHUR. 1949. "Living with Vesuvius," *Investment Company News.*

WILLIAMS, DAVID. 1947. *The 56-year Rhythm of American Business Activity* – a lecture delivered before the Henry George School of Social Science on April 6, 1947.

——————. 1959. "Business Cycle Forecasting," *Journal of Cycle Research.* Vol. 8; No. 2; April. pp. 39–63.

——————. 1961. "Sunspot Cycle Correlations," *Annals of the New York Academy of Sciences.* Vol. 95; No. 1; October 5. pp. 78–88.

——————. 1962. "Sunspot Cycle Correlations," *Cycles.* Vol. XIII; No. 4; April. pp. 93–98.

WILSON, B. B. 1930. See NORTON, L. J. and B. B. WILSON. 1930.

WILSON, LOUISE L. 1962-A. "A Possible 12-year Cycle in Cigarette Stock Prices," *Cycles.* Vol. XIII; No. 6; June. pp. 159–161.

———— . 1962-B. "What's Ahead for Soft Coal Production?" *Cycles.* Vol. XIII; No. 8; August. pp. 213–216.

WILSON, WINNIFRED P. 1936–38. See BLACKETT, OLIN W. and WINNI- FRED P. WILSON. 1936–38.

WINNICK, LOUIS. 1956. See GREBLER, LEO, DAVID BLANK and LOUIS WINNICK. 1956.

WOODIN, M. D. 1941. *Changes in the Prices of Apples and Other Fruits.* Cornell University Agricultural Experimental Station Bulletin 773; December. p. 6. As quoted in HADORN, ERWIN T. 1949. *Cycles in Economic Data: A Digest.* Riverside, Connecticut: Foundation for the Study of Cycles.

WOODS, M. V. 1946. "Stock Market Time – Cycles: A Knowledge Derived from the Past Makes Possible the Forecasts of Future Trends in the Affairs of Man," *Price Curve Bulletin and Studies in Market Trading.* No. 1.

WORKING, HOLBROOK. 1931. *Cycles in Wheat Prices, Wheat Studies.* Stanford, California. Food Research Institute. As quoted in HADORN, ERWIN T. 1949. *Cycles in Economic Data: A Digest.* Riverside, Connecticut: Foundation for the Study of Cycles.

WOYTINSKY, E. S. 1959. See WOYTINSKY, W. S. and E. S. WOYTINSKY. 1959.

WOYTINSKY, W. S. and E. S. WOYTINSKY. 1959. *Lessons of the Reces- sions.* Washington, D. C.: Public Affairs Institute.

WOYTINSKY, W. S. and ASSOCIATES. 1953. *Employment and Wages in the United States.* New York: The Twentieth Century Fund.

WRIGHT, WILSON. 1947. *Forecasting for Profit: A Technique for Business Management.* New York: John Wiley and Sons, Inc.

WYLIE, CHARLES CLAYTON. 1948. *The Solar Cycle in Temperature and Crops.* Ames, Iowa: University of Iowa. As reported by MORRIS, WILLIAM W. 1948. *Sunspot and Crop Production.* Madison, Wisconsin: William W. Morris.

YAMAMOTO, TAKEO. No Date. As reported by NISHIOKA, HIDEO. 1957. *Long Warm Weather Cycle Ahead: History of Cold and Warmth.* New York: International Economic Research Bureau.

YEATMAN, W. C. No Date. As reported by DEWEY, EDWARD R. 1950-C. "Cycles in General Business: The 3- to 3 1/2-year Waves, 1790– 1946," *Cycles.* Vol. I; No. 4; November. pp. 4–14.

ZIMMERMAN, ERICH W. 1951. *World Resources and Industries.* New York: Harper & Brothers Publishers.

PRECIS INDEX BY AUTHOR

A

Abel, Martin E.
795

Abramovich, Moses
1070

Abramson, Adolph G.
593, 983, 1169

Achinstein, Asher
643, 714

Adelman, Irma
668

Aftalion, Albert
1285

Allen, W.
876, 896

Andrews, Loring B.
82, 100, 213, 236, 416,
1265

Anonymous
311

Appel, Joseph
217, 218, 260, 261

Armstrong, C. E.
637

Ayres, Leonard
333, 488, 495, 515, 516,
519, 587, 602, 624

B

Babson, Roger W.
220, 244, 251, 457, 725,
785, 898, 1068, 1269

Barbour, Percy E.
43

Barger, Harold
868

B (continued)

Bartlett, Edwin B.
441, 458

Bassie, V. Lewis
756, 783, 840, 866, 1144,
1156, 1157

Bean, L. H.
117, 125

Benjamin, Earl W.
92

Benner, Samuel
60, 81, 131, 144, 381, 769,
1267

Bennett, K. R.
172

Bernstein, E. M.
253

Berry, Thomas Senior
240

Beveridge, William H.
203, 902

Bjorka, Knute
113

Blackett, Olin W.
268, 272, 286

Blank, David
841

Blau, L. W.
359

Blodgett, Ralph H.
1310, 1311, 1312, 1313, 1314,
1315, 1316, 1317, 1318, 1319,
1320, 1321, 1322, 1323, 1324,
1325, 1326, 1327, 1328, 1329,
1330, 1331, 1332, 1333, 1334,
1335, 1336, 1337, 1338, 1339,
1340, 1341, 1342, 1343, 1344

B (continued)

Bodfish, Morton
927

Bond, M. C.
29, 196

Bouniatian, Mentor
1254, 1259

Bowerman, Walter G.
583, 598

Bradley, P. D., Jr.
804

Brandow, George E.
697, 829, 830, 843, 881, 947,
979, 1161

Bratt, Elmer C.
245, 609, 662, 1045, 1170

Bressler, Raymond G.
161, 807

Bressman, Earl N.
108

Brinewell
1246

Brown, E. H. Phelps
536, 1215

Burns, Arthur Edward
612, 720

Burns, Arthur F.
329, 357, 465, 504, 507, 874,
995, 1007, 1008, 1067, 1345,
1347

Burton, T. E.
1252

Business Week
654, 663, 741, 742

C

Cairncross, A. K.
582, 858, 883, 962, 963, 1000,
1304

Campbell, Carlos E.
187

Card, Dana G.
94, 182

Cardozo, J. N.
728

Cassel, Gustav
1250, 1251

Cassetta, J. V.
172

Castle, D. S.
280, 365

Chambers, Edward J.
167, 633, 1079, 1142

Chapman, C. R.
1029, 1041, 1235, 1236

Clark, Hyde
1264, 1277

Clement, M. O.
606

Clough, H. W.
214, 746

Clough, Shepard Bancraft
226

Cochrane, Willard W.
118, 163, 178

Cole, Charles Woolsey
226, 746

Colean, Miles L.
911

D (continued)

Dewey, Edward R. (continued)
396, 397, 398, 399, 400, 401,
403, 422, 423, 426, 428, 429,
431, 438, 440, 443, 445, 448,
454, 455, 477, 532, 539, 544,
545, 546, 547, 549, 550, 551,
552, 553, 555, 556, 557, 558,
561, 562, 563, 565, 574, 589,
601, 613, 614, 766, 771, 773,
774, 817, 818, 819, 822, 826,
830, 831, 833, 849, 892, 894,
895, 920, 922, 928, 929, 930,
931, 935, 937, 939, 941, 943,
944, 948, 949, 951, 952, 953,
959, 960, 965, 966, 967, 968,
969, 970, 971, 972, 973, 974,
976, 986, 987, 988, 989, 990,
991, 992, 993, 994, 996, 997,
998, 999, 1004, 1005, 1006,
1016, 1017, 1018, 1020, 1023,
1024, 1038, 1039, 1042, 1059,
1060, 1063, 1065, 1073, 1074,
1075, 1076, 1077, 1078, 1080,
1081, 1082, 1083, 1084, 1085,
1086, 1087, 1088, 1089, 1090,
1091, 1092, 1093, 1094, 1095,
1096, 1101, 1102, 1103, 1104,
1105, 1106, 1108, 1109, 1110,
1111, 1112, 1121, 1124, 1125,
1128, 1129, 1130, 1131, 1132,
1133, 1134, 1135, 1136, 1137,
1138, 1139, 1140, 1158, 1159,
1178, 1179, 1180, 1181, 1182,
1183, 1184, 1185, 1186, 1187,
1194, 1199, 1200, 1201, 1202,
1219, 1223, 1224, 1225, 1227,
1240, 1241, 1264, 1283, 1307,
1308, 1309, 1353, 1359, 1361,
1363, 1366, 1374, 1375, 1380

DeWolff
242

Doane, William S.
358

Dodd, James Harvey
616, 748

D (continued)

Dorfman, Joseph
1255, 1256, 1258

Dorland, Jack A.
363, 366

Douai, Adolph
678

Downs, James C., Jr.
600, 891, 913, 914, 915, 916,
917, 918, 923, 1376

Dunbar, Veryl L.
350, 351, 353, 354

E

Eaton, Phillip
382

Einarsen, Johan
1117, 1118, 1119, 1120

Elliott, F. F.
104, 790

Encyclopedic Dictionary of Business
656, 747

Engels, Friedrich
1288

Ensminger, M. E.
13, 110, 195

Ernst, Harry
640

Estey, James Arthur
252, 626, 657, 718

Ezekiel, Mordecai
11, 109

F

Feig, J.
863

WAVE LENGTH INDEX

Page 411

SUBJECT INDEX

SUBJECT INDEX